REVIEWS

"Outstanding! Incredibly comprehensive yet thoroughly readabl[e] standard on how to rewrite a screenplay. *Gardner's Guide to Scr[eenplay: The] Rewrite* gives readers the big picture in the form of numerous story a[naly]ses and interviews with actual screenwriters, while using exercises and questions to push the writer deeper into plot, character, theme and dialogue."

Scott Myers, executive producer, Distillery Pictures and screenwriter of K-9, ALASKA and TROJAN WAR

Gardner's Guide to Screenplay: The Rewrite should be required reading for studio development executives and producers as well as the writers they work with. The amount of time and money this book would save them in "development hell" cannot be emphasized enough. The combination of Selbo's savvy as both a teacher of screenwriting and a working writer herself is evident from page one."

Bettina Moss, former HBO Films development executive, Head of the Professional Screenwriting MFA Program at National University.

"A fundamental, step-by-step, rewrite manual from an experienced screenwriter and teacher in full command of her craft, *Gardner's Guide to Screenplay: The Rewrite* shimmers with clarity, good sense, and a respectful tone. Employing an eleven-step story checklist and using numerous examples from successful films, Jule Selbo encourages writers to protect their material, stressing re-engineering over re-thinking…wise advice in an industry where the variety and volume of feedback can be confusing and overwhelming. "Rewrite" is a welcome and valuable resource for new and experienced screenwriters alike."

Dana Coen, screenwriter and co-executive producer of the prime-time series JAG and BONES

"As one who deals with what is known at the "final rewrite" or the third phase of moviemaking, editing the film, I found this work to be extremely comprehensive, enlightening and thorough on so many levels of storytelling. *Gardner's Guide to Screenplay: The Rewrite* succinctly brings all of the elements of building a tight story into sharp focus. It will become a reference prize for me for my work."

Paul Trejo A.C.E., film editor, THIEF (TV miniseries) GREEN STREET HOOLIGANS, TWIN PEAKS, CONEHEADS, RADIOLAND MURDERS

"Those not lucky enough to take one of Jule Selbo's classes have the next best thing in this book. *Gardner's Guide to Screenplay: The Rewrite* plunges the reader headlong into the process of re-writing and makes the voyage fun, fascinating and productive. From character to theme, plot to dialogue, she guides the writer with a sure hand toward making their good screenplay lean, mean and moving forward and great. A must read for anyone staring at a first draft."

Pat Verducci, screenwriter/director TRUE CRIME

"Selbo does a great job of combining her two selves – writer and teacher – into this helpful book that will surely keep you from letting your work sit on a shelf unfinished – or worse – arrive at an agent's office unreadable!"

Rosanne Welch, screenwriter, TOUCHED BY AN ANGEL, PICKET FENCES, Professor of Television Writing and New Media for Writers at UCLA Extension and Stephens College

"In her new book, Selbo takes the mystery and fear out of rewriting a screenplay. Selbo's engaging voice and matter-of-fact style asks both the novice and trained screenwriter to not only dig deeper, but she gives them the necessary tools to craft a rough draft into a marketable script. Her student examples as well as the wide range of film breakdowns provide extraordinary insight into creating real characters and story."

Kerry Madden, author of GENTLE'S HOLLER, LOUISIANA'S SONG, JESSIE'S MOUNTAIN, THE MAGGIE VALLEY TRILOGY

"Whether you're a seasoned pro or a struggling beginner, Jule Selbo's book shows all of us how to attack the fire eating dragon known as THE REWRITE. Her book gives every screenwriter the tools and courage to be a knight in shining armor."

Robert Engels, screenwriter TWIN PEAKS, FIRE WALK WITH ME, writer/ producer of television's ANDROMEDA, MONSTER SMASHER, SEA QUEST, TWIN PEAKS, WISE GUY and more.

"Filling up a blank page is easy when compared to having to identify and address the shortcomings in your own work. Jule has done screenwriters a great favor by providing a detailed and systematic approach toward attacking and improving their scripts. I'll be recommending Gardner's Guide to Screenplay: The Rewrite to all of my students."

Richard Lewis, Associate Professor Dept of Radio-TV-Film, The University of Texas at Austin

"This is 'as good as it gets.' A welcome guide to helping writers through the exciting process of polishing a first draft of a script and getting it ready for the marketplace. Selbo's book is clear. It is concise. It is challenging. Read the chapters. Do the exercises. Be inspired by the detailed explanations of how to make your script the very best it can be."

Bob Bland, screenwriting student

"Selbo's follow-up book to her Gardner's Guide to Screenplay: From Idea to Successful Script needs to be on every screenwriter's shelf- as well as on the shelf of producers, directors and film editors. The book focuses on the final polish of a story, how to make characters pop, how to illuminate theme as well as the original and exciting elements of the film story."

Craig Anderson, Producer, Television's ON GOLDEN POND, O PIONEERS, THE BALLAD OF LUCY WHIPPLE, and more.

GARDNER'S *guide to*

SCREENPLAY

The Rewrite

JULE SELBO

GG
C

GARTH GARDNER COMPANY

GGC publishing

Washington DC, USA · London, UK

Editorial inquiries concerning this book should be mailed to: The Editor, Garth Gardner Company, 5107 13th Street N.W., Washington DC 20011 or e-mailed to: info@ggcinc.com.http://www.gogardner.com

ISBN-13: 978-1-58965-052-7

Library of Congress Cataloging-in-Publication Data

Selbo, Jule.
Gardner's guide to screenplay : the rewrite / Jule Selbo.
    p. cm. -- (Gardner's guide series)
Includes bibliographical references.

  ISBN-13: 978-1-58965-052-7
  1. Motion picture authorship. I. Title.
  PN1996.S3848 2008

  808.2'3--dc22

                                    2008029153

Printed in Canada

ACKNOWLEDGMENTS

This was a wonderful book for me to write because it gave me the opportunity to re-examine so many great films written by great screenwriters – so first of all – thanks to the screenwriters who write the scripts that provide the initial step in the filmmaking process. Thanks for the amazing stories and complex characters you created. Many of you are mentioned in the book.

I would also like to thank my assistant, Mary Leona Fisher, for her diligent research, and my students and clients for their questions and amazing creative work. Thanks also to the Radio-TV-Film department at California State University at Fullerton for their support. Many offered advice, support, critiques and inspiration, and among them are Janet Blake, Dr. Chu, Lupe and Brenda of Carrows Writing Table, Mary Beth Whelan at Globe Photos, the Writers Bloc, L.A., and Mark and Lilliana Winkworth. And special thanks to Christina Edwards for her editing expertise and Anthony Mason at GGC.

TABLE OF CONTENTS

INTRODUCTION

When producers Cindy Chvatal, William Peterson, and Pete McAlevey called me and told me industry pro actress/director Lee Grant had signed on as director of my script *HARD PROMISES*, I was thrilled. Lee Grant had a reputation for doing excellent character-based films and bringing out a simple good story. Only a year before I had been hired to write *HARD PROMSIES* for Michael Douglas' company – then based at Columbia Pictures. This was my second studio assignment. So far *HARD PROMISES* had been a good experience. I had written a first draft, turned it in to the producers, got a series of notes that made sense, and made the script better. Quickly the studio gave the film a green light. Now it was time to work with the director. The producers arranged a time for Lee and I to meet and for me to get her notes. When I met Lee, she had a personal confrontational style that was intimidating. She questioned nearly every moment in the script and wanted me to defend it. After initially freaking out a bit, I realized what she was doing was asking me all the questions the actors would eventually be asking her as they worked on motivations for their characters. She pushed me to dig deeper into the characters; she wanted to make sure they were three-dimensional and relatable and flawed and complex. I tried to implement her suggestions, some enhanced the script – some notes did not improve the script. I was able to discuss the notes with her – those I agreed with and those of which I felt concern. Sometimes I could convince Lee to my way of thinking, other times she convinced me. Lee always listened. Working with her was exciting because of her inherent actor instincts, her ability to collaborate creatively and her point of view on the world of the story. This experience reinforced for me the truism that a rewrite can strengthen a piece of work if it is approached from a desire to clarify and illuminate the characters and existing story.

The script was soon ready for production. Lee requested that I be on the set in Texas as the cameras rolled, doing any re-writing necessary as the script got up on its feet.

Unfortunately, a few weeks into shooting there was a major disagreement between the producers and Lee and she was released from the project. Another director was brought in and I was sent home to Los Angeles. From that moment on, rewrites on the film were made by many involved in the film – but not by me. A few actors called, upset about the rewritten pages they found under their hotel doors in the morning. Unfortunately, as the writer, a thousand of miles away from the set, I was not in a power position and could do nothing. The next time I had anything to do with the film was when I saw a screening of it before it opened the Toronto Film Festival. An entire "B" story had been cut out, a minor character became an awkward running joke and other changes, to me, stuck out like sore thumbs. Many scenes still worked and the overall plot was intact – just not in the way I had envisioned it. It was a hard lesson to go through as a writer. Those in Hollywood know – the more fingers in the script-pie, the less likely a film will succeed on all levels.

Since that time I have gone through other production processes, some good and some bad, and learned to focus on the good. Most produced screenwriters have experienced similar scenarios. Some writers decide to become directors to protect their vision. This is a very smart thing to do because in feature filmmaking, at this time in its evolution (and it hasn't always been so), the director has more clout than the writer. If you have the inclination, talent and stamina, consider being a writer/director.

I learned a great deal from my first experience as a writer of a feature film that found its way before the cameras. Fortunately, as **HARD PROMISES** hit the movie theatres, I was also writing and producing for one-hour television dramas, where the writer has a more alpha position in the filmmaking hierarchy. The television writer can enjoy more control – and the pace of television production keeps the problems inherent in the "multiple-fingers-in-the-script-pie" down to a minimum. There is simply not <u>time</u>, in most cases, to do massive and continual rewriting.

Another memorable rewrite experience, from which I emerged a more skilled writer, was on a script for HBO's **PRISON STORIES: WOMEN ON THE INSIDE**. The script went through many rewrites. The initial story was about two young women from a tough and poor neighborhood – not criminals at heart, but desperate. They commit a robbery. They are caught and sent to prison. Most of the story takes place in the prison. The script explored their adjustment problems. I thought my first draft was packed with drama, action, events and interesting characters. When the executives' notes suggested I add two more major events, more obstacles and more drama, I initially thought there was no room. This was television; I had to hit a certain page count. But in working on the notes, I soon saw where my script was fat; there were dialogue exchanges that did not move the story forward and there were moments where mood was paramount – not action. By implementing the studio notes, I learned how to fill every second with elements that <u>pushed the story forward.</u> By the end the rewriting process, I had added drug addiction, pregnancy and a prison birth – and made the script more compelling – and remained at the same page count. This experience was instrumental in taking my approach to rewriting to a more sophisticated level; something I did not foresee as I was tearing my hair out trying to fulfill the notes.

One of my favorite rewrite experiences was working with Lindsay Duran, then an executive at Paramount Pictures on a script I had been hired to adapt Rachel Ingalls novel, *MRS. CALIBAN.* Lindsay went on to head production at United Artists, and her skills as a script analyst and ability to work with writers helped her earn that position. Lindsay's method was to sit the writer down and go, scene by scene, through the script and trim out anything extraneous to the forward movement of the story. The rewrite of this script caused the story to become a lean, emotional machine – and a lot more clear and compelling.

Another favorite experience was the years I worked with George Lucas on *YOUNG INDIANA JONES CHRONICLES.* Lucas, being a writer himself, respects the work of the writers. His notes on the first drafts of the scripts addressed pacing and character intention and thematic clarity. Since each writer on the series was responsible for their own episodes, each writer did their own rewrites. Once the scripts were ready to go before the cameras, Lucas expected the directors to <u>shoot the script.</u> Lucas' method of protecting the written material brought about the desired result – each story had a strong beginning, middle and end, compelling characters and strong, consistent thematic elements.

Working for Walt Disney Studios in their live action and animation divisions also added to my knowledge of the rewrite process. The teams of Disney executives are trained to be insistent on <u>bringing out the theme</u> of a script. In the rewrite phase of the script, each scene or sequence was shaped, in some way, to support the theme or anti-theme of the story. This work caused the stories to become more focused.

All screenwriters face the rewrite process – whether they are writing under the umbrella of a paycheck or on speculation. Sometimes the work is enjoyable – sometimes it is not. Take a look at John Gregory Dunne's 1997 novel, **MONSTER, Living off the Big Screen.** This book chronicles the multi-year journey he and his writing partner (his wife, Joan Didion), took while writing a first draft and subsequent drafts of the 1996 film *UP CLOSE AND PERSONAL.* Screenwriter William Goldman, in his book,

ADVENTURES OF THE SCREEN TRADE, reflects on the writing, rewriting and production process on his 1969 film, *BUTCH CASSIDY AND THE SUNDANCE KID.* Both books illuminate the writer's dilemma and the need to be able to deal with every new person (producer, actor, director, designer) who is brought into the collaborative process of filmmaking. Each person will have his or her bias on the film story and characters. It is the writer's job to protect his script while remaining open to any suggestion that could enhance the work. Dunne's book and Goldman's book make it clear that the focus of a script can get muddied with every "finger-in-the-script-pie." They make it clear that each writer must strive to hold onto the heart of his or her story and characters.

Note the number of writers' names on a film's credits. Each time you see an "and" in the credits means a new writer was brought on to rewrite the script before (or during) production.

The rewrite process can be fraught with problems. That is why is it important for the screenwriter to be clear on how to keep the process as clean as possible. A writer must commit to bringing out the story that the writer wants to tell (if it is your original screenplay) or the story that originally caught the eye of the producer or actor or director (if you are working on assignment) – and learn how to enhance – not just change – the components so as to not lose the heart of the piece.

The good news is – you have a first draft that is now ready for the rewrite. That's an accomplishment.

Now the fun can begin.

Chapter One

THINKING ABOUT YOUR REWRITE

First draft completed. Celebration over. Now what?

Should you send your script out into the marketplace? Should you put your script in an envelope and mail it into the world? Or convert it to a PDF file and press "send"?

No.

Wait.

First, consider if any elements of your screenplay can be improved. You want to make sure your script is the best it can be before you send it out. Why? Each script that is read at a production company or studio is logged and submitted for coverage.

Details of your script will be entered into a database. This information may be shared among various production companies and studios. Studios, in most cases, will not re-consider material after an initial "pass." You want to make a good impression. You must make sure you are putting your best work out there.

Spend the time it takes to improve your script. Even if your script doesn't get chosen for production (few are), you want your writing skills to impress so you can be put on the list of writers with a reputation for excellent storytelling, excellent character development and excellent dialogue. You want to become known as a screenwriter with a <u>voice</u> that is special.

Rewriting can be the most exciting task of being a screenwriter

The rewrite can be the most enjoyable part of working on a screenplay. After all, you have already created a story filled with interesting characters that are engaged in a strong plot. Your characters have their individual story arcs. You have created locations, dialogue, and visual storytelling elements. Even if your first draft is rough and there are many elements

Definition: *Coverage* is a story synopsis of submitted scripts done by readers who are employed by studios and production companies. Coverage also includes an assessment of the writing skills of the script's author.

you want to re-consider – you have the skeleton, muscle and sinew of your story already down on paper. Now it's time to "take your script" to the gym and make sure it's toned and shaped.

Commitment to the process is everything

You will meet people who don't understand the mental and physical demands that come with being a writer. After all, it looks easy; a writer imagines elements of a story and characters, gets in front of a computer and types out his ideas. How hard can that be? Only those who have attempted this feat appreciate the level of difficulty. It is, in most cases, hard work. Don't fall into the frustration trap. Don't worry that getting your script to a marketable level is taking more time that you expected. Trust me, it will take more time than you expect. Think about it. How difficult is it to become a top athlete? Many professional baseball players have natural talent, but learning and perfecting plays, sliding, bunting and batting takes practice. An athlete must stay in shape and sometimes running the requisite miles every day or regularly lifting weights can get old. However, steady and consistent work keeps the athlete competitive. Steady and consistent work will keep a screenwriter in the game. Steady and consistent work – every day.

Don't put off writing.

Don't wait for inspiration.

Commit to perspiration. Lift those weights whether you feel like it or not. Write every day. Commit to a consistent schedule.

Sometimes it can be a mental battle that keeps us from writing. We can convince ourselves that writing will happen as soon as the house is cleaned, the groceries bought, the "research" films seen, or books read. Or we use friends or family as excuses – telling ourselves that as soon as each is placated – then the writing will begin. We can convince ourselves that completing these things first will "clear our heads" and let us concentrate on the writing.

As you know, things keep coming up. Distractions will always be there.

Ignore them.

The most successful writers I know block out all distractions and set aside time to be incommunicado. Some refuse to answer the phone and don't respond to emails. They unplug the television. They put off lunches or dinners or meetings with friends or agents or studio executives until the writing is done. Some writers don't have the luxury of being totally incommunicado (because of family or other responsibilities) so they put aside the needed hours of every day to pursue the goal – getting the screenplay finished. A famous novelist put aside a certain number of hours every day to write. When his daughter "tested his love for her" by scheduling her wedding during his work hours, she was sadly reminded of his work ethic when he did not show up at the ceremony. Stephen Cannell, a successful screenwriter, producer and novelist (among his long list of credits are *ROCKFORD FILES, WISE GUY, GREAT AMERICAN HERO* and a series of Shane Scully mystery books and more) when speaking at a university writing seminar, told the students he begins writing at 4 am every morning, seven days a week and works at least five hours a day.

A writer needs to get obsessed with her project. When the story invades your dreams – that's good. When you take walks and you find yourself trying out dialogue (and don't notice the stares from passersby) – that's good.

Keep the momentum going. The script you recently completed reflects you now, where you are as a writer and a person now - your thoughts and points of view of people and the state of the world now. Finish your script while you are still in the same frame of mind.

Self-doubt is fine but second-guessing can be crippling

You want to always ask yourself these questions: Can it be better? Can I add more conflict? Is the character feeling deeply or just going through the motions? Are the supporting stories helping the protagonist's main story as much as possible? Is the story as focused as it can be?

Questions like these will push you to re-examine the work to which you have already committed lots of energy – and make it better.

While self-doubt can help a writer, second-guessing can be a crippler. It does no good to try and second-guess the marketplace.

Let's say you have completed a romantic comedy and the latest box office hit is a thriller. You hear through the writers' grapevine that all the studios want thrillers. Should that make you re-think your story?

No.

Question: What do I do after I've finished the first draft of my screenplay? I know there's work to be done but how do I go about it?

Answer: First things first. Celebrate. You've finished a first draft; you have a solid beginning, middle and end. This is a huge accomplishment. Many people want to be screenwriters but don't have the discipline and inspiration to complete a script. You do – you've proved it. So take a day or two to celebrate, kick back and let your draft rest. You want to come back to the work fresh. But don't get too comfortable – you want to get back in the saddle before you lose your momentum.

Development executives at studios and production companies are looking for good scripts they can put into a production pipeline. They are also looking for good writers. Stand by your story – if it's good, it will attract Hollywood's interest. Good executives know that what is hot on the screen right now will not necessarily be hot two to three years from now. (Once your film gets green-lit for production, the processes of pre-production, casting, shooting, post-production, marketing and opening on screens across the country, can take, on average, one to three years.)

Better or… just different?

You want your script to become <u>better</u> – not just <u>different</u>.

If this is a spec script (one written on <u>spec</u>ulation, meaning no one is <u>paying</u> you to write it), this script is all yours. You need to embrace the content, theme and vision, and stick to your original concept – the concept that propelled you to write the 100 pages that now sit on your desk.

Remember, if you ask friends or relatives or peers to read your script and they give you notes, <u>you are not bound to implement those notes.</u> You are the expert on your script. Thank your readers for their input and consider only the notes that work for you. Then rework your script as <u>you</u> see best.

There is danger in deciding to go for "different." The danger? It means you will be, essentially, writing another first draft. At the end of that draft you'll be in the same place you are now – facing a rewrite that will make the script market-worthy. If you do decide the script must be very "different," make sure the decision isn't just an excuse not to tackle solve-able problems in your first draft. Make sure you are not going for "different" because you are wrongly second-guessing yourself. Most problems are fixable. Most scenes or sequences can be massaged to better illuminate the story, characters and themes. Maybe you will add a new supporting story. Maybe you will excise or add a character. But, in most cases, it's a good idea to stick to the original concept – after all, it inspired you to write a first draft of 100 pages.

Remembers, all writers do rewrites. It's part of the craft. In most cases, <u>believe in your script and story</u> and simply commit to making your existing draft <u>better.</u>

Of course, if you are on assignment at a studio or production company and the executive or producer want "different," it is your job (unless you want to be released from the project) to give them "different."

The "HEAD" and "HEART" rewrite

There are two ways to look at the latest draft of your latest screenplay.

The first approach to the rewrite should be technical and can be called the "head" rewrite. This explores the clarity of the characters and plot and technical areas of your script. Do you have a clear protagonist? Is your antagonist strong enough? Are their desires and goals clear? Are there clear character arcs? Is your plot working? Is your "A" story and supporting stories properly balanced? How is your pacing? Have you trimmed all the fat by removing excess dialogue and unnecessary words from action lines and scene settings? Is the formatting perfect and does it make for an easy read? Some of the exercises and tips in this book will focus on the "head" rewrite and address these questions and other technical screenwriting tools.

After you have done the technical work on your latest draft, it's time to make sure the "heart" is working in the screenplay. The "heart" rewrite will explore these questions: Is your theme resonating? Is the author's point of view clear? Are all the characters tracked emotionally? Have you truly explored the reason you were drawn to tell this story? Are you playing it too safe? Are you trusting the audience? Are you challenging the audience? Some of the exercises and tips in this book will focus on the "heart" rewrite.

Let's begin.

Chapter Two

REVIEW THE BASICS

The first book of my series on screenwriting, Gardner's Guide to *SCREENPLAY: From Idea to Successful Script*, covers the basics of turning an idea into a full story worthy of being written as a screenplay. The book explores character development, elements of plot and theme and other necessities to be considered when writing your first draft. Let's review quickly so that we will have a common language in which to talk about the rewrite and polish of your screenplay.

Most studio executives, producers, directors, screenwriters – most people in the film industry – will talk about screenplays in relation to a THREE ACT STRUCTURE.

In the classic Act One, the screenwriter will:

- Set up genre and tone.

- Set up time and place.

- Introduce this protagonist and her normal life.

- Clarify the protagonist's overall want. This could be a conscious desire or unconscious need.

- Clarify the protagonist's most immediate goals. These are goals that may change or evolve throughout the story and are directly related to plot.

- Introduce the <u>problem</u> facing the protagonist in your story. What stands in the way of his reaching his goals?

- Introduce the protagonist's main nemesis: the antagonist.

- Clarify the antagonist's overall want. This could be a conscious desire or unconscious need.

- Clarify the antagonist's most immediate goals.

- Introduce supporting characters; these could include friends and foes.

- Explore the actions the protagonist takes to achieve her overall want and most immediate goals.

- Build Plot Point One – a shift in circumstances that causes the protagonist to realize that logical attempts to achieve her want/goals/needs will not suffice. The protagonist faces a brick wall – and must find new methods to achieve want/goals/needs.

In the classic Act Two, the screenwriter will:

- Open the world of the story. Let the problem affect a wider arena, a wider group of people.

- Reveal a new opportunity for the protagonist to achieve her goal. This could appear to be a welcome opportunity – or an unwelcome one. This opportunity changes the protagonist's world or methods and propels her into territory that is unfamiliar – either physically or emotionally or both.

- Explore reasons for protagonist's goals. Open up the protagonist for deeper exploration.

- Explore reasons for antagonist's goals. Open up the antagonist for deeper exploration.

- Construct obstacles, reversals and conflicts that are a constant in the protagonist's journey.

- Make sure the antagonist and protagonist are in conflict.

- Construct a midpoint, where the challenges of the task shift again and the stakes are raised.

- Continue to escalate conflict until the protagonist finds herself in a situation that feels like the deepest, darkest hell imaginable. Possibility of failure or giving up is real.

- Focus on the protagonist's decision to go into the climax (or not).

In the classic Act Three, the writer will:

- Construct a climax where the protagonist goes beyond her original abilities to achieve (or not) her overall want and immediate goals.

- Be sure to include the final elements of the supporting stories and characters in the climax.

- All supporting stories should come together to create the most conflict for the protagonist.

- Build a resolution where the outcome of the protagonist's journey is revealed.

- Feature the emotional and/or physical "new normal life" of the main character; a sense of the future.

A more thorough breakdown of the structure of a screenplay is what I have called the Eleven Step Story Structure. Most good film stories (most stories in general) will follow this Eleven Step template because it concentrates on character and how the character changes. Character is what is most important in any story. The plot could revolve around a love story, an adventure, a crime, a mystery, a disaster or any other genre of story – but that is only plot. It's the solid, exciting, original character's journey within the plot that will make your screenplay successful.

In your rewrite, it is paramount to examine your characters' journeys. If they are full, surprising, revelatory and fresh, your script will attract good actors. Good actors move films into the production channel. Characters - not plot - will get your film made.

ELEVEN-STEP STORY STRUCTURE

1. Character's Overall Want/Need and Why

2. Character Logically Goes For It

3. Character Is Denied

4. Character Gets Second Opportunity To Get Overall Want

5. Conflicts About Taking Advantage Of Second Opportunity

6. Character Decides To Go For It

7. All Goes Well

8. All Falls Apart

9. Character's Crisis

10. Climax

11. Truth Comes Out

How the Eleven Step Story Structure helps you make your film unique

No one wants films to be predictable. No one wants the structure to jump out at the audience. But audiences <u>do</u> want to be taken on a full and satisfying journey, they want highs and lows and twists and turns. They want to know <u>why</u> a character is on the journey; they want to invest in the outcome. So the screenwriter/storyteller's task is to provide the structure of a good story and handle story elements with a fresh point of view. Your point of view and ability to use and play with good structural elements can help make your film story original.

If you construct (or in the rewrite phase, re-examine your work) using the Eleven Step Story Structure as a creative map – your screenplay will feature characters with strong individual arcs and a plot that is driven by those characters. Your story will have a strong beginning, middle and end – and that is what is needed to satisfy an audience.

More in-depth details about how the Eleven Steps work

1. Character's Overall Want/Need and WHY.

Your main character needs to <u>want</u> something and the more he wants it (or needs it), the better. It's got to be important. It has to be major in his life. It has to be consuming.

Be sure you know the <u>emotional reason</u> for this overall want. You have to be specific. Consider 2006's Academy Award winning screenplay ***THE DEPARTED***; Colin Sullivan (portrayed by Matt Damon) wants <u>power and legitimacy</u>. Why? He grew up poor, was taken under the wing of a powerful criminal, and came to understand that power is important. However, Colin aches to rise above his background. He wants legitimate political power (he even chooses an apartment with a view of the state capitol building), he wants marriage to a good woman (he flirts with women with whom he can banter sexually but forges a relationship with a respected, well-educated, successful psychologist). All the <u>specific immediate goals</u> that he forms in the story reflect his <u>overall want</u> for power and legitimacy.

In 2006's ***BLOOD DIAMOND,*** Danny Archer (portrayed by Leonardo DiCaprio), thinks what he wants is wealth, but comes to realize what he <u>needs</u> is to embrace a connection, a sense of nationalism, a <u>purpose</u>.

Bruce Wayne (portrayed by Christian Bale) in 2005's ***BATMAN BEGINS*** wants justice. Why? He feels immense personal guilt concerning his parents' death; he seeks justice to alleviate the guilt.

The characters in 2005's **CRASH** all want connection. Why? Racial and family tensions are destroying their relationships.

2001's **SHREK** wants <u>love and acceptance</u>. Why? Because the ogre Shrek (voiced by Mike Myers) has no friends and he is lonely.

Clarice Starling (portrayed by Jodie Foster) in 1991's **SILENCE OF THE LAMBS** <u>needs</u> to confront her past in order to move on in life. Why? Her past contains humiliation and deep pain and a sense of guilt. She <u>needs</u> to forgive herself and embrace her future.

Loretta (portrayed by Cher) in 1987's **MOONSTRUCK** wants true love but is too afraid to embrace it because her first husband died shortly after their marriage. Her fear is her flaw; she is ready to settle for less than true love to ensure protection from being hurt again.

Jake Gittes (portrayed by Jack Nicholson) in 1974's **CHINATOWN** wants <u>respect</u>. Why? He wants to believe he can do the right thing and cleanse himself of guilt due to past experiences in Chinatown.

In 1942's **CASABLANCA**, Rick (portrayed by Humphrey Bogart) wants <u>connection </u>in his life. Why? He has disconnected himself from emotion because the love of his life walked out on him in Paris.

Check your script. Does your character have <u>one</u> (only one!) strong, emotional overall want? Yes, human beings want many things; we are complex. But you are telling a story to <u>make one point.</u> You are not telling a story that will inform all facets of humankind – you are exploring characters at a <u>specific time in their lives</u> where <u>one</u> desire or need is paramount.

Remember, you will write other scripts. There is no need to pile everything into one script.

In the script you are ready to rewrite now – ask yourself what does your main character want most <u>at this point in his life?</u> Does he need the respect of his father (and others) in order to move forward? Does she need to feel loved in order to feel confident enough to take on her nemesis at work? Does he need to believe in himself in order to feel lovable? What does your character <u>need</u> to be happy? Feel whole? Feel worthy? Find the emotional motor for your character.

This is the most important part of tackling a rewrite. Unless that <u>overall</u>

want is clear, you may have a hard time bringing out the <u>theme</u> of your story. You may have a hard time committing to a <u>point of view</u>. These are elements that you will need to embrace to make your script stand out.

Don't let your script straddle the fence

Decisions will free you. Commit to your story, theme and point of view. Don't think you can mask indecision. You can't. One of the most common complaints of studio readers is, "It's not clear what the protagonist wants." Clever dialogue or wild plot points will not save your script if the protagonist's want is not clear. How do you focus your protagonist's want? <u>Trim out the fat, the extra pounds put on by ancillary desires</u>. Your film story will feel crisper, cleaner, edgier if the protagonist's overall want and journey to attain that want is clear.

Consider 2006's **CASINO ROYALE**; James Bond's overall want is to feel love and acceptance. Yes, this is an action/adventure film and Bond is trying to save the world – but saving the world is the background <u>plot</u> for his <u>real pursuit</u> – love and acceptance. After all, once he falls in love and feels loved, he is ready to resign from his job. Bond's want of love and acceptance are paramount in this episode in the Bond series – and it is why the film won high praise. The film story is more than its <u>plot</u>; it is about the character's growth and change.

CASINO ROYALE (2006) Eva Green, Daniel Craig
- photo courtesy of Globe Photos

A student of mine was working on a story – she had a character, Mindy, who wanted to make a lot of money. The story was not working because Mindy's desire for money wasn't strong enough to get an audience interested in the character. The student needed to identify why Mindy wanted money – so that her desire had an emotional base. The student began to explore the emotional reasons why Mindy had this intense desire to make money. Finally the student identified the why. Mindy needed to prove to her mother that she was capable, talented and worthy of respect. Why? Mindy felt her mother's love was conditional, based on approval of Mindy's actions. Why? Her mother never praised her; Mindy's accomplishments were never acknowledged or praised. Why? The "why" question can go on and on as you explore the story, but in this instance, it became clear that Mindy's real emotional want was respect. Once the writer identified that emotional overall want, she could focus all her scenes; Mindy chafes when she doesn't get respect at the dry cleaners, when her boss hits on her and doesn't respect her as a colleague, when her boyfriend cheats on her and when her mother thinks she is a huge disappointment. Her need for respect stems from the relationship with her mother but permeates other relationships. Her need for respect fuels her desire for money. The audience begins to worry that Mindy will sabotage herself in all areas of her life while seeking respect. The script becomes focused on one thing – even as different areas of Mindy's life play out.

Take a look at your script. Commit your protagonist to a strong, emotional overall want. Good stories explore the human condition; neuroses, fears, deep desires. This is true for dramas, comedies, farces and fantasies – all genres. Committing to tracking this overall want throughout the script will raise the level of your screenplay.

2. Character LOGICALLY goes about trying to attain his Overall Want.

Your main character needs to pursue his overall want in a logical fashion before he takes any extreme action. If a character wants to become a successful singer/recording artist, is it the most logical thing to storm the stage at the Grande Ole Opry, kick the star off the stage and demand attention? No. Logically your protagonist could write songs, try to get an audition, make a recording of his work and try to get it into the hands of an agent or beg a radio host to play his work on the air. Only when all practical, logical options are used up and your protagonist is feeling angry and abused will he be ready to make a less obvious or acceptable choice that will change his life forever.

Question: If my script is now focused more on the immediate goals of my protagonist – to get money and to get the girl – is there an easy way to identify the overall want behind the pursuit of the immediate goals?

Answer: Sometimes the writing process will feel "easy," other times you may have to put in some time to identify overall wants and other elements in your story. The level of difficulty may change from script to script – some scripts will be easier to write than others. The best way to identify the overall want is to keep asking the question, why? When the answer starts to become emotional you may be getting close to the overall want. The overall want does not need to be (or should it be) unique; it is usually a base human need – love, respect, control, sense of family, etc. The overall want needs to be something to which the audience can relate.

If you don't have these logical steps, the audience will be asking, "If he wanted the job, why didn't he apply for it?" If he wanted a date with the girl, why didn't he ask her out? If he wanted to get justice, why didn't he go to the cops/lawyer/judge? Follow the <u>logic</u> of the story; that way you won't lose your audience. A character must pursue a few <u>logical steps</u> before resorting to an action that will test him in a new way. These logical steps are called <u>immediate goals</u>, and they will serve as the base of your plot.

Take a look at your script. Do you need to add a few scenes of your character logically pursuing his goal? Consider 2005's ***40-YEAR-OLD VIRGIN***. Andy Stitzer (portrayed by Steve Carell) wants love – someone with whom to share his life. His fellow employees translate this desire into a need for sex. Andy has no idea how to fulfill his overall want, so he <u>logically</u> allows his fellow employees to open up possibilities for him. Andy goes with his fellow employees to a club, lets himself get picked up (and then there is a reversal, the "sure thing" turns into a disaster). His attempts continue; they backfire. Logical steps <u>will not</u> work. The brick walls your character runs into are called <u>reversals</u>. After a series of reversals, Andy Stitzer decides to follow a new path. He pursues a woman that his friends don't consider a sure-bet – but she touches Andy's heart – and that feeling is what he is really after – love.

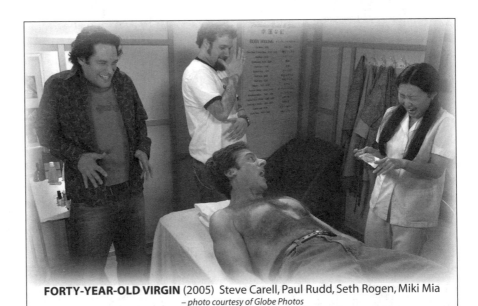

FORTY-YEAR-OLD VIRGIN (2005) Steve Carell, Paul Rudd, Seth Rogen, Miki Mia
– photo courtesy of Globe Photos

Gardner's Guide to Screenplay: The Rewrite

Consider 2006's bio-pic **MISS POTTER.** Children's book author Beatrix Potter (portrayed by Renee Zellweger) <u>wants to live life according to her own values and dreams</u>. How does she do that? Logically she refuses to marry the suitors her mother parades in front of her, she goes into the business world (not a normal thing for an proper British woman in the early 1900s) to get her stories published. She also makes friends with young people of a lower class and she falls in love with a tradesman, the publisher of her books. She is logically pursuing her goals and in doing so creates conflict with her mother. Conflict in a screenplay needs to be consistently present.

3. *Character is DENIED. All logical efforts have failed.*

Hopefully in a big and awful way. Or in an emotional or violent or funny way. The protagonist eventually needs to hit a large enough roadblock that will force him onto a new path that will lead to the accomplishment (or not) of his overall want.

Consider the denial of Billy Costigan (portrayed by Leonardo DiCaprio) in **THE DEPARTED.** This is a young man who wants <u>respect</u>. He wants to make up for his family's past failings, wants to prove to his step-family that he does not approve of their cold and elitist ways. He logically enters the police academy, does well and is considered a bright and promising candidate. In the scene where he faces Captain Queenan (portrayed by Martin Sheen) and Officer Dignam (portrayed by Mark Wahlberg) in hopes of getting a top assignment, Costigan is denied. He is humiliated, he is forced to relive his past pains, he is suspected of being a dirty cop – or at least planning to be a dirty cop. This powerful denial scene for the character forces Costigan to take on an assignment that will be challenging and life-threatening. He accepts the job to prove to his superiors that he deserves their <u>respect</u>.

Consider the denial in 2006's **THE QUEEN.** Queen Elizabeth (portrayed by Helen Mirren) plans to deal with Princess Diana's death in a quiet "family" manner. The public outcry for a forum in which they can grieve for their beloved princess denies Queen Elizabeth her privacy and the <u>control she desires</u>.

Bruce Wayne in **BATMAN BEGINS** is denied when he comes home from college with plans to attend the trial of the man who shot and killed his parents. Bruce (logically) plans on shooting the man in the courtroom to fulfill his personal need for revenge. Circumstances prevent Bruce from carrying out his plan. Frustrated and desperate to relieve his guilt, Bruce leaves Gotham and travels to the East where he finds new opportunities.

Consider *SHREK*. The audience knows that Shrek (voiced by Mike Myers) <u>needs</u> to connect with people, that he hates his loneliness. However, Shrek is lying to himself; he states that his <u>immediate goal</u> is to be left alone. He is <u>denied</u> when the Donkey (voiced by Eddie Murphy) moves into Shrek's house and the other Fairy Tale creatures won't leave him alone - their presence forces Shrek to connect with people and head out on the adventure of Act Two.

In 1997's *GOOD WILL HUNTING,* Will (portrayed by Matt Damon) <u>needs</u> to take a risk. He needs to get out of his comfort zone, use his mathematical talents to fulfill his potential. At the beginning of the film, Will makes it clear he is attached to his friends and familiar life. He is <u>denied </u>his comfort zone when he is arrested and released into the guardianship of the math professor.

The denial doesn't necessarily have to be a large event. But it does need to send your character down a new path. Consider 1992's *UNFORGIVEN.* Munny (portrayed by Clint Eastwood) has made a promise to his wife to give up violence and killing and live a good clean life. Even though she is dead at the beginning of the story, this promise looms large for Munny. His children are hungry, his hog farm is failing, and he is barely surviving. Munny is presented with an opportunity to kill to gain a financial reward – he says no. But when Munny's hogs get sick and his last hopes of making it as a farmer are dashed, Munny agrees to go back to violence to support his family. Munny is <u>denied</u> his desire to live up to the promise he made his wife – because his hogs got sick. Seems small, but it is the event that moves Munny into Act Two.

Exercise:

Take a look at your script. Does your protagonist face a series of obstacles or reversals as he logically goes about trying to achieve his want through the initial immediate goals? How is the larger denial different? How is it more life–changing? How does it move your protagonist into a new challenge in Act Two?

4. A SECOND OPPORTUNITY presents itself to the character.

Just when the denial makes all seem lost, or too difficult, or too unfair – an opportunity presents itself. A <u>new</u> way to achieve the goal is revealed.

<u>The second opportunity doesn't always have to seem like a good thing.</u> Does **THE DEPARTED's** Billy Costigan want to go undercover in the gang led by Frank Costello (portrayed by Jack Nicholson)? No. It's dangerous and nerve-wracking, but Billy has a deep, obsessive desire to prove himself. So he takes advantage of the opportunity. Does Belle in **BEAUTY AND THE BEAST** want to be a prisoner in the Beast's castle? No. But she must protect her father and, in retrospect, this opportunity does present the new life she desires. Remember, your character is on a journey, possibly not one of his or her choosing. Shrek does not <u>want</u> to go to the King to plead for a better life for the Fairy Tale creatures. Will, in **GOOD WILL HUNTING**, does <u>not</u> want to have to see a psychiatrist or be under the guardianship of the arrogant professor. However, the Second Opportunity events in these films <u>push</u> the characters into circumstances that will allow them to achieve their overall want.

In some cases, the second opportunity <u>will</u> look like a godsend. Consider Alvy Singer (portrayed by Woody Allen) in **ANNIE HALL.** He wants to pursue the opportunity of love with Annie Hall. Does Dobbs (portrayed by Humphrey Bogart) in 1948's **TREASURE OF SIERRA MADRE** see the opportunity to use his lottery winnings to finance a search for gold as a welcome opportunity? Yes. Your story will dictate how the character views this second opportunity.

Exercise:

> Take a look at the latest draft of your script. Can you heighten the danger (emotional or physical) of the second opportunity? Is your character gung-ho or reluctant? Make sure you emotionally track your protagonist. Let the audience in on how she feels. This could be done with a look, an action, a line of dialogue or a hint in the action line.

5. CONFLICTS INVOLVED in taking advantage of second opportunity.

If it's too easy, it's not good. Good stories need <u>conflict</u> and not just between the protagonist and the antagonist. The really good stories also deal with the protagonist's internal conflicts and personal conflicts with

Question: What about page count?

Answer: At the character's denial (Step #3), you could be on page 3 or 5 or 15 or 20. Don't worry about page count. However, if you have not yet reached your denial by page 30 you may be telling your story too slowly or the balance of your story may need adjustment. (See the Chapter on Balance.)

every character in the story. Conflicts can be emotional or physical – or both.

Take a look at your script. What's at stake for the main character if he accepts this second opportunity? Is there a moral conflict? Is he going behind his best friend's back? Is she making a pact with the devil? Is there physical danger? Is he going into territory where he doesn't have the necessary skills to survive? Is there emotional conflict? Is she nervous? Lying? Pretending? Is there a great possibility his heart could get broken?

This is an area that can be built up. The more conflicts, the more you'll have to play out as your story progresses in Act Two. You may have to go back into Act One scenes and adjust or add elements to enhance the amount of conflicts your protagonist will take with him into Act Two.

Consider the conflicts Billy Costigan in *THE DEPARTED* has about taking advantage of his second opportunity:

    – Being an undercover cop in Frank Costello's violent, criminal gang is not easy; there is the need to constantly lie, remember lies, and to pretend to be someone else.

    – His life is in danger.

    – His superiors in the police force don't trust him.

THE DEPARTED (2006) Leonardo DiCaprio, Jack Nicholson
- *photo courtesy of Globe* Photos

– Another cop is trying to find out his identity.

– He feels alone – and he is lonely.

– He feels as if he can trust no one.

– His mother is ill and close to death.

– He does not get along with his stepfather.

By focusing on and/or expanding the <u>conflicts</u> your character creates or faces at the top of Act Two, you can set up story elements that can play out throughout the act. When things are too easy, people tend to coast. When conflicts and problems arise, people are forced to react and this opens up opportunities for growth and change. Take a look at your script. Have you piled on the conflicts?

Check out the breakdowns at the end of the book to see how other films use Step #5 of the Eleven Step Story Structure – conflicts about taking advantage of the second opportunity – to help build conflicts that will play out in Act Two.

Exercise:

Make a list of the different areas of your protagonist's life – work, friendships, romances, family, enemies, allies and other areas. Under each area make another list – what are the conflicts that could present themselves to the protagonist if he takes advantage of this second opportunity? Work these conflicts – they will enrich your script. Make sure you are letting each play out as Acts Two and Three play out.

6. Character's decision TO GO FOR IT.

The protagonist decides – despite all the conflicts that arise about taking advantage of this second opportunity – that she <u>must take advantage of the second opportunity</u> to continue to pursue her <u>overall want.</u> Or, she decides she <u>cannot</u> take advantage of the opportunity and circumstances beyond her control propel her into Act Two. Be aware that if you have a character that decides <u>not</u> to go forward and lets circumstances (or fate) take over, she may look passive and weak. Audiences, for the most part, do not maintain a strong interest in passive characters.

Caution: Don't switch the character's overall want mid-stream. Yes, your story may go down various paths and <u>immediate goals</u> may change as the plot unfolds, but the strong <u>emotional overall want</u> should not change.

Take a look at your script. Are you staying consistent? Are you still focused on <u>one</u> overall want?

Often this <u>decision</u> step is a "taken for granted" step because the story is tumbling forward quickly. Sometimes the character has no choice. Sometimes it's an active choice and the protagonist embraces the new opportunity.

The <u>reluctant hero</u> is a staple in many stories. Consider **THE DEPARTED** (Billy Costigan doesn't want to go undercover but…) **THE GODFATHER** (Michael Corleone doesn't want to be part of the family business but…) **KRAMER VS KRAMER** (Ted Kramer doesn't want to be a single father but …) **SHREK** (Shrek doesn't want to go see the King but…) **BEAUTY AND THE BEAST** (Belle doesn't want to be a prisoner in the castle but…). The protagonists of these films are reluctant – they do not <u>want</u> to enter the journey before them, but they do.

The <u>misguided hero</u> decides to do the <u>right</u> thing for the <u>wrong</u> reasons; consider 2006's **BLOOD DIAMOND** (Danny Archer agrees to help prisoner Soloman Vandy escape persecution in hopes of gaining personal wealth) or the Beast in **BEAUTY AND THE BEAST** (Beast agrees to let Belle change places with her prisoner father in hopes of personal salvation).

The <u>anti-hero</u> decides to do the <u>wrong</u> thing for the <u>right</u> reasons; consider **UNFORGIVEN** (Munny agrees to kill again in order to support his family), 1975's **ONE FLEW OVER THE CUCKOO'S NEST** (McMurphy takes his fellow inmates on a joy ride and pretends to be unbalanced so he will not be sent back to a prison work farm).

The <u>straightforward hero</u> (1963's **THE GREAT ESCAPE,** 2000's **ERIN BROKOVICH,** 2000's **THE GLADIATOR,** 2001's **LEGALLY BLONDE**) can be fearful, sure of failure, have a date to do something else, think he is doing something immoral or unethical… but knows that if he or she does not take action, right will not win out. These protagonists want the world to be fair and honest and will continue down their paths doing the right thing for the right reasons.

Take a look at your draft. Have you skipped this opportunity to make sure your hero is <u>actively</u> deciding to enter (or not) the most life-changing act of his life?

7. ALL GOES WELL (…usually for a very short time).

It's a good idea to give your protagonist a sense that reaching his goal is possible. Let him get close. Or be successful in some way. Perhaps he gets close to the bad guys. Or the first date goes well – for a moment or two.

If you are spending more time here, you may want to consider adding an underlying tension. Take a look at 1998's **SHAKESPEARE IN LOVE** where tension is constant because the true identity of Violet (portrayed by Gwyneth Paltrow) could be discovered at any moment or 1979's **KRAMER VS KRAMER** where Ted (portrayed by Dustin Hoffman) is learning to be a good father but problems at work and in the custody proceedings are making his life difficult. You can also take a look at 1993's **MRS. DOUBTFIRE** where newly divorced Daniel (portrayed by Robin Williams) is able to be close to his children and learning to be responsible – but the fact that he is pretending to be someone else could be exposed at any moment. Make sure there are obstacles and increasing tensions even as the protagonist is getting closer to his goal.

Take a look at your script. If things are going well for too long, you may be in danger of losing your audience because they will cease to <u>worry.</u> Keep the audience off balance. They <u>need to worry</u> that things will not turn out well for the protagonist. Tease them with a taste of near-success, but the protagonist's attainment of his overall want must remain elusive.

8. ALL FALLS APART.

This is the part of your story where your character is tested in a way he has never been tested before. Physically and emotionally. In most screen stories, this section will feature a series of disastrous events. Elements of the main plot, subplots, and relationships you've set up are now working aggressively <u>against your protagonist</u>. The protagonist gets misunderstood, gets beaten up, loses love, gets cheated on, has his boss come down on him, has parents disown him, breaks a leg, loses a battle, loses a spaceship, plans go awry… <u>everything</u> falls apart. People, promises. Weaknesses become real and scary liabilities….

There may still be ups and downs. Obstacles and reversals are a constant in good storytelling. Consider 2006's **PURSUIT OF HAPPYNESS**, the story of man (portrayed by Will Smith) who faces extraordinary challenges caring for his son as he relentlessly pursues a successful business career. The film is a series of events that bring the protagonist to situations that <u>exceed</u> his worst nightmares. This film spends nearly 75% of its screen time

Question: What about film stories where the protagonist chooses not to take advantage of the second opportunity but is thrust into it by circumstances?

Answer: Stories like *ALICE IN WONDERLAND*, where the protagonist stumbles into Act Two are viable, but beware of fate driving your story. Stories work better when the protagonist is making active choices to engage in reaching his goal.

in the ALL FALLS APART area. Most action films spend a large percentage of their time here. In most romances, this area of the story explores every possible thing that could go wrong in a relationship. Consider 2005's romantic-comedy *MUST LOVE DOGS*; Sarah Nolan (portrayed by Diane Lane) is a woman reeling from a failed marriage. Her husband left her for another woman. Jake (portrayed by John Cusack) is still in deep emotional pain because his wife left him. Both have friends/siblings trying to get each back on the "dating track." Sarah and Jake meet early in the film story and connect for a brief moment; and then ALL FALLS APART in their romance until the final moments of the film. The ALL FALLS APART section takes up at least 40% of the film and the audiences begin to <u>worry</u> that these two people will never connect romantically.

MUST LOVE DOGS (2005) Diane Lane, John Cusack
- photo courtesy of Globe Photos

Exercise:

Take a look at your script. Make a list of at least five <u>more</u> things (large and small) that could fall apart for your protagonist. Catapult him into that deepest, darkest hell. Make her worst nightmare come true.

9. CHARACTER'S CRISIS.

This is one of the most important sections of your script. It is the area that will define your protagonist. The crisis point is a <u>decision</u> that your protagonist will make to enter (or not) the climax – the situation where he will be sorely tested emotionally or physically – or both. Will the main character be able to make the strong/difficult decision against incredible odds in the midst of great conflict? Will she put her own judgment above others? Will he give up? <u>The crisis point is a decision.</u> Will the protagonist give up or go forward? Keep your protagonist <u>active</u>. Remember, passive protagonists, in most cases, are not very interesting. Let your protagonist <u>decide</u> (or <u>decide not to</u>) head into the climax.

Without a clear definition between the ALL FALLS APART and the CLIMAX, a story can lose a sense of propulsion and stay on one level. You want variation. You want clear turning points. The audience wants to see <u>why</u> the protagonist is willing to enter this last test. Let the crisis show that your character has changed on some level. Let the crisis be marked with a <u>decision</u> and help prepare the audience for the fireworks of the upcoming climax.

Exercise:

Take a look at your script. Make sure your character is making a decision in the crisis moments. Give him something to decide between – safety or danger, following his heart or following his head. Does he need to choose between love or money? Trust or mistrust? Will she be willing to die for her beliefs? If you need to go back to prior sequences and adjust story points to support the need for this decision, do it. Perhaps a few story elements will need to be adjusted. Perhaps a supporting character's role needs to be adjusted. Work longhand in the margins of the hard copy of your script and explore the possibilities.

10. THE CLIMAX.

The main character goes that extra mile to defeat the antagonist in pursuit of her goal. It could be a courtroom scene, it could be a fierce battle in space, the championship basketball game, a chess match, racing against time to save the world, a series of scenes or sequences that bring lovers together or making it through enemy territory to reach a border that leads to freedom.

The climax <u>needs</u> to be the most difficult (physically and emotionally) test of the protagonist in the entire story. There is a reason why many stories spend a good amount of time in this area – the audience, at this stage of the story, is invested in the character's desires. There should be a great possibility for defeat. Remember, you want the audience to <u>worry</u> about the outcome – will the protagonist reach his goal or not?

Exercise:

Take a look at your script. Note how much time you spend in the climax. Check off the scenes that keep the tension rising. Make notes in the margins of the pages; think of ways to make the conflicts and obstacles of the climax even more difficult.

Check your script. Does the protagonist realize something new about himself in the climax? Is the audience still receiving new information? Is the plot still unfolding? The climax needs to be more than a physical contest; it should also include emotional and psychological elements.

Exercise:

Read through your climax again. Ask yourself: Is there a moment when the protagonist realizes something new about himself? Does your protagonist have an epiphany during the climactic scenes? Does this moment give him the strength to commit to the final surge needed to attain his goal?

11. THE TRUTH COMES OUT.

After the final test (climax) has ended and the bad guys have been bested (or not) there are the details to be revealed to ensure that the audience understands the <u>new</u> situation in which your protagonist finds himself. Has he accepted love and is he now happily married? Does she have the respect of her father and is now head of the corporation? Has he found peace and now lives on a country farm? Is he heartbroken and ready to take revenge against the bad guys?

What is the future for your protagonist? Give a sense of what lies ahead....

Exercise:

Take a look at your script. Make sure your main characters' feelings and states of mind are clear. If you have not constructed a sequence that reveals a sense of your protagonist's future, do so now. Give a sense of the "new normal life" of your main characters.

Overlay of the Eleven-Step Story Structure onto the Three Act Template

In order to further illuminate our common language, let's overlay the Eleven Steps onto the classic Three Act Template. Remember, there is no need to hit certain page counts; however, the story steps are of great importance. Make sure you have you included all the basic steps of good story.

- **ACT ONE:** *Steps 1-3; Character's Overall Want and Why, Character Logically Goes for It and the Character is Denied.*

- **ACT TWO:** *Steps 4-9, Character's Second Opportunity to Achieve Overall Want, Conflicts About Taking Advantage of the Second Opportunity, Decision to Go for It, All Goes Well, All Falls Apart and finally, the Crisis.*

- **ACT THREE:** *Steps 10-11, Climax and Truth Comes Out.*

It's not necessary to employ the classic page count demands of the Three Act template. (Act One 1-25 pages, Act Two 26 to 75 pages, Act Three 76 to 100 pages.) Stories need to be told in different rhythms.

If you follow the Eleven Steps, you will have every element you need in your screen story. You can choose to spend more time (number of pages) in one area or another, on whatever you think are the most compelling elements. Your Denial (Step #3) could be on page 5 or page 30. Things could start Falling Apart (Step #8) in a major way very quickly. The Climax (Step #9) could be short or long. You decide the rhythm of your story.

The most important thing to remember is that you, the writer, are in charge. You hold the key to a story that reflects your view of the world. The way you tell your story is your choice – and there is no right or wrong choice. It all comes down to what works. And what works is a screenplay that focuses on the characters' journeys and leads the reader (and eventually the audience in the theater) down an emotional and exciting path that illuminates a change in the emotional and physical lives of your main characters.

CHAPTER SUMMARY

- The Eleven Steps contains all the classic story structure elements and allows the writer greater freedom than the page count guidelines of the Three Act Template.

- The protagonist's overall want must be set up early in the story. The overall want reflects the emotional need of the protagonist.

- The protagonist's immediate goals (how he moves towards attaining his overall want) help shape the plot.

- No matter what structure the writer employs, a full story is necessary to completely satisfy the audience.

Chapter Three

FIRST TEN QUESTIONS
AND MORE

Writers can get very attached to their work. After all, you've put in weeks, months, maybe a year into the first draft of your screenplay. It represents your sweat and angst and joy. That's great, but <u>now is the time to step back and pretend someone else wrote the script.</u>

> *REWRITE TIP: Print a hard copy of your first draft. Put it in a safe place. Also back up the draft on your computer, make sure you have it on a separate disk or drive. Computers and files can get corrupted or fail, get lost or destroyed. You want to know that you can always access your work – or at least re-type it if all technology fails.*

Now, let's get to work.

Answer these questions

1. What Genre (s) are you working in?

Most films will be a combination of genres; 2002's **SPIDERMAN** is a drama and a fantasy <u>and</u> an action/adventure as well as a romance <u>and</u> coming-of-age film story. 2005's **WALK THE LINE** is a drama and a bio-pic <u>and</u> a romance and features music. Most film-goers will choose the film they wish to view by its genre. Each genre has certain inherent elements and audiences will consciously or unconsciously have certain expectations. An audience paying to see **WALK THE LINE** will be disappointed if Johnny Cash's music is not featured; an audience attending **SPIDERMAN** will be expecting special effects and action sequences and will feel cheated if the film does not fulfill those expectations.

What is the overriding genre in your film story? What genres are introduced in the supporting stories? (Chapter 4 explores, in depth, the expectations of various genres.)

2. Is your story irreverent, serious, sarcastic, ironic, dark or light in tone?

Most films will strive to stay consistent in tone. A dark, "R" rated comedy might have edgier characters, locations and plot points than a "G" or "PG" rated film story written to appeal to a family audience. Dramas that appeal to older, conservative women's groups will not, in most cases, explore violent themes with tongue-in-cheek irony. Dramas that appeal to college students may employ sarcasm, irony and dark themes. Consider three of 2006's well-received films in the dramatic genre; each employs a different tone: *THE DEPARTED* is edgy and violent. *THE QUEEN* has a reflective and controlled tone. *MISS POTTER* employs a softer, romantic, and quietly determined tone.

Some writers are chameleons and are adept at writing scripts in various tones. Other writers choose to stick to the one tone in which they feel most comfortable and make a name for themselves in the industry as an "edgy" drama writer or as a "family action-adventure drama" writer – or whatever tone (and genre) they choose to master.

3. What story are you telling? Can you focus it into a logline?

Logline example: THE GODFATHER is a drama about Michael, the resourceful and determined son of a powerful Mafia leader who wants to break away from his family to live a legitimate "American Dream." When rival mob families attempt to murder his father and his family comes under attack, Michael goes on a violent journey to discover that family honor outweighs his desire for legitimacy.

Exercise:

Fill in the details of your film story into this template: (NAME OF FILM STORY) is a (GENRE) about (NAME OF PROTAGONIST AND TWO ADJECTIVES OR SHORT PHRASES THAT DESCRIBE HIM/HER) who wants (IMMEDIATE GOAL). When (PLOT POINT) and (ANOTHER PLOT POINT) happen, (NAME OF CHARACTER) goes on a journey to discover (THE THEME). THE THEME IS WHAT THE PROTAGONIST COMES TO REALIZE OR LEARN THAT RELATES TO HIS/HER OVERALL WANT.

By filling in the details of your story into the logline template, you will be forced to focus your story on its basic components. After you have polished your logline, adjust it to reflect the tone of your story (if it's a comedy – let the logline reflect that, if it's ironic – let the logline reflect that…). Let your logline reflect your personal style.

4. What is the Dramatic Question of your story?

The dramatic question of **WALK THE LINE** is: Will Johnny Cash win June Carter's trust and love before he self-destructs? The dramatic question of 2005's **BROKEBACK MOUNTAIN** is: Can the love of these two men triumph in a world full of prejudice? The dramatic question of 2006's **CHILDREN OF MEN** is: Can Theo retain his faith in humankind and save the future? The dramatic question of 2007's **BOURNE ULTIMATUM** is: Will Jason Bourne find the genesis of his training and expose government corruption?

Exercise:

Write the dramatic question of your story. Keep it focused on your protagonist and on the main question you are exploring. If this is difficult, or if you have a run-on question that includes too many disparate elements, you may want to look at your story and ask if you are trying to explore too many story ideas.

5. Is there a strong Beginning, stronger Middle and resonating End?

Do the character stories, especially the protagonist's story, constantly move forward? Do the main characters stories have clear turning points? Is the plot always moving forward? Does the plot have clear turning points? See Chapter __ on PLOT to take a closer look at strengthening the events in your story.

6. Is your protagonist driving the story? Is the antagonist a strong and present force?

Make sure your protagonist is making choices and is staying active. Make sure your protagonist is at the center of the story. Check your script to make sure the antagonist is a constant force, mentally or physically – or both.

7. Does your protagonist change as the story progresses?

What changes in your protagonist's life? His moral center? His beliefs? His

Definitions:
DRAMATIC QUESTION: The main question posed by the plot of the story as it affects the protagonist.

PLOT: The sequence of events that move the main characters on the journey towards attaining their overall wants and goals.

PROTAGONIST: The main character that the audience invests in emotionally as he strives towards his goal. The character that changes or causes the most change in the story.

ANTAGONIST: The character that gets in the way of the protagonist achieving his or her goal.

connections with people? His job? His ability to commit or disconnect? His view of the world?

Exercise:

Fill in the blanks and then adjust the short paragraph below to reflect your story.

The main character NAME, in this GENRE begins as a _____ and _____ person. He/She ends the story having learned _____ and is forever changed. He/She is now _____ and will live his/her life _____.

Consider how those blanks can be filled in for protagonist, Miles, in 2005's **SIDEWAYS:** The main character, Miles, in this dark comedy, begins as a depressed, angry, stalled man who fears risk-taking. Miles ends the story having learned that he can't live in the past – that risk in love and life is necessary – and he is forever changed. He is now able to put his past behind him and move forward, with hope, into the future.

Exercise:

Chart your protagonist's change from the beginning of the film to the midpoint and to the end of the film story.

Example: This charts the protagonist's journey in 2005's SIDEWAYS.

BEGINNING: Miles is lying to himself and all he meets as he starts on his journey.

MIDDLE: Miles sees the possibilities of the future, but his lies and low self-esteem stand in his way

END: Miles accepts and tells the truth and is able to take the first steps to move on in life.

8. Do all your "B" and "C" stories concern or affect the "A" story of the protagonist?

"B" and "C" stories are fantastic storytelling tools, they can help fill out the life of the protagonist, advance character, reveal theme or give you an opportunity to add a supporting genre to balance out the over-riding genre. Make sure all your supporting stories reflect or affect the protagonist's story.

9. Is your Theme resonating throughout the story?

Audiences or script readers may identify different themes in the same film story because the story will affect each individual in a singular fashion. But it is important for the writer to personally identify an overriding theme in his script.

Examples: A theme of 2007's dumber-than-dumb comedy **BLADES OF GLORY** could be: Without learning to work together, true greatness can not be accomplished. A theme for 2006's Academy Award nominated **CHILDREN OF MEN** could be: Without hope, mankind cannot survive. A theme for 2000's **GLADIATOR** could be: Without facing one's demons, there can be no peace.

Definitions:

THEME: The unifying moral or emotional truth or hypothesis the writer is exploring. Theme usually relates to the main character's revelation about life – or about himself.

AUTHOR'S POINT OF VIEW: The screenwriter's commitment to exploring an underlying truth or world as he sees it..

Exercise:

Fill in the blanks and commit to the theme of your story.

Use the template: Without _____ there can be no _____. Once you have filled in the blanks, ask yourself if your theme is something you personally believe. Can you embrace the truth of the statement and prove it in your story?

10. Is the Author's Point of View clear?

This is your point of view, your bias on the actions of the characters, your sense of what is right or wrong or good or bad or acceptable or unacceptable. A screenwriter needs to commit to a point of view. Do you feel that love is worth dying for? Do you feel that patriotism is good? Do you feel that the world is corrupt but there is hope for the future? Do you feel the existence of true love is bogus and a only a product of advertising? Do you think there is nothing worth the sacrifice of your existence? Any point of view is valid; it is your point of view.

Post your genres and tone, main characters arcs, theme and point of view near your workstation. Use them as a reminder of the basics of your story. Your task is to make sure you have explored various ways of illuminating your main character – and to make sure your supporting stories serve as a mirror of your main character's change and that your theme and point of view resonates.

The story is built around characters

The screen story should be built around a protagonist in whom the audience can invest sympathy and/or empathy. The protagonist should face obstacles that loom large in his life. A strong antagonist should stand in the protagonist's way and try (for selfish or evil or well-meaning reasons) to keep the protagonist from achieving his goal.

Before you worry about page count or final format check, make sure your screen story is working at capacity.

The easiest way to approach the script into which you have just poured your heart and soul is to simply investigate it rationally. Take the emotions out of it for a week.

Commit to focusing on the craft of screenwriting.

Some technical things to do

1. Make a hard copy of your latest draft. Use a marker to highlight each scene's slug line.

2. Count the number of scenes in your script. Technically, a new scene begins every time a location – or time of day – changes.

3. Write the total number of scenes in your script on the top of a sheet of paper. The number of scenes doesn't really matter (remember, every script will have its own rhythm, pacing and style) but this count will help you assess the balance of your script.

4. Count the number of scenes in which your protagonist appears. Make a note of this on your sheet of paper.

5. Count the number of scenes in which your antagonist appears. Make a note of it.

6. Calculate the percentage of scenes in your script that include your protagonist. Do the same for the antagonist.

Example:

Total number of scenes in screenplay	*= 96*
Number of scenes in which protagonist appears	*= 84*
Number of scenes in which antagonist appears	*= 60*

In this equation, the protagonist is in 90% of the scenes. The antagonist is in just under half of the total number of scenes. What is the optimal percentage? Unfortunately (actually – fortunately) there is no perfect equation for a perfect balance. This exercise is a tool to illuminate the balance and focus of your script. If your protagonist is in less than 85% percent of the scenes, ask yourself if you have inadvertently allowed a "B" story or supporting character to grab the focus of the story? Ask yourself if your protagonist is active enough? Are things happening <u>to him</u> and not <u>because of him?</u> Is your protagonist driving the story?

Again, there is no perfect percentage related to the antagonist's amount of screen time. However, if your antagonist is not in at least half of the scenes of the film story, ask yourself if the character is working at capacity.

MORE THINGS TO THINK ABOUT

Your style of storytelling

There are many ways to tell a story, but let us concentrate on two of the most common – the <u>closed style</u> and the <u>open style</u> of storytelling. This refers to how the story is told – through the experiences of one or two characters or through the omniscient view of the storyteller. In most cases, you want to make sure your script is one or the other. This is a technical check; you will want to look at every scene in your script.

The Closed Story

Many film stories are told through the experiences of the protagonist. <u>The audience does not know anything the protagonist does not know.</u> The audience learns and is able to piece together story points (elements of plot, character motivations, clues, repercussions of events) as the protagonist puts them together. This is sometimes referred to as the "first person point of view." The audience's judgment of events and supporting characters will be influenced by the point of view of the protagonist.

The horror film, 1968's ***ROSEMARY'S BABY***, is clearly Rosemary's story. Rosemary (portrayed by Mia Farrow) wants the perfect life – a successful loving husband, a fabulous NYC apartment and a child. The screenwriter puts Rosemary in nearly 100% percentage of the scenes and the audience experiences the story through her eyes. All the supporting stories are focused on Rosemary and her desire for a child, her fertility and, ultimately, her pregnancy. Her husband (portrayed by John Cassavetes), the man who loses his soul in the story, does not appear in scenes where Rosemary is not present. The Satanists (portrayed by Ruth Gordon and Sidney Blackmer) are in only a few scenes sans Rosemary; notably a scene where they witness the aftermath of a young woman's suicide. This suicide focuses more of their attention on Rosemary. Their supporting story serves up plot points that force a stronger focus on Rosemary as the center of the film – and as the person through whom the audience experiences the story.

GOOD WILL HUNTING (1997) Minnie Driver, Matt Damon, Ben Affleck
- photo courtesy of Globe Photos

Protagonist Jake Gittes (portrayed by Jack Nicholson), in 1974's ***CHINATOWN*** is in over 95% of the scenes. The audience comes to understand the vagaries of the murder mystery and the family secrets of incest through his eyes. ***CHINATOWN*** is an excellent example of <u>closed</u> storytelling.

Consider 1997's **GOOD WILL HUNTING**. Will (portrayed by Matt Damon) drives the film; the world is seen through his eyes. It's Will's apartment, Will's view of the arrogant Harvard students, and Will's view of the court system, the psychiatrists, the Harvard math program, his love interest, and the business world that wants to possess his talents. Will is in over 90% of the scenes and the audience learns of events as he does.

2006's **MISS POTTER:** the character of Beatrix Potter is in nearly 98% of the scenes of the film; the audience experiences events as she does.

2006's **PURSUIT OF HAPPYNESS**: the character of Chris Gardner is involved in nearly 98% the film, the audience experiences events as he does.

2006's **CHILDREN OF MEN,** the protagonist, Theo (portrayed by Clive Owen), is in nearly 100% of the scenes in the film. His through-line is clear; he has lost a child and that emotional loss, added to the fetid state of the world, has destroyed his marriage. He longs for a sense of family – and specifically for his dead child. All the scenes in the film support Theo's story. It's through his eyes that we come to realize the first tragedy of the film; the youngest person in the society has just died and the future of the human race is now in greater jeopardy. Theo visits his friend, Jasper (portrayed by Michael Caine) and laments the loss of human connection. When Theo's ex-wife abducts him, it is clear Theo wants their old life back. He can't understand how his wife can get over the death of their child and concentrate only on politics. When Theo is given the task of protecting the only pregnant woman in the society, his task resonates on many levels. Theo delivers the baby and gives his own life to ensure the baby's safety. The audience experiences the story as Theo experiences it.

2006's **BLOOD DIAMOND** allows the audience into two worlds, those of the protagonist, smuggler Danny Archer (portrayed by Leonardo DiCaprio) and the main supporting character, South African worker and eventual prisoner Solomon Vandy (portrayed by Djimon Hounsou). The audience experiences the story through the eyes of these two characters and when their lives intersect, Danny's story and experiences take precedence.

When two characters share a film story

1967's *IN THE HEAT OF THE NIGHT,* 1987's *LETHAL WEAPON,* 1989's *WHEN HARRY MET SALLY,* 1993's *SLEEPLESS IN SEATTLE* and 2006's *NOTES ON A SCANDAL* are strong examples of films that feature two

Question: What if I am writing a story that equally tracks two protagonists?

Answer: Consider 2006's THE QUEEN. This is a story of two protagonists dealing with repercussions of Princess Diana's death. The structure is interesting because each serves as the other's antagonist. Queen Elizabeth (portrayed by Helen Mirren) clearly wants the Royal Family to deal with Diana's death in a private manner. Tony Blair (portrayed by Michael Sheen) is convinced that the Royal Family (specifically the Queen) needs to connect with the British people's grief so the country can heal from the tragedy. One of the two main characters is in nearly every scene – and the film is at its best when they share the screen.

IN THE HEAT OF THE NIGHT (1967) Sidney Poitier, Rod Steiger
- *photo courtesy of Globe Photos*

strong characters, each with a full individual journey. It's a good idea to view the films or read the scripts of the film stories closest to your project to learn more about the craft of screenwriting.

WHEN HARRY MET SALLY: This very smart romantic comedy features two characters, Harry (portrayed by Billy Crystal) and Sally (portrayed by Meg Ryan), in the classic boy meets girl, boy gets girl, boy loses girl, boy has to get girl back scenario. However, a twist is added – boy and girl become best friends. The audience experiences the story through their experiences, either individually (with friends) or together (with each other). Note how the supporting stories focus on what is happening to the relationship of Harry and Sally.

NOTES ON A SCANDAL: Selfish and manipulative Barbara (portrayed by Judi Dench) and naïve, restless Sheba (portrayed by Cate Blanchett) share this film. Each has strong back-stories and active scenes that focus on each of their lives. One or the other main character is always on screen. Each scene furthers the tension of their relationship. The film is at its best when the two women are on screen together, (approximately 75% of the story). Note how the screenwriter does not take us into the life of Sheba's husband or the life of her high school lover or the lives of the teachers in the school– the knowledge of their lives is revealed only as it relates to the stories of Sheba and Barbara.

Exercise:

> Check your script. If you are embracing a Closed Story structure, make sure all scenes are structured to feature your protagonist and that all scenes are structured so that the audience learns of events through his eyes only. If you have designed a story where two main characters serve as the base of your closed story, make sure all the scenes are structured so that the audience learns of events through their eyes only.

Some film stories may feature a secondary character telling the main character's story. This is also a closed story; everything that happens in the story must be seen or experienced by the character that is telling the story. The audience's judgment of events and supporting characters will be influenced by the point of view of the storyteller.

The Open Story

Many films are told in the open style, with an omniscient storyteller. This style features the strong protagonist and concentrates on the particular journey of the protagonist, but allows the screenwriter to cut between characters and locations and follow the events in various characters' lives that will affect the protagonist. This can be referred to as "third person" storytelling. The screenwriter is able to explore the inner thoughts and motivations of several characters.

The romantic drama, 1942's *CASABLANCA*, is clearly Rick's story but the audience is privy to private moments in other characters' lives that affect Rick's story. Rick (portrayed by Humphrey Bogart) owns a nightclub in the North Africa town of Casablanca. Although Rick was once a political activist in Paris, he now refuses to take sides in the war; Allies and Germans are both accepted in Rick's nightclub. Political refugees also fill Rick's club, all hoping to obtain exit visas to escape the war's oppression. Rick is in nearly 90% percentage of the scenes of the film. The screenwriters made sure the supporting stories illuminate Rick's character or revolve around him. Ilsa (portrayed by Ingrid Bergman) appears in only a few scenes where Rick is not physically present and those scenes are focused on Rick — she continually asks — what does Rick think? Where is Rick? What will Rick do? Ilsa's husband, Laszlo (portrayed by Paul Heinreid) has a political agenda; however, it is explored only as it relates to Rick's lack of commitment to a cause. Captain Renault (portrayed by Claude Rains) is a pivotal character that is focused on trying to understand and predict Rick's actions. The opening sequence sets up the world and the inciting incident of the story – all constructed to make Rick's entrance <u>important</u>; everyone wants to know where Rick is, what Rick will do, what will Rick think of the events unfolding – and most importantly, as the story moves forward, what will Rick decide to do with the letters of transport he has agreed to hide? However, note how the screenwriters have <u>opened</u> the world – the audience is privy to scenes between Captain Renault and the Germans, to scenes between Ilsa and her husband Laszlo, to scenes where desperate characters attempt to gain the transit papers that will get them out of Casablanca. *CASABLANCA* is an example of an open story.

GHOSTBUSTERS (1984) Bill Murray, Dan Aykroyd, Harold Ramis
- photo courtesy of Globe Photos

The protagonist of 1984's *GHOSTBUSTERS* is Dr. Peter Venkman (portrayed by Bill Murray). He drives the story, he is the one who gets his pals fired from the University, he heads up the Ghostbusters team, he is the one who falls in love. Peter is featured in approximately 75% of the scenes. This may seem low, but note how every scene that does not feature Peter increases the problems Peter will have to eventually face. Using the omniscient style, the screenwriter can open his story to the audience – <u>so the audience knows more than the protagonist.</u> In *GHOSTBUSTERS*, the audience gets to know Peter's love interest, Dana (portrayed by Sigourney

Weaver), witness her home life, meet her the neighbor who has a crush on her, Louis (portrayed by Rick Moranis), and see Dana's possession (and Louis' possession) by the demon. The audience knows that Peter's romantic interest and his professional interest will eventually be affected by the demon possessions. The audience sees the hiring of Winston (portrayed by Ernie Hudson), some of the scientific trials by Peter's partners (portrayed by Dan Aykroyd and Harold Ramis), the machinations of the antagonist Walter Peck (portrayed by William Atherton) and the emotional life of the secretary (portrayed by Annie Potts). The plot points in these supporting stories put Peter in more jeopardy – and the audience enjoys waiting to see how Peter will react to the repercussions of each new event.

1997's *TITANIC:* The audience experiences the film story in the omniscient style – as a voyeur. Each character is carefully set up. Jack (portrayed by Leonardo DiCaprio) has his story; he wins passage on the ship in a poker game, he has dreams to make a new life for himself in America and falls in love with a socialite, Rose, on the ship. Rose (portrayed by Kate Winslett) has her story; she has a controlling mother (portrayed by Frances Farmer) who wants her to marry for money. Rose's controlling fiancé (portrayed by Billy Zane) has a mean streak and considers Rose his possession. The screenwriter gives these antagonists their scenes – alone and together – where they plot to control Rose. There are also "B" stories that have individual arcs; newly-rich Molly Brown (portrayed by Kathy Bates) gains respect, ship designer Thomas Andrews (portrayed by Victor Garber) falls into despair as his ship goes down.

2003's *PIRATES OF THE CARIBBEAN, CURSE OF THE BLACK PEARL* is also told in the open style. Elizabeth (portrayed by Keira Knightly) is in approximately 70% of the scenes; Will Turner (portrayed by Orlando Bloom) is in approximately 55% of the scenes. Jack Sparrow (portrayed by Johnny Depp) is in approximately 60% of the scenes. This is a film that strives to balance three characters and their individual stories; but it is Elizabeth's story that remains most prominent. Act One introduces each character individually. When Act Two kicks into gear, the three main characters find themselves in close proximity and their stories directly affect one another. The audience understands each of their aims and enjoys the anticipation of their stories intersecting.

Question: What about films that feature parallel stories of two main characters?

Answer: 2006's **THE DEPARTED** follows parallel stories of two cops; one corrupt, one not. They are both undercover in their individual situations. Both try to appear to be something they are not. They both embody classic protagonist story elements – strong overall wants, strong back stories, antagonistic forces, adversity, challenges, a chance at love (with the same woman) crises and climaxes. Their stories do not directly intersect until Act Three, but they become aware of the other in Act Two and affect each other's stories. Each story takes up nearly equal percentage of screen time and is at its best when the two main characters are in direct conflict. **THE DEPARTED** also follows the story of Frank Costello, the head of the Irish gang. The audience is privy to his plans, his desires and elements in his life.

Exercise:

Go through your script – if you can flesh out main supporting characters without taking the focus from the protagonist's story, put in the time to do it. Your script will be richer and you will be able to attract actors that relish playing well-drawn supporting characters.

Both the closed and open styles of storytelling are valid and both work well. Make sure you know which you are using. The balance of a story can be thrown out of whack if the audience becomes accustomed to a closed style and then suddenly a scene or sequence takes them out of the protagonist's point of view. The balance of a story can also be thrown off if the audience has become accustomed to the open style and then the screenwriter fails to track the events and characters as they affect the protagonist's story.

CHAPTER SUMMARY

- Approaching the rewrite of your screenplay from a technical aspect can help identify the strengths and possible weaknesses in your story.

- The protagonist needs to drive the story. His journey will be clearer if there is a definite beginning, middle and end.

- Balance is important in your script. Balance the "A" and "B" and "C" stories as well as characters and supporting characters and genres.

- A closed story is told from the protagonist's vantage point.

- An open story is told from an omniscient vantage point.

Chapter Four

GENRE EXPECTATIONS

A film-goer, searching the internet or newspaper for what is playing at the local Cineplex or choosing the film to watch on the home television or computer, will consciously or unconsciously, choose to view a film that reflects his or her favorite genre. That film-goer will <u>expect certain genre criteria to be met,</u> and if the criteria are not met, he may feel dissatisfaction and disappointment. Therefore, the screenwriter must find ways to fulfill all the basic elements of his chosen genres in order to satisfy the audience – and then surpass audience expectations to achieve the greatest story success.

A list of the most common genres

Action	Horror
Adventure	Musical
Buddy	Period
Biography	Mystery
Comedy	Romance
Coming of Age	Science Fiction
Crime	Thriller
Drama	Western
Dumber than Dumb	War
Epic	Historical
Film Noir	Satire
Fantasy	Farce
Disaster	Fish Out Of Water
Sports	Road

Question: Is it a good idea to try to fit a screen story into one specific genre?

Answer: No. Most films are genre hybrids and employing just one genre might cause your film story to lack dimensionality. However, it is a good idea to understand the basic elements of your overriding genre so that you can satisfy the expectations of the audience.

Most films will have an "over-riding" genre that sits clearly in the "A" story of the film, the story that relays the primary journey of the protagonist. The supporting stories that help illuminate the protagonist's journey, the "B" stories, may sit in another genre altogether and in most cases – this is a very good idea. In the rewrite phase, a screenwriter should know how to assess the <u>balance</u> of genres in his screenplay to technically approach an evaluation and enhancement of his creative work.

Remember that most movies are a combination of genres

CASABLANCA (1942) Romance/Drama/War/Historical

SUNSET BOULEVARD (1950) Drama/Coming of Age/Romance/Crime

SHANE (1953) Western/Drama

SPARTACUS (1960) Drama/Period/Historical/Coming of Age

TOOTSIE (1982) Comedy/Romance

BACK TO THE FUTURE (1985) Sci-Fi/Action-Adventure/Coming-of-Age/Comedy

BEAUTY AND THE BEAST (1991) Animation/Fantasy/Romance

MEN IN BLACK (1997) Action/Comedy/Buddy/Science Fiction

SHALLOW HAL (2001) Dumber Than Dumb/Romance/Comedy

TRAINING DAY (2001) Buddy/Action/Crime/Drama

LEGALLY BLONDE (2001) Comedy/Fish Out Of Water/Romance

SHREK (2001) Comedy/Romance/Satire

ADAPTATION (2002) Drama/Coming of Age

TROY (2004) Historical/Biography/Adventure/War/Romance/Drama

MILLION DOLLAR BABY (2004) Drama/Sports

MEAN GIRLS (2004) Teen/Coming-of-Age/Drama

FANTASTIC FOUR (2005) Sci-Fi/Crime/Drama/Romance

SIDEWAYS (2005) Buddy/Comedy/Romance

THE QUEEN (2006) Historical/Drama

LITTLE MISS SUNSHINE (2006) Comedy/Drama

300 (2007) Action/Drama/History/War

HAIRSPRAY (2007) Musical/Comedy/Period

YOU KILL ME (2007) Drama/Romance/Coming-of-Age/Satire/Crime

THE GOLDEN COMPASS (2007) Fantasy/Drama/Coming of Age

One of two genres, drama or comedy, form the base of most stories.

In general terms, the drama genre explores its subject matter in a more emotionally realistic and serious manner. Drama investigates human frailties, disappointments, lost hopes and dreams and tragedies of life. The story revolves around an everyday, normal person; the everyman or the everywoman. In order for the story to be deemed dramatic, the everyman protagonist must want to accomplish his goal in an overpowering, all-consuming way. The possibility of failure must be real and the consequences of failure must be of great significance.

Comedy, generally, explores its subject matter in a more emotionally exaggerated and/or light-hearted manner. Characters in comedies may be a bit off center or have exaggerated personalities; they may be too intense, too romantic, too nervous, too passive, too aggressive, too social, too anti-social, too smart, and too insecure. A sense of absurdity that will tickle the audience's funny bone can be employed to good use. Comedy can (and should) also explore deep feelings, deep needs and deep desires; the protagonist must want what he wants in an all-consuming way. However, for the story to be deemed comedic, the methods and attitude of the protagonist need to illicit a humorous response.

It's clear the subject matter of a film can be handled in various ways. Consider four films revolving around the world of soccer; 2007's family drama *GRACIE*, 2005's broad comedy *KICKING AND SCREAMING*, 2002's coming-of-age drama/romance *BEND IT LIKE BECKHAM*, and 2001's action/comedy/martial arts film *SHAOLIN SOCCER*. The genres you have chosen will appeal to specific audiences. Be clear about your over-riding genre and the supporting genres you are using in your screenplay; commit to them and satisfy the criteria that make up each genre.

Caution: If you straddle the fence too much and try to hit too many core audiences by hitting too many genres, your story may be unfocused and fail to attract anyone.

There's no definite guideline to help determine how many genres are too

Question: What if I have both dramatic and comedic elements in my script?

Answer: You should know the over-riding base genre. In many dramas, characters can employ a humorous turn of phrase or the story could contain an action sequence meant to illicit a chuckle, but the story is still based in the drama genre. 2006's **THE DEPARTED** often breaks the tension of the story with humor, but the film is based in the drama genre.

There is "dram-edy"; a combination of drama and comedy with more emphasis on the drama. There is also the "comedy-drama" with more emphasis on the comedy. These hybrids can work well, but you must commit to fulfilling the criteria of the strongest genre. Know which genre base takes precedence in your story. If you don't, the audience may not be able to jump on board the story train.

many genres in one script. However, you can check out the balance of the genres in your story and come to a personal conclusion concerning which genre choices aid you in telling the story you have set out to tell – and which genres may be added – or which genres may be extraneous.

Remember, it's your story. Your personal style of storytelling is what will make your script stand out.

Make sure you have fulfilled the elements in your over-riding genre

Let's first look at the comedy genre and the genres that are most often matched with comedy.

COMEDY

Characters in comedies may be a bit off center or have exaggerated personalities; they may be <u>too</u> intense, <u>too</u> romantic, <u>too</u> nervous, <u>too</u> passive, <u>too</u> aggressive, <u>too</u> social, <u>too</u> anti-social, <u>too</u> smart, <u>too</u> insecure (and so on). In most cases, the situations in which the characters find themselves are also heightened to gain comic effect. There are juxtapositions of scenes that keep the characters off-guard. The author can play with a sense of absurdity or adjust the level of reality.

 If you are working on a comedy script, have you explored all elements in your script to make sure they are pushed to just the right comic level?

There are dumber-than-dumb comedies (the film tradition goes back to Keystone Kops, W.C. Fields, the Marx Brothers). The comedy is broad and catches the audience off guard with its physical and verbal humor. Take a look at the work of these screenwriters: Mel Brooks (*BLAZING SADDLES, HIGH ANXIETY, ROBIN HOOD MEN IN TIGHTS*), the early work of Woody Allen (*BANANAS, SLEEPER),* Harold Ramis and Douglas Kenney (*ANIMAL HOUSE, CADDYSHACK)* Jim Abrahams and David Zucker (*AIRPLANE),* Peter and Bobby Farrelly (*DUMB AND DUMBER, SHALLOW HAL)* and Christopher Guest and Eugene Levy (*BEST IN SHOW, WAITING FOR GUFFMAN).* 2006's *BORAT*, written by Sacha Baron Cohen and Anthony Hines, is a good example how the dumber-than-dumb comedy genre can be lifted into political satire and employ a strong author's point of view.

There are more reality-based comedies; consider the work of screenwriters

Robert Riskin *(IT HAPPENED ONE NIGHT, MR. DEEDS GOES TO TOWN)*, James Brooks *(AS GOOD AS IT GETS, STARTING OVER, BROADCAST NEWS)*, the later work of Woody Allen *(ANNIE HALL, A MIDSUMMER NIGHT'S SEX COMEDY)*, Larry Gelbart *(OH GOD!, TOOTSIE)* Richard Curtis *(FOUR WEDDINGS AND A FUNERAL)*, Leslie Dixon *(OUTRAGEOUS FORTUNE)*, Elaine May *(HEAVEN CAN WAIT, A NEW LEAF)* and the many films penned by Neil Simon. The characters in these comedies exist in a real world but confront outrageous or out-of-character situations. The characters are relatable, but also have comedic quirks reinforced through comedic exaggeration.

There are black comedies; comedies that take a poke at politics, mores, ethics or the world in which the comedic characters inhabit. Serious plot points and themes are massaged and turned upside down for comedic effect. Consider 1964's political satire **DR. STRANGELOVE** and 1971's coming-of-age black comedy **HAROLD AND MAUDE** and 2007's dark romantic comedy **YOU KILL ME.** Dark comedies and satires engage the audience through laughter but also hope to make the audience consider the world in a new way.

In each genre and genre hybrid, I have listed examples of film stories that can be read or viewed for inspiration. You will see that a few films are on two or more lists – they may successfully fulfill the criteria of several genres. If, in your rewrite, you want to expand your exploration of a certain story line in your screenplay, identify the genre of that story line and read or view the films listed in that genre.

Listed below are successful comedies. Which of the films listed are closest to your story in tone and character? Study these films; be inspired by their strengths.

DUCK SOUP (1927) written by Arthur J. Jefferson and H.M. Walker

A NIGHT AT THE OPERA (1935) written by George S. Kaufman, story by James Kevin McGuinness

SOME LIKE IT HOT (1959) written by Robert Thoeren and Michael Logan

DR. STRANGELOVE (1964) written by Stanley Kubrick and Terry Southern and Peter George, based on the novel by Peter George

ODD COUPLE (1968) written by Neil Simon

HAROLD AND MAUDE (1971) written by Colin Higgins

YOUNG FRANKENSTEIN (1974) written by Gene Wilder

9 TO 5 (1980) written by Patricia Resnick and Colin Higgins, story by Patricia Resnick

FAST TIMES AT RIDGEMONT HIGH (1982) written by Cameron Crowe

A FISH CALLED WANDA (1988) written by John Cleese and Charles Crichton

MRS. DOUBTFIRE (1993) written by Randi Mayem Singer and Leslie Dixon, based on the novel by Anne Fine

THE FULL MONTY (1997) written by Simon Beaufoy

SHREK (2001) written by Ted Elliott and Terry Rossio and Joe Stillman and Roger S.H. Schulman; based on the book by William Steig

LEGALLY BLONDE (2001) written by Karen McCullah Lutz and Kirsten Smith, based on the novel by Amanda Brown

SCHOOL OF ROCK (2003) written by Mike White

NAPOLEON DYNAMITE (2004) written by Jared and Jerusha Hess

KICKING AND SCREAMING (2005) written by Leo Benvenuti and Steve Rudnick

BLADES OF GLORY (2007) written by Jeff Cox & Craig Cox and John Altsculer & Dave Krinsky

SUPERBAD (2007) written by Seth Rogen and Evan Goldberg

* Note how many of these comedies embrace a coming-of-age element.

COMEDY/ACTION

Stories in this genre must contain basic tenets of comedy as well as employ the criteria of the <u>action</u> genre. The action genre demands sequences featuring the protagonist in a physical and moral interplay between good and bad forces. The action genre will use combat, stunts, car chases, explosions and other physical feats; therefore, the story must support the <u>need</u> for physical challenges. The physical action needs to be integral to the story – it must <u>advance</u> the story. Random action sequences that are designed just to use special effects or to wow an audience with physical feats or camera moves, can slow down your film and put you in danger of losing your audience.

If you are writing in this genre combination, take a look at your script. Make sure the character arc and plot live in the heightened, exaggerated (slightly or greatly) comedic world. Then look at the elements that support the action genre. Do you have enough physical scenes? Have you found the most original action sequences? Consider how location, props, vehicles, natural and unnatural physical obstacles can be used for more outrageous and singular comedic chases or comedic battles – the "set pieces" of your film.

Important questions: Is your protagonist involved in the action sequences? Do the action sequences allow for your protagonist's comedic turns? Do the action sequences contribute to the protagonist's change and growth? Have you committed to the "moral" interplay between the good and bad forces? Is it absolutely clear how the action sequences move the protagonist's story forward?

Because it is important to set up your over-riding genre at or near the beginning of your film, many action films will open with a rock'em-sock'em action sequence. In many cases, this falls flat because the audience is not yet invested in <u>character</u>. If you are convinced your script should start with an action sequence, consider making it short (one to one and half pages) – or better yet – make sure the sequence <u>clearly</u> reveals your protagonist <u>and</u> his desires while the action is progressing.

Listed below are successful comedy/action films. Which of the films listed are closest to your story in tone and character? Study these films; be inspired by their strengths.

THE GENERAL (1927) written by Clyde Bruckman, Al Boasberg and Buster Keaton

CHARADE (1963) written by Peter Stone

SMOKEY AND THE BANDIT (1977) written by Hal Needham and Robert L. Levy

CADDYSHACK (1980) written by Brian Doyle-Murray and Harold Ramis

GHOSTBUSTERS (1984) written by Dan Aykroyd and Harold Ramis

Question: How many action sequences should be in an action film?

Answer: There are no rules. However, a story development person may point to the "triad theory," that all things are better in "threes." If you want your script to fit into the action genre, check to see if you have at least three strong action sequences in your film story.

Definition: **"Set piece"** is the term used to describe action sequences that are large and prolonged and accelerate in physical difficulty.

BACK TO THE FUTURE (1985) written by Robert Zemeckis and Bob Gale

BEVERLY HILLS COP (1984) written by Danilo Bach and Daniel Petrie Jr.

FARGO (1996) written by Joel and Ethan Coen

MEN IN BLACK (1997) written by Lowell Cunningham and Ed Solomon

RUSH HOUR (1998) written by Ross LaManna and Jim Kouf

GALAXY QUEST (1999) written by David Howard

O BROTHER, WHERE ART THOU? (2000) written by Ethan Coen

KUNG FU HUSTLE (2004) written by Stephen Chow and Xin Huo

HOUSE OF FURY (2005) written by Stephen Fung and Yui Fai Lo

BANDIDAS (2006) written by Luc Besson and Robert Mark Kamen

COMEDY/ADVENTURE

Adventure is the search or the quest for something that seems unattainable. The goal of the adventure could be a treasure (consider the *INDIANA JONES* films) or a political ideal *(THE ADVENTURES OF ROBIN HOOD)* or search for sense of self *(ALICE IN WONDERLAND)* or any quest that, when taken on, will force the protagonist into physical situations and mental challenges that test every fiber of his being.

The most important element in your script is still the strong character arc. Millions of chases and special effects will not make for a successful film story; the focus on a character's personal journey is still of utmost importance.

Take a look at your script. Is the reason your protagonist goes on an adventure quest strong enough? Will the success or failure of the quest change your protagonist's life forever? Have you taken time to set up the main character before propelling her on the journey so the audience cares about the outcome? The adventure genre often works well with the action genre. If you are using an action sequence, ask yourself if you have found the most original action sequences. Are they designed to get your protagonist closer to the treasure or reason for the adventure quest? Are your characters still at the forefront? Do the action sequences allow for the character's overall want to remain clear?

Listed below are successful comedy/action/adventure films. Which of the films listed are closest to your story in tone and character? Study these films; be inspired by their strengths.

ROMANCING THE STONE (1984) written by Diane Thomas

THE PRINCESS BRIDE (1987) written by William Goldman

MIDNIGHT RUN (1988) written by George Gallo

SHANGHAI NOON (2000) written by Miles Millar and Alfred Gough

EMPEROR'S NEW GROOVE (2000) written by David Reynolds, story by Chris Williams and Mark Dindal and Roger Allers and Matthew Jacobs

MONSTERS INC (2001) written by Andrew Stanton, Daniel Gerson, Robert L. Baird, Rhett Reese, Jonathan Roberts, story by Peter Docter, Jill Culton, Jeff Pidgeon and Ralph Eggleston

FINDING NEMO (2003) written by Andrew Stanton, Bob Peterson and David Reynolds

PIRATES OF THE CARIBBEAN, CURSE OF THE BLACK PEARL (2003) written by Ted Elliott and Terry Rossio

NATIONAL TREASURE, BOOK OF SECRETS (2007) written by the Wibberlys

COMEDY/COMING OF AGE

This genre explores a character's reaching a new sense of self, maturity, respectability or prominence. The protagonist at the beginning of the story is, in most cases, in a quandary concerning his or her purpose in life. He may not understand <u>why</u> life is making its difficult demands. The protagonist could be exploring a moral dilemma, a crisis of self-identity, or ethical crisis. On the journey, the protagonist eventually experiences an epiphany and, in most cases, comes out with a stronger sense of purpose and identity.

The chronological age of the main character does not matter. He could be a teen or twenty-something or much older. It's the maturation, the new sense and understanding of self and purpose that is most important. One could argue that most films embrace the coming-of-age genre because characters, in good stories, change and grow.

Basic criteria of the coming of age film story: Examination of the unenlightened protagonist that includes a look at his normal life and the reasons he has not matured or gained a sense of self. The protagonist might desire a change but experience an inability to find the right path. The protagonist, given the chance to begin his metamorphosis, often may not recognize that this is the opportunity he needs. The character, usually in Act Two, gains new knowledge but rejects the new life it offers – usually out of fear of risk or because of commitments to others. The protagonist, usually in Act Three, has to dig deep and take an <u>emotional risk</u> to embrace a new maturity.

Check your script. Does your character start naïve and end wise? Or start jaded and become more able to embrace sentiment? Or does she start happy and end angry and disenchanted? This genre calls for a strong change in character, a gaining of knowledge of the world and – more importantly – knowledge of self.

COMEDY/ FISH-OUT-OF-WATER

One could argue that all films use elements of the fish-out-of-water genre. The name of the genre is self-explanatory: a protagonist, used to "swimming" in his normal life, is forced to learn how to survive in new surroundings. This genre demands that the writer first set up the "normal life" of the protagonist – if this is not accomplished, the reader/viewer will not understand the difficulties the protagonist faces in being a neophyte in a foreign territory. The learning process is paramount, and a perfect opportunity to create comedic situations. Remember, exaggeration is key. Is your character trying hard to learn, or trying hard <u>not</u> to learn?

Consider the story elements of *ALICE IN WONDERLAND.* Alice goes through the looking glass and finds herself in a mad, outlandish world. She must find her way out, but she cannot until she comes to an understanding of her world. *WIZARD OF OZ, TOOTSIE, MEN IN BLACK* and other films all fall into this genre combination.

Take a look at your script. Can you enhance or add elements to the new situation or territory or world your protagonist finds himself in Act Two? Can you increase the difficulty for your protagonist in understanding new situations or in becoming proficient in newly needed skills?

COMEDY/ROMANCE (ROMANTIC COMEDY)

Romance is key. The classic romance structure: Boy meets girl, boy wants girl, boy gets girl, boy loses girl, boy realizes his life is empty without girl, boy strives to get girl back, boy gets girl back (or not). If you have not addressed each element in the classic romance structure, you are in danger of not having your audience care about your lovers.

Comedy is, of course, necessary. However, to truly fall into the romantic comedy genre, the story needs to focus on the love elements. In most cases, the lovers are kept apart until the very end of the film story. In most cases, the two lovers do not appreciate each other at the outset of the film story. In most cases, both lovers have to change in order to make the romance work. If you are writing a romance and the lovers do not have trouble getting together, you may want to take another look and consider adjusting your script. If there is not comedy in the situations that keep the two lovers apart, you may want to take another look and consider adjusting your script.

Are the stakes high enough? Does the story concern <u>true</u> love? Flirtations and affairs, in most cases, <u>are not big enough canvasses</u> for the audience to invest their care and worry.

Variations on the classic structure are always fun. Consider 2004's *50 FIRST DATES* (boy meets girl, boy wants girl, boy gets girl, boy loses girl over and over and over due to her short term memory loss, boy realizes his life is empty without girl, boy has to cleverly strive to get girl back over and over again, boy gets girl (over and over and over again).

Which of the films below are closest to your story in tone and characters? Study their strong points.

IT HAPPENED ONE NIGHT (1934) written by Samuel Hopkins Adams and Robert Riskin

THE PHILADELPIA STORY (1940) written Donald Ogden Stewart, based on play by Philip Barry

THE LADY EVE (1941) written by Preston Sturges, story by Monckton Hoffee

THE APARTMENT (1960) written by Billy Wilder and I.A.L. Diamond

CHARADE (1963) written by Peter Stone

ANNIE HALL (1977) written by Woody Allen

VICTOR/VICTORIA (1982) written by Blake Edwards and Hans Hoemburg

SPLASH (1984) written by Brian Grazer and Bruce Jay Friedman

MOONSTRUCK (1987) written by John Patrick Shanley

THE PRINCESS BRIDE (1987) written by William Goldman

BULL DURHAM (1988) written by Ron Shelton

WHEN HARRY MET SALLY (1989) written by Nora Ephron

SOMETHING ABOUT MARY (1989) written by Ed Decter and John J. Strauss

SHAKESPEARE IN LOVE (1998) written by Marc Norman and Tom Stoppard

KISSING JESSICA STEIN (2001) written by Heather Juergensen and Jennifer Westfeldt

BRIDGET JONES'S DIARY (2001) written by Helen Fielding and Richard Curtis

50 FIRST DATES (2004) written by George Wing

MUST LOVE DOGS (2005*)* written by Gary David Goldberg based on a novel by Claire Cook

ONCE (2006) written by John Carney

ENCHANTED (2007) written by Bill Kelly

DRAMA

Drama reflects the human frailties, disappointments, lost hopes and dreams and, sometimes, the tragedies that can be part of everyday life. The dramatic story revolves around <u>an everyday, normal person;</u> the everyman or the everywoman.

Dramatic stories should explore deep feelings, deep needs, deep desires. In order for the story to be deemed dramatic, the protagonist must want to accomplish his goal in an overpowering, all-consuming way. The possibility of failure must be real and the consequences of failure significant. Does your story involve the need for survival? Or peace of the psyche? The future of a family? The acceptance of love? Take a look at your script. Are the stakes high enough? Does it concern life or death? Or retaining or losing one's soul? Happiness or certain despair? The end of life as one knows it?

Use the Eleven Step Story Structure to make sure you are fulfilling the criteria of a good dramatic story. Check your story – have you dealt with each step to ensure you have a complete story?

Which of the films listed below are closest to your film story in tone and characters? Study these films for inspiration – there's nothing better than reading a film script or watching good films with an eye to making yours better.

THE GRAPES OF WRATH (1940) written by Nunnally Johnson, based on the novel by John Steinbeck

TREASURE OF SIERRA MADRE (1948) written by John Huston, based on novel by B. Traven

STREETCAR NAMED DESIRE (1951) written by Tennessee Williams

MARTY (1955) written by Paddy Chayefsky

HUD (1963) written by Irving Ravetch and Harriet Frank, Jr., based on a novel by Larry McMurtry

NETWORK (1976) written by Paddy Chayefsky

THE DEER HUNTER (1978) written by Michael Cimino and Deric Washburn

ORDINARY PEOPLE (1980) written by Alvin Sargent, based on a novel by Judith Guest

SOPHIE'S CHOICE (1982) written by Alan Pakula and William Styron, based on the book by William Styron

DANCES WITH WOLVES (1990) written by Michael Blake, based on his novel

THE SHAWSHANK REDEMPTION (1994) written by Frank Darabont, based on a short story by Stephen King

UNFORGIVEN (1992) written by David Webb Peoples

GOOD WILL HUNTING (1997) written by Matt Damon and Ben Affleck

AMERICAN BEAUTY (1999) written by Alan Ball

MILLION DOLLAR BABY (2004) written by Paul Haggis, based on stories by F.X. Toole

TRANSAMERICA (2005) written by Duncan Tucker

NOTES ON A SCANDAL (2006) written by Patrick Marber, based on the novel by Zoe Heller

ZODIAC (2007) written by James Vanderbilt, based on a book by Robert Graysmith

MARGOT AT THE WEDDING (2007) written by Noah Baumbach

THE SAVAGES (2007) written by Tamara Jenkins

DRAMA/ACTION

The classic drama genre employs an everyman or everywoman as the protagonist of the story. The protagonist needs to face challenges that seem beyond his or her capabilities. The protagonist has to dig deeper than he or she ever thought possible in order to attain his or her goal.

The necessary requirement of an action film is physicality – chases, battles, gunfights, fight scenes or other physical feats. The physical challenges work best when the protagonist is up against insurmountable odds.

Don't forget to explore the moral interplay between the "good" and "bad" characters or story elements. Perhaps you want to let your protagonist – or the antagonist – question himself. Perhaps there is no absolute "good" or absolute "bad" and the right thing to do is not always clear. Exploring the moral questions that the story brings to light will strengthen the story and the audience's investment in the outcome of the story.

This combination of genre is often paired with the crime genre or the mystery genre.

THE MAN WHO SHOT LIBERTY VALANCE (1962) written by James Bellah and Willis Goldbeck, story by Dorothy Johnson

MANCHURIAN CANDIDATE (1962) written by George Axelrod from the novel by Richard Condon

BULLITT (1968) written by Alan Trustman and Harry Kleiner, based on the novel by Robert L. Fish

TAKING OF PELHAM ONE TWO THREE (1974) written by Peter Stone, based on the novel by John Godey

APOCALYPSE NOW (1979) written by John Milius and Frances Ford Coppola

TOP GUN (1986) written by Jim Cash and Jack Epps Jr. based on an article by Ehud Yonay

DAYS OF THUNDER (1990) written by Robert Towne

CHILDREN OF MEN (2006) written by Alfonso Cuaron & Timothy J. Sexton and David Arata and Mark Fergus & Hawk Ostby, based on the novel by P.D. James

DRAMA/ADVENTURE

Adventure is the search or the quest for something that seems, initially, unattainable. The goal of the adventure could be a treasure or a political ideal *(James Bond's quest in 2006's **CASINO ROYALE)** or search for sense of self *(BATMAN BEGINS)* or any quest that, when taken on, will force the protagonist into physical situations and mental challenges that test every fiber of his being.

The most important element in your script is still the strong character arc. Millions of chases and special effects will not make for a successful film story; the focus on a character's personal journey is still of utmost importance.

Take a look at your script. Is the reason your protagonist goes on the adventure quest strong enough? Will the success or failure of the quest change your protagonist's life forever? Have you taken time to set up the main character before propelling her on her journey so the audience cares about the outcome?

Adventure and action often go hand in hand. Have you found the most original action sequences? Are you characters still at the forefront? Do the action sequences allow for the character's overall want to remain clear?

Elements of crime, mystery and political intrigue are often plot elements in the action/adventure arena.

Take a look at these films listed below. The tone of the stories will vary, but all are examples of the action/adventure genre.

*CAPTAIN BLOOD (*1935) written by Casey Robinson, based on book by Rafael Sabatini

BRIDGE OVER A RIVER KWAI (1957) written by Michael Wilson and Carl Foreman, based on the novel by Pierre Boulle

NORTH BY NORTHWEST (1959) written by Ernest Lehman

BUTCH CASSIDY AND THE SUNDANCE KID (1969) written by William Goldman

SUPERMAN (1978) written by Mario Puzo, David Newman and Leslie Newman and Robert Benton; based on characters created by Jerry Siegel and Joe Shuster

RAIDERS OF THE LOST ARK (1981) written by George Lucas and Philip Kaufman

JURASSIC PARK (1993) written by Michael Crichton

HARRY POTTER AND THE SORCERER'S STONE (2001) written by Steve Kloves, based on book by J.K. Rowling

PIRATES OF THE CARIBBEAN, CURSE OF THE BLACK PEARL (2003) written by Ted Elliot and Terry Rossio

BOURNE IDENTITY (2004) written by Tony Gilroy and W. Blake Herron, based on a book by Robert Ludlum

BATMAN BEGINS (2005) written by David S. Goyer and Bob Kane

CASINO ROYALE (2006) written by Neal Purvis and Robert Wade based on the novel by Ian Fleming

DRAMA/CRIME

The drama genre focuses on the everyman or everywoman put into a situation that challenges his moral and physical being. The crime genre must include the set up of the law and order of the day, the breaking of the law by a commitment of a crime, the repercussion of the crime (who does it affect and why), the investigation of the crime to narrow the field of suspects, an examination of the motives of the criminals and the apprehension (or not) of the perpetrator. The protagonist is sometimes an investigator (a professional – cop or detective or private eye) or a private citizen who has to take the pursuit of justice into his or her own hands. To fully satisfy the criteria of crime/drama, the writer should consider exploring the power relations in the society as well as the moral flexibility of the law and the moral code of the perpetrators of the crime.

If you are writing in the drama/crime genre, take a look at your script. You may have hit all the criteria of the drama/crime genre in a non-linear order, depending on how your story is set out – remember nothing has to adhere to a strict structure. However, if you find that you are missing one or two elements of the drama/crime criteria, consider working those areas in this rewrite phase.

The film stories listed below do not hang on huge action sequences. These crime stories tend to be more cerebral; battles of wills rather than weapons. Many "film noir" films fall into this genre. Film noir (meaning black film or cinema) is a label given to the American films of the 40's (mostly shot in black and white) that explore the protagonist's struggle to find morality in an immoral world.

MALTESE FALCON (1941) written by John Huston, based on the novel by Dashiel Hammett

DOUBLE INDEMNITY (1944) written by Billy Wilder and Raymond Chandler based on the novel by James M. Cain

ON THE WATERFRONT (1954) written by Budd Schulberg based on articles by Malcolm Johnson

TOUCH OF EVIL (1958) written by Orson Welles, based on a novel by Whit Masterson

THE GODFATHER (1972) written by Mario Puzo and Francis Ford Coppola, based on novel by Mario Puzo

THE VERDICT (1982) written by David Mamct, based on novel by Barry Reed

INTERNAL AFFAIRS (1990) written by Henry Bean

GOODFELLOWS (1990) written by Nicholas Pileggi

A FEW GOOD MEN (1992) written by Aaron Sorkin

SE7EN (1995) written by Andrew Kevin Walker

THE USUAL SUSPECTS (1995) written by Christopher McQuarrie

BREACH (2007) written by Adam Mazer and William Rotko and Billy Ray

FRACTURE (2007) written by Daniel Pyne and Glenn Gers

DRAMA/CRIME/ACTION

This combination of genre is popular and very commercial. It has inherent plot conflict because, in most cases, it involves life and death situations. This genre often centers on one or more murders. It certainly involves exploration of criminal actions or the loss of important elements that make a human's life bearable.

Let's review the crime genre criteria: A set up of the law and order of the day, the breaking of law, the repercussions of the crime (who does it affect?) the crime investigation, apprehension (or not) of the criminal. To fully satisfy the criteria of crime/drama, the writer must explore the power relations in the society as well as the moral flexibility of the law and the perpetrators of the crime.

Review the requirements of an action genre: The story must include physical sequences such as chases, battles, gunfights, amazing fight scenes or other physical feats. The genre is elevated when the moral interplay between good and bad forces is explored.

The writer must build in sequences that will become set pieces to impress the audience. 2007's *BOURNE ULTIMATUM* is a series of set pieces – action sequences built to put the protagonist, Jason Bourne, up against unbelievable challenges. He does not take on one assailant at a time, but two or three or more. He not only has to steal a motorcycle to make an escape, but he has to hotwire it and then maneuver it up and down steep steps and winding, narrow streets. At one point, Bourne manages to abscond with a police car and after a wild chase in a parking structure, drive off the roof of the structure, crash into multiple cars on the street below and he still is able to escape. Yes, all a bit unbelievable and over the top, but, depending on the tone of your story, you may want to push your action sequences to the extreme.

Remember to make each individual task or action fraught with difficulty. Nothing can be easy.

The drama component of action/drama demands that an <u>everyman or everywoman protagonist with a strong personal story</u> is at the center of the story. The writer must make the audience care about the personal story as well as the action-packed plot. Jason Bourne is, at his core, an everyman. He has incredible skills but he is a lost soul searching for his true identity; he does not want to be a killer, he simply wants to know why and how he has become a hunted man. 1993's *THE FUGITIVE* fulfills the drama/crime/action criteria. Upstanding Dr. Kimble (portrayed by Harrison Ford) is an everyman who wants to find his wife's murderer and understand the reasons for her death.

Consider *THE GODFATHER*. Michael (portrayed by Al Pacino) is introduced as the <u>everyman.</u> Yes, he is the son of a powerful Mafia Don but Michael has chosen the everyman life; he wants to stay out of the family business, he's served in the military, he's planning to enter the legitimate business world and marry a woman who is not Italian. His everyman status lets the audience relate to him, empathize with his situation and care about his dreams. If Sonny (portrayed by James Caan) had been chosen to be the protagonist of the story, the story may not have attracted such a large audience. Sonny is not an everyman – he is a criminal, an adulterer, he's hot-headed and unreliable. The basic element of the drama genre – the <u>relatable</u> everyman facing great challenges and risking failure – is well-used in this film.

Consider these films below. The tones of the film stories vary, but all are good examples of films in the drama/crime/action arena.

SERPICO (1973) written by Waldo Salt and Norman Wexler, based on the book by Peter Maas

LETHAL WEAPON (1987) written by Shane Black

DIE HARD (1988) written by Jeb Stuart, based on the novel by Roderick Thorp

THE FUGITIVE (1993) written by David Twohy, characters created by Roy Higgins

IN THE LINE OF FIRE (1993) written by Jeff Maguire

SPEED (1994) written by Graham Yost

L.A. CONFIDENTIAL (1997) written by Brian Helgeland, based on the novel by James Ellroy

TRAINING DAY (2001) written by David Ayer

MAN ON FIRE (2004) written by Brian Helgeland, based on the novel by A.J. Quinnell

THE DEPARTED (2006) written by William Monahan, based on the film *WU JIAN DAO* by Siu Fai Mak

BLOOD DIAMOND (2006) written by Charles Leavitt, based on a story by Charles Leavitt and C. Gaby Mitchell

DRAMA/MYSTERY

The classic criteria of the mystery genre: An event takes place that is inexplicable. The reasons for it cannot be readily or fully explained. This event could be a murder, a theft, a kidnapping, an out-of-character decision, an alien encounter or other event that is of inexplicable origin.

A mystery must include secrets or unexplained events or unknown elements that remain unsolved or concealed throughout most of the story. A mystery may center on characters' secrets and hidden agendas, or natural or man-made mysterious challenges. In the classic mystery, the audience is given clues (where, why, who, how, when) and is able to put them together as the protagonist puts them together. In some cases, the story is constructed to be a "closed" story – the audience "solves" the mystery as the protagonist does. In the "open" structure, the audience may know the identity of the killer or criminal before the protagonist and enjoys the tension that builds as the protagonist discovers the truth.

An important element in the drama/mystery genre is identifying the consequences of solving of the mystery. Once the puzzle is completed, does an unexpected element reveal itself and make the puzzle more interesting or diabolical or have more far-reaching implications than first imagined? Is the whole _more_ than the sum of the parts?

One-hour American television, in the last decade, has mastered the telling of the simple crime tale. Television shows like **LAW AND ORDER** and **CSI** set up the crime in the first moments of the hour. The investigators gather clues and identify suspects and work to facilitate the arrest and conviction of the criminal. The audience learns little about the private lives of the investigators because the focus is on the "whodunit" – and a little bit about the "why" of the criminal. Feature films need to go deeper. The length of a feature film gives the screenwriter an opportunity to add thematic elements and interesting emotional and/or psychological arcs for the main characters. The film audience wants a full story experience and a sense that the story has deeper ramifications than a simple crime "whodunit." Consider 2000's **ERIN BROKOVICH**. Erin (portrayed by Julia Roberts) investigates a mysterious claim and uncovers layers of untruths about a California power company accused of polluting a city's water supply. The ramifications of her actions affect many people and a community as well as her own boss, friends, lover and children – and her sense of self-esteem. Make sure many areas of the protagonist's life are explored – and as the story unfolds, a change is forced upon the character. Feature films scripts need to be more that just the solving of the mystery – they must also center on a character that changes.

Again, <u>drama</u> is highlighted in this genre. The everyman or everywoman character is put into a situation to solve (or be affected by) the mystery. This is not the genre for super-heroes; the heroes are ordinary people who face extraordinary situations. Personal challenges of a physical or emotional nature must come into play.

If you are working in the mystery genre, put the films below on your viewing list. All are excellent examples of the mystery/drama. Note that many of these films include elements of crime.

TO KILL A MOCKING BIRD (1962) written by Horton Foote, based on the novel by Harper Lee

REBECCA (1940) written by Philip MacDonald, based on the novel by Daphne Du Maurier

PSYCHO (1960) written by Joseph Stefano, based on the novel by Robert Bloch

IN THE HEAT OF THE NIGHT (1967) written by Stirling Silliphant, based on the novel by John Ball

CHINATOWN (1974) written by Robert Towne

SECRET WINDOW (2004) written by David Koepp based on the novel by Stephen King

THE LIVES OF OTHERS (2006) written by Florian Henckel von Donnersmarck

DRAMA/ROMANCE

Romance must revolve around love relationships. In most cases, the ability of the lovers to get together is always in question and the lovers are kept apart as long as possible in the film story. Because of the demands of the drama genre, there should be a relatable everyman or everywoman element to the characters. Even 1995's *THE AMERICAN PRESIDENT* (written by Aaron Sorkin) sets up its main characters, the President of the United States and a Washington lobbyist, as people with ordinary desires for love and companionship even though they are in high-powered careers.

Remember the seven criteria of the romance genre: boy meets girl, boy wants girl, boy gets girl, boy loses girl, boy realizes life is meaningless without girl, boy strives to get girl back, boy gets girl back (or not). Have you examined each step in the romance process? Have you found surprises within the steps? <u>How</u> does boy meet girl? (Or girl meets boy or any combination.) <u>How</u> does boy discover that he does, indeed, really want the girl? Does it take him a long time to realize this? What actions does he have to take to win the girl? <u>How</u> does he lose the girl? What difficulties arise as he strives to get the girl back? Is she now engaged to someone else? Does she despise him? Does he resent her even as he is trying to get her back? Find the singular ways to show how <u>your particular character</u> will fulfill the romance in the story.

CASABLANCA (1942) Paul Henreid, Humphrey Bogart
- *photo courtesy of Globe Photos*

Check that you have fulfilled the Eleven Step Story Structure and fulfilled the drama genre story criteria. Then ask: Are the stakes in your story high enough? Does the story concern <u>true</u> love? Are you embracing the idea that the ability to love and be loved is needed for a person to feel truly complete? Are you accepting the deep need of your character for love? Rick, in *CASABLANCA,* is a functioning person at the beginning of the film story, but he is unhappy, unfeeling and disconnected. The story unfolds and the audience comes to an understanding of his great love for Ilsa and the emotional damage he suffered due to their unsuccessful love affair. When Ilsa re-enters his life, Rick transforms and becomes a man who can admit to feelings and also re-connect with the world. Love has "saved" him from an uncommitted life. Will your main characters be destroyed physically or emotionally if character flaws or vagaries of plot keep them apart? Is the plot consistently working against them? Keep the stakes high. Make sure the audience can sense the consequences of failure; you want the audience to root for your lovers.

Which of the films listed below are closest to your screenplay in tone and characters? View the ones that relate and be inspired.

GONE WITH THE WIND (1939) written by Sidney Howard, based on the novel by Margaret Mitchell

CASABLANCA (1942) written by Julius and Philip Epstein and Howard Koch, based on the play by Murray Burnett and Joan Alison

DOCTOR ZHIVAGO (1965) written by Robert Bolt, based on the novel by Boris Pasternak

ALICE DOESN'T LIVE HERE ANYMORE (1974) written by Robert Getchell

LOVE STORY (1970) written by Erich Segal

OUT OF AFRICA (1985) written by Kurt Luedtke adapted from writings of Karen Blixin

THE ENGLISH PATIENT (1996) written by Anthony Minghella, based on the novel by Michael Ondaatje

SENSE AND SENSIBILITY (1995) written by Emma Thompson, based on the novel by Jane Austen

MONSTER'S BALL (2001) written by Milo Addica and Will Rokos

SECRET LIVES OF DENTISTS (2002) written by Craig Lucas, based on the novel by Jane Smiley

THE NOTEBOOK (2004) written by Jan Sardi and Jeremy Leven, based on the novel by Nicholas Sparks

ETERNAL SUNSHINE OF THE SPOTLESS MIND (2004) written by Charlie Kaufman

UPSIDE OF ANGER (2005) written by Mike Binder

BROKEBACK MOUNTAIN (2005) written by Larry McMurtry and Diane Ossana, based on the short story by E. Annie Proulx

AWAY FROM HER (2007) written by Sarah Polley, based on the short story by Alice Munro

DRAMA/THRILLER

A thriller features a protagonist who is almost constantly at risk. High stakes, sometimes non-stop action, sudden twists are often elements of successful thrillers. A sense of danger permeates the whole story. A thriller, in most cases, lets the audience <u>know</u> (or suspect) the identity of the nemesis. Oftentimes, it is not the mystery that drives the story, but the drive to apprehend the villain or villains before they can strike again. The protagonist is often pitted against an antagonist who is out to destroy the protagonist's life, his community or his world.

Psychological thrillers focus on a battle of wills or on a battle to control a person's mind. Take a look at 1944's *GASLIGHT* or 1968's *ROSEMARY'S BABY* or 2000's *WHAT LIES BENEATH*.

Remember, the drama genre maintains that the focus is on the everyman; an ordinary person pulled into extraordinary circumstances.

The director Alfred Hitchcock is known as a master of the drama/thriller. The writers he employed shared his passion. Hitchcock's protagonists are set up quickly as an everyman or everywoman; in 1960's *PSYCHO,* Marion Crane (portrayed by Janet Leigh) is an ordinary employee who, frustrated, steals from her boss because she wants to start a new life with her cash-strapped boyfriend who spends his earnings on alimony to an ex-wife. In 1959's *NORTH BY NORTHWEST*, Roger Thornhill (portrayed by Cary Grant) is an ordinary advertising executive mistaken for a government agent. He is pulled into a web of spies and intrigue. In 1940's *REBECCA,* the shy ladies' companion (portrayed by Joan Fontaine) falls in love with a man with a past and as she unravels the truth, her life becomes endangered. In 1946's *NOTORIOUS*, a society girl (portrayed by Ingrid Bergman) wants to prove her patriotism after her father's arrest as a traitor. She agrees to become a spy and while she is undercover, it's clear that any false move could cause her demise and the demise of the government's operation.

Check your script. Does your main character have elements of the everyman/everywoman? Can the audience relate to the protagonist as he is pulled into an extraordinary situation that tests his moral fiber or his sanity or his life?

NORTH BY NORTHWEST (1959) Cary Grant, Eva Marie Saint
- photo courtesy of Globe Photos

As in the mystery/drama genre, there is a fine line to walk in your storytelling; are you telling the audience too much so they lose interest because they are ahead of the story? Or are you not telling the audience enough, causing confusion and ultimate disinterest?

Take a look at the films listed below.

REAR WINDOW (1954) written by John Michael Hayes, based on the short story by Cornell Woolrich

VERTIGO (1958) written by Alec Coppel and Samuel A. Taylor, based on the novel by Pierre Boileau and Thomas Narcejac

NORTH BY NORTHWEST (1959) written by Ernest Lehman

THE FRENCH CONNECTION (1971) written by Ernest Tidyman, based on the novel by Robin Moore

JAWS (1975) written by Peter Benchley

TAXI DRIVER (1976) written by Paul Schrader

ALIEN (1979) written by Dan O'Bannon and Ronald Shusett

FATAL ATTRACTION (1987) written by James Dearden

MISERY (1990) written by William Goldman, based on the novel by Stephen King

THE SILENCE OF THE LAMBS (1991) written by Ted Tally, based on the novel by Thomas Harris

CAPE FEAR (1991) written by James R Webb and Wesley Strick, based on the novel by John D. MacDonald

PRIMAL FEAR (1996) written by Steve Shagan, based on the novel by William Diehl

THE EDGE (1997) written by David Mamet

MEMENTO (2000) written by Christopher Nolan, based on the short story by Jonathan Nolan

MYSTIC RIVER (2003) written by Brian Helgeland, based on the novel by Dennis Lehane

THE CONSTANT GARDENER (2005) written by Jeffrey Caine, based on the novel by John le Carre

SYRIANA (2005) written by Stephen Gaghan, based on the book by Robert Baer

There are other genres that you may be using in combination with drama or comedy and other supporting genres. Remember, you may be using two, three or four genres and you want to fulfill the expectations of each of them. Read on and find the genres that are of most interest to you.

BIO-PIC

The film biography is a story based on a person, living or dead, and includes the elements in his or her life that are deemed dramatic and story-worthy. The best bio-pics, in most cases, do not try to tell a person's story from birth to death but focus on a certain section in a person's life – usually a pivotal time that caused a life-changing moment. 2005's *WALK THE LINE* (drama, bio-pic, romance) focuses on Johnny Cash's need to bring

June Carter into his life. 1984's **AMADEUS** (drama, bio-pic, coming of age) focuses on Mozart's time at the Royal Court and rival Salieri's actions aimed at destroying Mozart. 1993's **SCHINDLER'S LIST** (drama, bio-pic, war) focuses on Schindler's life during World War II. 1982's **GANDHI** (drama, bio-pic, political, coming of age) covers many years, but focuses on <u>one</u> element of Gandhi's life – the reasons for and his desire to help free India from British rule. 2001's **ALI** (drama, bio-pic, coming of age) focuses on Muhammad Ali's life-changing trip to Africa.

Most bio-pics will be based in the drama genre. If you are working on a bio-pic, check your script. Have you found the dramatic thread for this story? It's not enough to simply give the facts of a person's life; you must construct the story so that it builds in intensity and shows how and <u>why</u> the protagonist experienced a great change and the <u>results</u> of that change.

2006's **CAPOTE** is a bio-pic that centers on Truman Capote's writing of his masterpiece novel **IN COLD BLOOD.** The book is based on a true crime that took place in Kansas in 1959, the senseless murder of a family in their farmhouse. After setting up the interest of Truman Capote (portrayed by Phillip Seymour Hoffman) and his decision to travel to Kansas to interview the people affected by the crime, the audience learns of a long friendship with fellow novelist Harper Lee (portrayed by Catherine Keener). The audience also learns that Capote has a lover. When Capote and Harper Lee arrive in Kansas, the audience is introduced to law enforcement officer Alvin Dewey (portrayed by Chris Cooper) – and the murderer, Perry Smith (portrayed by Clifton Collins, Jr.). Capote forges unique relationships with these new characters. The audience is primed and interested in seeing how these relationships play out. However, midway through the film, the story switches focus and these characters no longer serve the story. Capote's character arc is truncated because the arcs of these relationships (or "B" stories) are not fully explored. Capote's ultimate "loss of soul" – when his obsession with getting his book published takes over – does not resonate as much as it could have because the supporting characters have fallen out of the story – thus the audience does not witness the personal consequences of the protagonist's actions. This film is focused on forging an understanding of Capote's character and how this event changed his life forever. By not completing the arcs of the "B" stories onscreen, the audience misses a sense of completion of the story the film set out to tell. The words on the screen at the end of the story tell the audience that this event was life-changing for Capote. Stories can be told in many ways – but if you can <u>show</u> the consequences and not rely on written words at the end of the film to tell

Question: What does a writer do when the biography of a person – or an exploration of certain events of an actual person's life – doesn't fit a nice, neat "story" arc?

Answer: Once you have identified the event or events that you are exploring in a true story of a person's life, find the theme that resonates for you in the story. Why is this event important? What will the audience learn from it? If the theme in CAPOTE is "without perspective, one can lose what's most important in life," how could you visually show this theme to be true?

the audience the outcome of the story – consider writing the scenes that will complete the story.

Take a look at your script. Does it need to be more focused? Are you including <u>only</u> the biographical information necessary to understand your protagonist at <u>this</u> life-changing time in his life? Are you including <u>only</u> the characters that are necessary in <u>these</u> moments of her life? One of my students was working on a bio-pic of an artist's life. He became so enamored of characters in the artist's large family and of elements in the artist's childhood and other ancillary components of the artist's experiences that he could not focus on the most interesting part of the dramatic story he wanted to explore; the destruction of talent when one comes under the hypnotic control of an evil mentor. The heart of his story was compelling and had universal appeal to an audience. However, the details of the historical figure's life that did <u>not </u>inform or affect the "A" story distracted the audience from focusing on the bones of the story. Many details (despite their uniqueness) needed to be expunged in order to tell <u>one</u> story. After drafts that were unfocused and episodic, the writer finally focused on the main story and time frame. And the script came together.

Ask yourself: Are you starting your bio-pic story as close you as can to the inciting incident, the moment that changed your protagonist's world and set her on the path to a major change? Have you remained focused on the <u>one</u> important area of the protagonist's life?

Check out the films listed below for inspiration.

THE LIFE OF EMILE ZOLA (1937) written by Heinz Herald and Geza Herczeg, based on the novel by Matthew Josephson

SPIRIT OF ST. LOUIS (1957) written by Charles Lederer and Wendell Mayes and Billy Wilder, based on the book by Charles A. Lindbergh

LAWRENCE OF ARABIA (1962) written by Robert Bolt, based on writings by T.E. Lawrence

RAGING BULL (1980) written by Paul Schrader and Mardik Martin, based on the book by Jake LaMotta, Joseph Carter and Peter Savage

COAL MINER'S DAUGHTER (1980) written by Loretta Lynn and Thomas Rickman

AMADEUS (1984) written by Peter Shaffer

GANDHI (1982) written by John Briley

MALCOLM X (1992) written by Arnold Perl and Spike Lee, based on the book by Alex Haley and Malcolm X

SCHINDLER'S LIST (1993) written by Steven Zaillian, based on the book by Thomas Keneally

ERIN BROCKOVICH (2000) written by Susannah Grant

POLLOCK (2000) written by Barbara Turner and Susan Emshwiller, based on the book by Steven Naifeh and Gregory White Smith

A BEAUTIFUL MIND (2001) written by Akiva Goldsman, based on the book by Sylvia Nasar

FRIDA (2002) written by Clancy Sigal and Diane Lake and Gregory Nava and Anna Thompson, based on the book by Hayden Herrera

AVIATOR (2004) written by John Logan

RAY (2004) written by Taylor Hackford, story by Taylor Hackford and James L. White

THE MOTORCYCLE DIARIES (2004) written by Jose Rivera, based on the book by Ernesto 'Che' Guevara and Alberto Granado

WALK THE LINE (2005) written by Gill Dennis based on the book by Johnny Cash

GOOD NIGHT, GOOD LUCK (2005) written by George Clooney and Grant Heslov

PURSUIT OF HAPPYNESS (2006) written by Steven Conrad

Question: Since bio-pics are based on facts, how does the screenwriter remain true to what really happened while trying to fashion a complete story?

Answer: Some writers take liberties, some writers find artistic ways to fulfill the story. Whichever way you approach the specific needs of your bio-pic, keep in mind that audiences have come to see a complete story. Documentaries will approach the biography in a completely different fashion – the screenwriter of a bio-pic must find the thematic through line and create a film with a strong beginning, middle and end.

BUDDY

The criteria of the buddy genre have much in common with the romance genre. Buddy A (let's call him Bill) meets Buddy B (let's call him Sam). Bill decides he wants to become buddies with Sam, the two become buddies, there is an altercation and the relationship goes sour or they get separated, Bill realizes that life isn't complete (or he can't accomplish his goal) without Sam, so Bill strives (against great odds) to save and/or reunite with Sam. The buddies get back together (or not). Buddy films have been popular since the beginning of film stories – take a look at the *LAUREL AND HARDY* comedies as well as the Bob Hope and Bing Crosby comedies and the Jerry Lewis and Dean Martin comedies. Buddy films based in the drama genre include 1990's *INTERNAL AFFAIRS* and 1987's *LETHAL WEAPON* or

THE WEDDING CRASHERS (2005) Vince Vaughn, Owen Wilson
- *photo courtesy of Globe Photos*

1991's *THELMA AND LOUISE* or 2005's *THE WEDDING CRASHERS* are all good examples of buddy films. Each of these films uses different genre combinations, but each fulfills the criteria of the buddy genre.

If you are writing in this genre, take a look at the films below.

LAUREL AND HARDY IN TOYLAND (1934) written by Frank Butler and Nick Grinder

PARDNERS (1956) written by Sidney Sheldon, based on a story by Mervin Houser and Jerry Davis

BUTCH CASSIDY AND THE SUNDANCE KID (1969) written by William Goldman

THE MAN WHO WOULD BE KING (1975) written by John Huston and Gladys Hill, based on a story by Rudyard Kipling

ROMY AND MICHELE'S HIGH SCHOOL REUNION (1997) written by Robin Schiff

SHANGHAI KNIGHTS (2003) written by Alfred Gough and Miles Millar

YOU ME AND DUPREE (2006) written by Michael LeSieur

BLADES OF GLORY (2007) written by Jeff Cox & Craig Cox and John Altsculer & Dave Krinsky

SUPERBAD (2007) written by Seth Rogen and Evan Goldberg

COMING OF AGE

The coming of age genre explores a character's reaching a new sense of self, maturity, respectability or prominence. The protagonist, in most cases, is in a quandary concerning his or her purpose in life, or lack of understanding of why life makes difficult demands. The protagonist could be exploring a moral dilemma, a crisis of self-identity, or ethical crisis. On the journey, the protagonist experiences self-revelation and, in most cases, comes out with a stronger sense of purpose and identity.

The chronological age of the main character does not matter. He could be a teen or twenty-something or much older. It's the maturation, the new sense and understanding of self and purpose that is most important. One could argue that many films embrace the coming-of-age genre because all characters, in good stories, change and grow and gain a new understanding of the world or self.

NATIONAL VELVET (1944) written by Helen Deutsch based on the novel by Enid Bagnold

REBEL WITHOUT A CAUSE (1955) written by Stewart Stern, story by Nicholas Ray, and adaptation by Irving Shulman

LAST PICTURE SHOW (1971) written by Larry McMurtry and Peter Bogdanovich, based on novel by Larry McMurtry

SUMMER OF '42 (1971) written by Herman Raucher

AMERICAN GRAFFITI (1973) written by George Lucas and Gloria Katz and Willard Huyck

STAND BY ME (1986) written by Raynold Gideon, based on the novel by Stephen King

SOME KIND OF WONDERFUL (1987) written by John Hughes

LION KING (1994) written by Irene Mecchi and Jonathan Roberts

THE KARATE KID (1984) written by Robert Mark Kamen

CIDER HOUSE RULES (1999) written by John Irving

THE PRINCESS DIARIES (2001) written by Gina Wendkos, based on the novel by Meg Cabot

LEGALLY BLONDE (2001) written by Karen McCullah Lutz and Kirsten Smith based on a novel by Amanda Brown

REAL WOMEN HAVE CURVES (2002) written by Josefina Lopez, teleplay by George LaVoo and Josefina Lopez

BEND IT LIKE BECKHAM (2002) written by Gurinder Chadha, Guljit Bindra, and Paul Mayeda Berges

40-YEAR-OLD VIRGIN (2005) written by Judd Apatow and Steve Carrell

ONCE (2006) written by John Carney

THE NAMESAKE (2006) written by Sooni Taraporevala, based on the novel by Jhumpa Lahiri

KNOCKED UP (2007) written by Judd Apatow

JUNO (2007) written by Diablo Cody

DISASTER

The disaster genre has great potential for box-office success because tales of large-scale destruction bring with it opportunities for life and death situations, huge emotional stakes – and of course – great opportunities for special effects. Disasters are calamitous event; floods, earthquakes, snowstorms, tornadoes, hurricanes, train or airplane crashes, burning buildings, sinking ships or other disasters.

There are disaster films that are based on historical facts, there are this-could-really-happen disaster films and there are disaster/fantasy films. Film stories embracing the disaster genre must be paired with a strong base genre, in most cases this is the drama genre. Disaster films often include a cautionary element or lesson; one must always be prepared, one must take care of the environment or one must not skimp on the maintenance of equipment, or one must not rely on machines when human watchfulness could be more effective. Often families or peers learn the importance of love or kindness or understanding, or lovers learn that petty problems mean nothing in the face of death. The everyman/everywoman character in drama works well in disaster films because the audience can immediately buy into "that could be me" and empathize on a deep level.

At the base of the really good disaster films are great characters that go on a journey of self-discovery and change.

AIRPORT (1970) written by George Seaton based on the novel by Arthur Hailey

POSEIDON ADVENTURE (1972) written by Wendell Mayes and Stirling Silliphant based on the novel by Paul Gallico

THE TOWERING INFERNO (1974) written by Stirling Silliphant

JURASSIC PARK (1993) written by Michael Crichton and David Koepp, based on the novel by Michael Crichton

BACKDRAFT (1991) written by Gregory Widen

TITANIC (1997) written by James Cameron

INDEPENDENCE DAY (1996) written by Dean Devlin and Roland Emmerich

ARMAGEDDON (1998) written by Jonathan Hensleigh and J.J. Abrams, based on a story by Robert Roy Pool and Jonathan Hensleigh

DAY AFTER TOMORROW (2004) written by Roland Emmerich and Jeffrey Nachmanoff

UNITED 93 (2006) written by Paul Greengrass

ENSEMBLE

The ensemble genre focuses on the individuals in a group of characters. Each character has a story with a beginning, middle and end. Each person's story contributes to the larger umbrella story that holds the film together. Consider 1963's **THE GREAT ESCAPE**, the tale of World War II Allied soldiers in a German prison camp. Each character has a specific task in the exciting escape attempt and their actions affect the other characters. 2006's **LITTLE MISS SUNSHINE** features members of a family who each have a specific goal to accomplish as well as roles to play in the family's journey to get its youngest member to a beauty pageant.

If you are working on an ensemble piece, count the number of main characters you have constructed. Take a look at the arcs for each of the characters. Do they each have an Eleven Step Story arc? Does each character go through a change? Do the characters affect the others' journeys? When working in this genre, it is imperative to use your technical skills to track each character.

There are ensemble films that take place over one day or night – consider the 1998 teen flick **CAN'T HARDLY WAIT** or 1999's twenty-something angst film **200 CIGARETTES**. Consider the time frame of your script. Would the tightening of the time frame be advantageous to your story? Remember, a shorter time frame can raise the intensity of the needs for characters.

There are ensemble films constructed so that by the end of Act Two, all the stories merge for one all-encompassing event such as a wedding or graduation or funeral or dinner party or physical challenge. This enables the writer to bring theme, plots and points of view together, raise the conflict and satisfy the audience who wants to see how the disparate characters will work together (or not).

Ensemble films must be paired with other genres. Be clear about your base genre. Is it drama or comedy? Have you added a thriller or horror genre? If so, have you met the criteria of the genres?

GRAND HOTEL (1932) based on a play by Vicki Baum and William A. Drake

DINNER AT EIGHT (1933) written by Frances Marion and Herman Mankiewicz, based on play by George S. Kaufman and Edna Ferber

THE GREAT ESCAPE (1963) written by James Clavell based on novel by Paul Brickhill

STALAG 17 (1953) written by Donald Bevan and Edmund Trzcinski and Billy Wilder

12 ANGRY MEN (1957) written by Reginald Rose

NASHVILLE (1975) written by Joan Tewkesbury

DINER (1982) written by Barry Levinson

SWINGERS (1996) written by Jon Favreau

THE BIG CHILL (1983) written by Barbara Benedek and Lawrence Kasdan

SCREAM (1996) written by Kevin Williamson

I KNOW WHAT YOU DID LAST SUMMER (1997) written by Kevin Williamson, based on a novel by Lois Duncan

X–MEN (2000) written by David Hayter, story by Tom DeSanto and Bryan Singer

LITTLE MISS SUNSHINE (2006) written by Mike Arndt

EPIC

An epic tale deals with extraordinary circumstances, people and events. Many epic films canvas an extended period of time. Many attempt to look at the sociological background of the story, how the affairs of the world contribute to the actions of the characters. The most successful epic films work on various levels; they are dramatic stories focusing on humans' challenges and determinations as well as investigations of political arenas. Many are based on history, many are cautionary tales. Many have a poetic nature with strong universal themes.

BIRTH OF A NATION (1915) written by Thomas F. Dixon Jr.

GONE WITH THE WIND (1939) written by Sidney Howard, based on the book by Margaret Mitchell

THE TEN COMMANDMENTS (1956) written by Aeneas MacKenzie and Jesse Lasky Jr. and Jack Gariss and Fredric M. Frank, based on various novels

BEN HUR (1959) written by Karl Tunberg, based on novel by Lew Wallace

SPARTACUS (1960) written by Dalton Trumbo based on the novel by Howard Fast

LAWRENCE OF ARABIA (1962) written by Robert Bolt from the writing of T.E. Lawrence

*CLEOPATRA (*1963) written by Joseph L. Mankiewicz, Ranald MacDougall and Sidney Buchman

GANDHI (1982) written by John Briley

LORD OF THE RINGS TRILOGY (2001-2004) written by Fran Walsh and Peter Jackson based on the novel by J.R.R. Tolkein

EPISODIC

The episodic genre has been growing in popularity in the post millennium years. Some may point to television as the cause because audiences are accustomed to following multiple stories and multiple characters whose lives may never intersect in various television series.

In the episodic genre, three or more separate stories are told, each with a beginning, middle and end of its own. The most successful films in this genre will feature a unifying element and theme.

If you are writing in this genre, take a look at the films listed below. Note how the stories relate – even though they do not always intersect.

TRAFFIC (2000) written by Stephen Gaghan based on the miniseries Traffik by Simon Moore

THE HOURS (2002) written by David Hare based on the novel Michael Cunningham

CRASH (2004) written by Paul Haggis and Bobby Moresco

BABEL (2006) written by Guillermo Arriaga

FANTASY

The fantasy genre will always attract an audience. Fantasy uses magic or supernatural forms as a primary element of plot. Settings are otherworldly and must be clearly drawn; rules of the society and mores and beliefs of the characters must be clear. The strictures of a writer's imagination are the only boundaries. The fantasy genre needs to be paired with other strong genres to fully engage the emotions of the audience.

If you are writing in the fantasy genre, are you using elements of drama? Or are you focusing on elements of comedy? Is there a mystery in the mix? Does your fantasy have thriller elements? Note how 1939's *THE WIZARD OF OZ* brings an ordinary farm girl, Dorothy, into an extraordinary world, Oz, (elements of drama) and puts her on a quest to get the Wicked Witch's broomstick (elements of adventure) and brings her to understand there is "no place like home" (elements of coming-of-age). 1993's *GROUNDHOG DAY* is set in an everyday comedic world (which keeps repeating itself) and has strong romance elements. Phil Connors (portrayed by Bill Murray) needs to experience the same events over and over until he begins to appreciate those around him. 1995's *TOY STORY* lives in a fantastical world where toys talk, feel, move and have full lives outside of the humans' interaction with them. Woody (voiced by Tom Hanks) wants respect and appreciation). His problems are drama-based problems and explore the relatable need to have a place in the world. *TOY STORY* is a well-balanced film; it employs comedy, buddy, adventure, action and just a hint at romance.

If you are writing in the fantasy genre, take a look at the films listed below. Note the strong points of each film and be inspired.

THE WIZARD OF OZ (1939) written by Noel Langley, based on novel by L. Frank Baum

STAR WARS (1977) written by George Lucas

BRAZIL (1985) written by Terry Gilliam and Tom Stoppard

E.T. THE EXTRA TERRESTRIAL (1982) written by Melissa Mathison

LEGEND (1985) written by William Hjortsberg

LABYRINTH (1986) written by Jim Henson and Dennis Lee

EDWARD SCISSORHANDS (1990) written by Caroline Thompson, story by Tim Burton

HOOK (1991) written by James V. Hart and Malia Scotch Marmo and Nick Castle, based on story by J.M. Barrie

GROUNDHOG DAY (1993) written by Danny Rubin and Harold Ramis

TOY STORY (1995) written by John Lasseter and Pete Docter and Andrew Stanton and Joss Whedon and Joel Cohen and Alec Sokolow

BIG FISH (2003) written by John August based on the novel by Daniel Wallace

PAN'S LABYRINTH (2006) written by Guillermo del Toro

THE GOLDEN COMPASS (2007) written by Chris Weitz, based on the novel by Philip Pullman

HORROR

Horror films have been a favorite genre of large audiences since the silent film era. Audiences like to feel the adrenalin rush, they like to shriek and gasp and be taken off guard. If you have a love of this genre, embrace it. It is commercial.

Horror films feature plots where <u>evil</u> forces, events or characters invade the everyday world and upset the social order. The characters are psychologically challenged as well as physically threatened. Sometimes the forces of evil can be of supernatural origin. The best horror films raise the terror bar by sparking the viewer's imagination with original horrific situations that feed into psychological fear. The audience must feel that just under the surface of normality, there is a world that is dangerous, evil and could be pervasive if unleashed.

Most horror films will be based in the drama genre. Remember, a great protagonist is still at the heart of every film story. If that protagonist has a goal, a dream, or a mission and then – suddenly – horrific elements get in his way – then the story will take off. If the protagonist has a lot to lose – perhaps his sense of self, a loved one or a family member – the film story will resonate at a deeper level. The audience must understand and empathize with the characters while they are stalked or disfigured, terrified or brought to the edge of madness.

SCREAM (1996) Drew Barrymore
- photo courtesy of Globe Photos

Horror fans accept that vampires, in most cases, are part of the aristocracy. They're usually portrayed as immortal, wealthy, secluded and live on the blood of others to survive. Werewolves are shape-shifters (man to animal) and, in most cases, represent man's inability to control his animal nature. They lack control and, in most cases, do not respond to reason. Zombies are undead corpses. The term is taken from the Afri-Caribbean culture. Some storytellers purport that zombies walk the earth because there is no more room in hell. Some zombies become re-animated through powerful sorcery (voodoo) or through contamination from other zombies or through airborne viruses or radiation from faraway planets. Some zombies can infect humans at an alarming rate (usually through biting) and are especially difficult to kill. Film reviewers and analysts often point to psychopathic characters like Jason Voorhees *(1980's FRIDAY THE 13th)* and Leatherface *(1974's TEXAS CHAINSAW MASSACRE)* and Michael Myers *(1978's HALLOWEEN)* as representations the failure of society to protect good, solid and well-meaning people from the various bullies of the world.

Science fiction, thriller, crime and mystery are favorite genre partners of the horror genre.

If you are writing in the horror genre, know that your core audience has high expectations. Take a look at these examples of well-executed horror tales and be inspired.

DRACULA (1958) written by Jimmy Sangster based on the novel by Bram Stoker

PYSCHO (1960) written by Joseph Stefano based on the novel by Robert Bloch

WHATEVER HAPPENED TO BABY JANE (1962) written by Lukas Heller based on the novel by Henry Farrell

ROSEMARY'S BABY (1968) written by Roman Polanski, based on the novel by Ira Levin

THE EXORCIST (1973) written by William Peter Blatty

TEXAS CHAINSAW MASSACRE (1974) written by Kim Henkel and Tobe Hooper

HALLOWEEN (1978) written by John Carpenter and Debra Hill

THE SHINING (1980) written by Stanley Kubrick based on the novel by Stephen King

THE EVIL DEAD (1983) written by Sam Raimi

NIGHTMARE ON ELM STREET (1984) written by Wes Craven

THE LOST BOYS (1987) written by Janice Fischer and James Jeremias

HELLRAISER (1987) written by Clive Barker

I KNOW WHAT YOU DID LAST SUMMER (1997) written by Kevin Williamson based on the novel by Lois Duncan

SCREAM (1996) written by Kevin Williamson

THE GRUDGE (2004) written by Stephen Susco

SCI FI

Science fiction stories should have their roots in science. The writer's imagination can extrapolate and vamp on scientific fact, but the fun of this genre is its proximity to some scientific truth or hypothesis that science is exploring.

One of the first story-based films was 1902's *A TRIP TO THE MOON,* written by George Melies, inspired by the novels by Jules Verne and H.G. Wells. It is the story of a group of scientists who build a rocket ship, fly to the moon and confront moon creatures. Science fiction visionary Jules Verne, author of *JOURNEY TO CENTER OF THE EARTH* and *20,000 LEAGUES UNDER THE SEA* and other sci-fi tales was a master of extrapolating wonderful "what if" stories based on scientific hypotheses. Novelist H. G. Wells' science fiction work still inspires, recent films based on his work are *WAR OF THE WORLDS, TIME MACHINE* and *INVISIBLE MAN.* Michael Crichton, author of *JURASSIC PARK, SPHERE, TWISTER* and *ANDROMEDA STRAIN* (and more) has built a career on imagining what could happen if scientific theories or facts were stretched, turned upside down or misused. Mary Shelley's 1818 novel, *FRANKENSTEIN*, was inspired by the scientific explorations into electricity. A sci-fi comedy like *GHOSTBUSTERS* uses ectoplasm, electricity and lots of science mumbo-jumbo to create its world.

If you are writing in the science fiction genre, take a look at the films listed below. The science fiction audience, like the horror film audience, tends to be passionate and knowledgeable about their genre – therefore <u>you</u> must be knowledgeable.

THE DAY THE EARTH STOOD STILL (1951) written by Edmund H. North, based on story by Harry Bates

THE FORBIDDEN PLANET (1956) written by Cyril Hume, story by Irving Block and Allen Adler

2001: A SPACE ODYSSEY (1968) written by Stanley Kubrick and Arthur C. Clarke, based on novel by Arthur C. Clarke

ALIEN (1979) written by Dan O'Bannon

STAR TREK VI: THE UNDISCOVERED COUNTRY (1991) written by

Nicholas Meyer & Denny Martin Flinn, story by Leonard Nimoy, Lawrence Konner and Mark Rosenthal, based on characters by Gene Roddenberry

TWELVE MONKEYS (1995) written by David Webb Peoples & Janet Peoples, based on film by Chris Marker

THE IRON GIANT (1999) written by Tim McCanlies and Brad Bird, based on book by Ted Hughes

THE MATRIX (1999) written by Andy Wachowski and Larry Wachowski

DONNIE DARKO (2001) written by Richard Kelly

SERENITY (2005) written by Joss Whedon

WESTERN

Some writers on genre will insist that a true western must be set in the American West between 1840 and 1900. Traditionally, the western film's protagonist is a semi-nomadic cowboy or gunslinger who must identify and eventually commit to his own morality in a lawless open territory and learn to survive against great odds.

 Other studies on genre will point to the essence of the western genre; the outsider arriving in a lawless land who struggles to find or hold onto his moral center and survive against the violence of the community and his antagonists. 1987's *ROBOCOP* and the early *STAR WARS* (Episodes 4 and 5) are often referred to as sci-fi westerns.

The revisionist western genre is one focused on the outsider, often an anti-hero (the protagonist doing the wrong thing for the right reasons). The protagonist's overall want is, in most cases, justice; he is seeking a personal justice through revenge.

For the sake of simplicity for the screenwriter, it might help to make a distinction between films that fulfill the criteria of the classic western genre and other films that employ various genres and just happen to take place in the western area of the United States and feature actors who wear cowboy hats. The 1963 drama, *HUD,* takes place in Texas and its main characters own a cattle ranch. However, its story elements are not based in the western genre – it is pure drama, with a coming of age story for one of its main supporting characters. 1971's *THE LAST PICTURE SHOW* takes place in Texas, but it, classically, cannot be classified as a western. Both of these well-made films would not fit in the classic western genre.

Classically, the true western genre explores the problems of western expansion and the building of lawful communities out of chaos. The classic western film features characters (sometimes saddled with a violent past) with a restless nature that are seeking revenge or a place to call home. Sometimes these characters are successful at settling down, sometimes they are not – and, at the end of the story, they move on and continue their search for revenge or redemption.

Take a look at a few of the classic westerns.

STAGECOACH (1939) written by Dudley Nichols, based on a story by Ernest Haycox

HIGH NOON (1952) written by Carl Foreman, based on a story by John W. Cunningham

SHANE (1953) written by A.B. Guthrie Jr. , based on novel by Jack Schaefer

THE SEARCHERS (1956) written by Frank Nugent, based on novel by Alan LeMay

RIO BRAVO (1959) written by Jules Furthman and Leigh Brackett, based on a story by B.H. McCampbell

THE MAGNIFICENT SEVEN (1960) written by William Roberts, based on a screenplay *THE SEVEN SAMURAI* by Akira Kurosawa and Shinobu Hashimoto and Hideo Oguni

THE WILD BUNCH (1969) written by Sam Peckinpah and Walon Green

BUTCH CASSIDY AND THE SUNDANCE KID (1969) written by William Goldman

THE BIG JAKE (1971) written by Harry Julian Fink and Rita M. Fink

THE GOOD, THE BAD AND THE UGLY (1966) written by Agneore Incrocci & Furio Scarpelli and Luciano Vincenzoni & Sergio Leone

UNFORGIVEN (1992) written by David Webb Peoples

ONCE UPON A TIME IN MEXICO (2003) written by Robert Rodriguez

OPEN RANGE (2003) written by Craig Storper, based on a novel by Lauran Paine

THE WILD BUNCH (1969) Ben Johnson, Warren Oates, William Holden, Ernest Borgnine
- photo courtesy of Globe Photos

Make sure you are getting the most out of your genres

Knowing that you have elements of different genres in your story will help inform the rewrite. Go through your script and check to see if you have satisfied the criteria of each genre. Make sure the <u>over-riding</u> genre gets the most screen time. Make sure each supporting genre is fully realized.

Compare the satisfying, genre-rich 2001's ***OCEAN'S ELEVEN*** with the disappointing 2007's ***OCEAN'S THIIRTEEN***. ***OCEAN'S ELEVEN*** used four genres to balance the film story; drama (an everyman, Danny Ocean (portrayed by George Clooney) has a strong, intense desire to reach his goal), crime (identifying, planning, executing), action (set pieces that feature chases and exciting infiltration of dangerous territory) and romance (boy re-connects with girl, boy wants girl, boy feels girl is still in love with him, boy loses girl, boy feels as if life is meaningless without girl, boy works to get girl back, boy gets girl). It's clear why ***OCEAN'S ELEVEN*** worked on many levels and satisfied a wide audience. ***OCEAN'S THIRTEEN*** was not as critically successful because it concentrated on the crime genre (identifying, planning and executing) and the action genre. The "romance" was a fake romance. The drama genre elements were not fully explored because the <u>reason</u> for the heist was one step removed from the protagonist. The coming of age "B" story concerning Linus (portrayed by Matt Damon) and his father did not have a complete arc. Without a successful balance of other genres, a story is in danger of feeling thin. Consider using various genres to fill out the lives of your main characters.

The heart of the genre

A writer who becomes known as a master of a specific over-riding genre is in high demand. There are lists at the studios of writers who know how to handle science fiction, or action/adventure or comedy or stories steeped in historical fact or other specific genres.

A producer, wanting to sell a project of a certain genre to a studio, will often try to interest one of these writers before darkening the studio executive's door. Adding a writer of this caliber to the project will assure the executive, if she decides to fund the project, that the script will meet <u>the basic criteria of its genre</u> and thus bring it closer to being a viable project to green-light for production.

The adage, "a writer should write what he knows," is not just referring to characters, locations or situations. More importantly, it applies to the genre the writer knows – and appreciates. There is no reason to assume a writer will be a master of all genres. Every screenwriter should identify the genres that he understands and appreciates. Write in the genre that excites you the most.

Film-going audiences are demanding. Genre-motivated film audiences are even more demanding. A screenwriter must <u>know</u> the world of horror to write successfully in that genre. The horror aficionado is a fan of the great horror films and great horror writers from Edgar Allan Poe to Stephen King to Anne Rice to Dean Koontz and more. You cannot disappoint your audience.

What makes you, the writer; respond to the films in the genre you are exploring? If you are writing in the mystery genre, are you a mystery fan? Have you read or viewed the best films in this genre? Have you read fiction and non-fiction in this genre? Have you studied how the best in their craft reveal clues while keeping the reader or audience invested in character change? Is the emotional investment of each character strong enough? Does each character serve a purpose? What do you, personally, find the most pleasurable elements of the mystery genre? Gathering clues? Setting up red herrings? Investigating possible motives that reveal something about human nature? It's now time to put yourself in the mystery-loving audience – go through your script scene by scene and ask yourself if you are delivering a story that deepens its mystery elements at every turn. Make sure you have not taken any short cuts or taken the easy way out.

If you have chosen to write in the romantic comedy genre, remind yourself of the elements that appeal to you about this type of film. Is it the lengths people will go to attain love? Is it the absurdity of the actions that cause highly emotional moments to unfold? Is it the notion that even the mighty can fall when the desire for love kicks in? Or that love conquers all and knows no boundaries? Most will agree that love can bring great joy – and great sadness. Have you written scenes that will evoke laughter? Scenes that illuminate heartache or heartbreak? Is there room for joy and is there a room for tears? Take a look at your script scene by scene. Have you gotten to the <u>truth</u> (as you see it) concerning the necessity of loving and being loved.

If you have chosen to write in the science fiction genre, remind yourself of its appeal. What scientific fact or hypothesis sparked the idea for your story? Is it the excitement of creating a new world? Is it creating new rules that people must live by? Are you striving to create the best society you can imagine? Or the worst? Have you explored the light and dark sides of the story? Science fiction aficionados (the ones you want to excite) are very demanding. Most will have read all the great sci-fi authors such as Ray Bradbury, Isaac Asimov, Charles Stross, Richard Morgan, Peter Watts and more. You should be as knowledgeable as your audience.

The classic western film revolves around an outsider who enters a lawless society or world and <u>reluctantly</u> agrees to help restore order. The protagonist needs to face personal difficulties or demons in order to be successful. Have you explored the basics? Have you raised the stakes? Have you added your voice, your ideas, and your point of view?

If you are passionate about a certain genre, study the good – and some of the bad – films in that genre. Take notes. What makes the good films better than the others? How does a film fulfill the genre expectations and then <u>rise above the basics</u> and become a great film? Consider paying homage to the genre – in your own original way.

Find the heart of the genre for yourself. Now, in the rewrite phase, you must totally commit to allowing your passion for the genre (have fun with it, embrace it, know it) become evident.

Write the film genre better than anyone else.

CHAPTER SUMMARY

- Most films are a combination of genres.

- Most films should have a strong over-riding genre.

- "B" and "C" stories are often in a different genre than the "A" story.

- Each genre has inherent elements and criteria that need to be met in order for the story to work at full capacity.

- If your story seems thin, consider the addition of "B" story that pays tribute to a genre different than the genre of your "A" story.

Chapter Five

BALANCE:
A KEY TO A GOOD SCRIPT

Most of us strive for balance in our lives; a good job, someone special with whom to share events, friends, intellectual stimulation, physical exercise, entertainment, rest and activity, spiritual pursuits. There is a balance in our perception of events; days when things seem to go well and days when things seem to go badly. Some people thrive on living in an area of the world where there is a balance of seasons. Some people seek to balance their year by knowing fishing cycles, hunting seasons or school regimens.

Most of us are <u>not</u> striving to live a life holed up in a remote cabin and dedicating 100 percent of our energies exploring an intimate relationship with one person. Or spending 24 hours a day, 7 days a week chained to a work desk. Or using every minute of every day exercising – or in church – or hanging on the beach having a good ol' time. Most of us strive for a balance that suits our personality. Every person's perfect balance will be different – but balance in life does aid in creating a sense of satisfaction.

Every film story needs to strive to find its perfect balance.

How does one achieve balance in a film story? Again, because screenwriting is a craft <u>and an art</u>, there are <u>no rules</u> one can follow to achieve balance. But when a script is well balanced, the reader and the audience can sense it.

Most serious drama is better when injected with some humor. Many horror stories use bits of comedy to relieve tension. Supporting stories of romance or familial conflict can raise the stakes of a protagonist in a drama or comedy. A coming-of-age element (self-revelation, maturation and change) can add texture to a strong drama. Every comedy needs to explore the dramatic needs of the protagonist.

Consider dramas like 1974's *CHINATOWN*, 1985's *OUT OF AFRICA*, 1995's *SE7EN,* 2001's *TRAINING DAY, 2005's CRASH* and 2006's *THE DEPARTED*. Each of these films feature strong dramatic stories, each of them have memorable moments of humor and romance. A few of them have action sequences. A few also embrace the mystery and crime genres.

These films have achieved a satisfactory balance and have proven they give satisfaction to the audience by their box office and critical successes.

Consider comedies like 1984's *GHOSTBUSTERS* and 2003's *SCHOOL OF ROCK.* These comedies explore the dramatic needs of the protagonist; to be loved, to fit in and to prove one's worth. There are also elements of romance in each of these film stories; in *GHOSTBUSTERS,* Dr. Peter Venkman (portrayed by Bill Murray) falls in love with musician Dana (portrayed by Sigourney Weaver). In *SCHOOL OF ROCK,* Dewey Finn (portrayed by Jack Black) takes the principal of the school (portrayed by Joan Cusack) out for drinks and there is possibility of romance. Comedy is at the forefront but the stories are balanced with supporting genres that help to create well-balanced films.

Balancing supporting genres in your "B" and "C" stories can raise your film story to a higher level. Consider films that are out of balance such as 1938's *BRINGING UP BABY* where the comedy hi-jinks and quirks of the characters are at a constant fever pitch and not one character feels based in reality. After the release of the film, director Howard Hawks, one of the most prominent filmmakers of the mid-20th century, in an interview about the film, lamented the choices that were made in script and production. He noted that there were no normal people in the film story; that all the characters were eccentric. Hawks said if he could do it over, he would make sure to keep a few characters as "every people' so the audience could better enjoy the outrageous situations and characters.

BRINGING UP BABY (1938) Cary Grant and Katharine Hepburn
- photo courtesy of Globe Photos

Dumber-than-dumb comedies such as 2006's **TALLADEGA NIGHTS** and 2007's **BLADES OF GLORY** are films not grounded in any dramatic reality. They are in danger of tiring their audience with a constant level of absurdity. Dumber-than-dumb is a valid and successful genre, but consider the best of them all: **ANIMAL HOUSE.** This classic 1978 well-balanced film presents characters that range from bizarre and outrageous to naïve to straight-laced to manipulative and focused. There are dumber-than-dumb comedic scenes, there is a bit of romance, there is a coming-of-age story tucked into the film. **ANIMAL HOUSE** stands out in the wild dumber-than-dumb comedies because it finds a balance by employing a variety of genres.

Howard Hawks, in a 1971 interview with Joseph McBride and Michael Wilmington in *Sight and Sound*, pointed out that if the comedy filmmaker pushes a funny main title and funny antics on the audience at the outset, the film is telling the audience – LAUGH. Hawks felt this was entertainment suicide. Over Hawks' nearly five decades of film directing, he found the well-constructed comedies should <u>first</u> get the audience involved in the character and his or her problem – and <u>then</u> introduce the opportunity for laughter. Take a look at 1982's **TOOTSIE**. The opening sequence features Michael Dorsey's commitment to acting; his teaching, his auditioning, his passion for getting his friend's play into production, his inability to attract women. The <u>tone</u> suggests lightness, but the scenes set up the character's serious overall want. Consider 2006's comedy **LITTLE MISS SUNSHINE**; the opening sequences set up each of the family members' strong and serious <u>desires</u> (overall wants). It's not until all the characters come together around the dinner table and the inciting incident (the phone call that alerts the family to 7-year-old Olive's opportunity to compete in the beauty pageant and sets the plot in motion) that the audience really begins to laugh.

1945's drama, **THE LOST WEEKEND**, has a similar problem to **BRINGING UP BABY**; only its relentless tone is dramatic hopelessness. The story revolves around Don Birnam (portrayed by Ray Milland), who is an alcoholic and has no desire to battle his addiction. His brother tries to help, his fiancé tries to help, Don is judged and found wanting by most of the characters in the film. All the characters are ardent and humorless. Compare **THE LOST WEEKEND** with 1995's **LEAVING LAS VEGAS,** a more successful story about an alcoholic who has no desire to reform. This latter film has a strong supporting genre; <u>romance</u>. As Ben (portrayed by Nicolas Cage) focuses on killing himself with alcohol, the love story heats

Question: What does it mean to "balance" a script?

Answer: Each element, from genre to character to plot points need to be employed and explored in a way that will focus the story on the protagonist's journey and illuminate the most resonate theme. An audience will recognize, consciously or subconsciously, a well-balanced screen story.

up. Sera (portrayed by Elizabeth Shue) does not save her lover but she loves him and in doing so, <u>comes of age</u> herself. The tragic ending is inescapable, but the engagement of the audience is at a higher level because these added genres give a sense of balance to the story.

Consider 2003's **PIRATES OF THE CARIBBEAN, CURSE OF THE BLACK PEARL**. Its over-riding genre is drama/action/adventure – but it is well balanced with the romance between Elizabeth (portrayed by Keira Knightley) and Will (portrayed by Orlando Bloom). There is also intrigue (politics of the time), fantasy (ghosts) and comedy. Jack Sparrow (portrayed by Johnny Depp) provides most of the comedy. The two **PIRATES OF THE CARIBBEAN** sequels are not as critically successful because the balance of genres, as well as the balance of the main characters' screen time (making it unclear who the main protagonist is) and the balance of the "B" and "C" stories are not as satisfying. This lack of balance throws off the focus on the **PIRATES** sequels and keeps the audience from engaging emotionally in a through-line for the major character.

PIRATES OF THE CARIBBEAN: DEAD MAN'S CHEST (2005) Keira Knightly, Johnny Depp
- photo courtesy of Globe Photos

Consider the story elements of 2005's unbalanced **BATMAN BEGINS**. Its over-riding genre is action/adventure. There are elements of humor, but not consistent enough to balance the dramatic "A" story. The "B" story suggests a romantic possibility between Bruce Wayne and Rachel but is unsatisfying because the two do not have a clear arc and there is no heat or passion in their relationship. Remember the seven elements that make up a solid romance story. (See Chapter 4 on genre). Note how many elements are missing in this lackluster attempt at fulfilling a complete romantic story line. The "C" story of friendship and allegiance between Bruce Wayne and his butler, Alfred, does not have a strong arc. Another "C" story relating to the business of Wayne Enterprises does not contain enough elements to make the two characters, Bruce's ally (portrayed by Morgan Freeman) and Bruce's paternalistic nemesis (portrayed by Bruce Davis) satisfying.

Consider 2006's ***NOTES ON A SCANDAL***. This dark, intense drama about an older woman's dangerous obsession with a younger fellow schoolteacher is well balanced with humor, forbidden romance and mystery. 2006's blockbuster hit, ***BORAT, CULTURAL LEARNINGS OF AMERICA FOR MAKE BENEFIT GLORIOUS NATION OF KAZAKHSTAN*** about Borat (portrayed by Sacha Baron Cohen), a man who comes from Kazakhstan to America to experience Western culture and decides that he must travel across the country to meet a sexy female TV star, is a comedy well balanced with dumber-than-dumb comedy, a sense of danger, a point of view of the world and political satire. Because it is well balanced, the film caught the imagination of a wide audience.

Exercise:

Check your script. List the overriding genre of your "A" story. Note your "B" and "C" stories. What are their overriding genres?

Balancing Story Elements

Film industry executives place scripts into categories. Labels like "high concept" and "low concept" and "soft" and "edgy" and "major release" or "big opening weekend" are attached to film stories and screenplays that come across the executives' desk.

There are "high concept" and "low concept" stories.

Examples: 1996's ***TWISTER*** (a tornado wreaks havoc, tornado chasers to the rescue.), 1975's ***JAWS*** (a shark attacks Martha's Vineyard and a new sheriff, who is afraid of water, must lead an unlikely crew of shark-chasers and save the town). Other high concept films include ***GLADIATOR*** (a Roman General is forced into slavery and the only way he can avenge the death of his Emperor and family is to become Rome's premiere gladiator),

TITANTIC (true love triumphs as the most expensive and elite ocean-crossing ship crashes into an iceberg and sinks on its maiden voyage), *WALK THE LINE* (Johnny Cash rises to fame and only the love of his life can save him from personal destruction), *SNAKES ON A PLANE* (the title tells us all) and others.

There are successful high concept stories and successful low concept stories; both are well respected. It is interesting to note that most award winning films tend to be "low-concept" films, such as 1976's *NETWORK,* 1995's *THE USUAL SUSPECTS,* 1996's *FARGO,* 2000's *ALMOST FAMOUS,* 2005's *SIDEWAYS,* 2003's *LOST IN TRANSLATION,* 2005's *CRASH,* 2006's *LITTLE MISS SUNSHINE,* 2006's *THE DEPARTED* and more.

"Soft" and "Edgy" films

There are "soft" and "edgy" films; these terms reflect the <u>tone</u> of the execution of the script.

There are very successful "soft" film stories: 2006's *DREAMGIRLS* (featuring various entertainers striving for personal happiness), 2006's *DEVIL WEARS PRADA* (an intelligent, college-educated young woman chooses to follow a career path that is true to her nature), 2005's *WALK THE LINE* (Johnny Cash works to get June Carter to fall in love with him), 2004's *THE NOTEBOOK* (a pampered young woman needs to be strong enough to go against her loving but controlling mother so she can commit to true love), 2003's *UNDER THE TUSCAN SUN* (a beautiful woman is re-awakened to love while she restores a Tuscan house), Pixar's 1995 *TOY STORY* (a well-cared for toy needs to be able to re-instate the respect of his peers), 1993'S *MRS. DOUBTFIRE* (a man needs to prove to his wife and children – and to himself – that he can be a good father and learn responsibility). The tone of a "soft" film comes from its characters and their desires. Most of the protagonists are "at risk" in an emotional way and do not, in most cases, face life or death situations. They wish to better themselves and their lives and it is only their own neuroses or well-meaning friends or family (not outside violence or evil or destructive forces or "politically incorrect" desires) that cause problems.

The term "edgy" refers to the tone or level of challenge (physical and emotional), and choice of action taken by the characters that inhabit the story. Many edgy films explore life and death issues, challenges caused by evil or powerful forces, difficult lives and desires. Successful "edgy" films

Gardner's Guide to Screenplay: The Rewrite

include 1933's ***TROUBLE IN PARADISE*** (a woman explores the reason why society accepts men if they engage in sexual affairs before marriage, but not women – this film was a shocker of its day), 1956's ***THE SEARCHERS*** (a man needs to rise above his hate and prejudice to rescue someone who will always remind him of what he despises most), ***THE GODFATHER*** (a man needs to remain good while committing evil deeds) and 1995's ***SE7EN*** (a man needs to keep his moral center when confronted and manipulated by true evil).

2006's ***LITTLE MISS SUNSHINE*** has soft and edgy elements. The soft elements include the basic love of the family for each other. The plot is soft; there is no inherent violence involved in the story of the family's journey. The edginess in the script comes from the frank discussions about sexuality, suicide, Grandpa's drug addiction and the dashed dreams of all the characters. The contemporary feel of the characters, the reality of their personal and desperate situations give the film elements of "edgy."

Some production companies, agents and film executives will use the term "soft" to describe a film story they deem to be old-fashioned in tone or character action or motivation. If you are a fan of 1940s and 1950s films and have written a story that harkens back to the sensibilities of those times, it may be time to look at your script closely. Perhaps you need to consider updating the sophistication and worldliness of your characters? Perhaps you need to make sure your story feels like it is a reflection of the present-day world fabric – even if you are setting it <u>in</u> a by-gone era. Consider what <u>today's</u> audience will take away from a period story.

Tone needs to be consistent

The screenwriter can also work to achieve a sense of balance by keeping a consistent tone throughout a script. Check to see if your tone is consistent by examining:

      1. Story elements

      2. Genre demands

      3. Character choices

      4. Pacing

Whatever your genre elements, keep the tone of the writing consistent. The <u>humor</u> in ***THE DEPARTED*** is dark, always on the offensive and

Question: What about films like (2003-2004's) KILL BILL, Volume I and II? How are the genres elements balanced in the film story?

Answer: Many critics agree that Volume II is the more satisfying film in this two-part story. Why? Because it is more balanced. There is the drama of the story; The Bride clearly wants a new life – she wants to be married, have her child and begin a peaceful life working in a record store. However, there is a sense of doom that pervades the story from the outset. There is humor in the wedding rehearsal scenes. There's a romance in The Bride and Bill's interaction; it's not pure love, it's twisted and dark, but the romantic overtones are evident. And when violence occurs, it hits hard.

testosterone-driven. The humor in *FINDING NEMO* is bright, self-deprecating, entertaining and non-threatening. The humor in *LITTLE MISS SUNSHINE* is more complex but consistent; it is built around honesty – as each character states what is really on his or her mind. The juxtaposition of the expected and unexpected creates the humor.

The violence and crime in *THE DEPARTED* is overt. It stems from anger, fear and thirst for power. It's a way of life. It's explored physically and verbally. People die on screen, there is lots of blood and the audience knows this world is unfair, dirty, twisted. One must kill to save oneself. The violence in *FINDING NEMO* involves the natural cycle of life. It's not personal. The sharks have appealing personalities; they are just hungry, they do not thirst for ultimate power or ultimate destruction. The violence in *LITTLE MISS SUNSHINE* is softer in tone. Grandpa dies quietly. Dwayne's quiet but violent reaction to his color blindness is character-driven; it is not aimed to hurt others. The family's protection of young Olive at the beauty pageant is handled with humor, they are not out to destroy the pageant – just to save a beloved member of the family from feeling judged and possibly rejected.

The drama in *THE DEPARTED* is edgy and desperate and extends outward. The focus is on survival, a deep-seated need for a father figure and a need for validation of self-worth and a need to feel loved. There is a level of extreme desperation. The loss of one's soul is possible; the loss of one's life is possible. Stakes are extremely high. The drama in *FINDING NEMO* is focused on the examination of self. Nemo's father, Marlin, is on a quest to save his son – and in doing so – Marlin faces the flaws in his own character. The drama in *LITTLE MISS SUNSHINE* revolves around family members coming to understand each other and reaching out to comfort each other in times of need. Because this is a story about the coming together of a family – the drama is in the right place.

Balance in your choice of characters

Personalities, views of the world and how the characters act and react must stay consistent in style within your script but they should also contribute to the balance of your story. Are all your characters in the "same" world? Yes, you will have characters that are more serious than others, or sillier, or more nervous, or more romantic – and you don't want all your characters to believe in the same things. You want your characters to create conflict with each other – but you also want them to belong in the same world. A violent, power-hungry murderer like **THE DEPARTED's** Frank Costello (portrayed by Jack Nicholson) with his immediate goal of supplying stolen goods to known criminals, does not belong in a film story like **DEVIL WEARS PRADA.** If you needed a violent, power-hungry character in this PG-13 film that is exploring "you are what you wear," the <u>tone</u> of the character and his goals would be different.

Imagine the serious, world-rests-on-my-shoulders persona of Michael Corleone in **THE GODFATHER.** This is <u>not</u> the tone of character needed in a film like **LITTLE MISS SUNSHINE.** Of course this seems totally obvious, but many student scripts will attempt to do too many things, attempt to be too many things. Commit to the specific world of <u>one</u> script and the tone of <u>one</u> story. Remember, if you are screenwriter, this is not the only script you will write. There is no need to pile everything into one script.

A student of mine is building a story about a woman (let's call her Sue) who is the head of a large corporation. She is successful and charming. A terrorist organization tries to blackmail her (she did something illegal some years ago) into producing equipment that could be used in a terrorist strike. In order to combat the terrorist plot, Sue decides to go <u>undercover as a man</u>. She gets herself a job in the bad guys' world. There, she falls in love with a male undercover agent (neither knows the other is undercover). Now, <u>dressed as a man</u>, Sue finds herself in a difficult position to woo and win her love. The film, which began as a dark drama, suddenly switched gears and became a romantic comedy. The student was having problems working out the plot sequences in Act Two. Why? Because the story was trying to cover too many bases – and be too many things. Once the student committed to the over-riding genre and balanced the story, characters and elements to satisfy that genre, the film story became more balanced – and easier to write. If you find that your script is switching gears from genre to genre – ask yourself if you need to identify the over-riding genre.

If you are writing a film in the tone of 1942's **CASABLANCA**, accept that a crazy, wild friend who only wants to bed women and pursue a tap-dancing career may not be a necessary character in this story of political intrigue and self-sacrifice. Save that tap dancer for another film story that you may write a year from now– or ten years from now. There is an appropriate sense of humor in **CASABLANCA**. It comes from characters and the situations that contribute to moving the story along – and stays consistent with the genre and intent of the film.

Of course, you may be breaking new ground in the use of tone and character/

Answer (cont'd): Each character has a well-rounded persona – soft, dark, violent, funny, and twisted. However, The Bride, as the protagonist, is a strong dramatic heroine, she wants what she wants in a myopic way (to avenge the loss of her child), the audience buys into its supreme importance. The audience knows that The Bride will be forever damaged if she is not successful. And literally, after being buried alive, she rises from the dead to accomplish her goal.

genre balance and may not want to limit or edit yourself in any way. It's wise to keep in mind that genres are always evolving. Film expectations and story-telling techniques are always changing. Follow your muse. Knowing the tenets of well-crafted screenwriting is important, but you should never dismiss your own style and voice.

IMPORTANCE OF BALANCING CHARACTERS

Balancing the screen time of your characters

It is important to commit to your protagonist. In most cases, that means he or she will have the most screen time of any character in the film story. This makes sense because it is the protagonist's journey that should be most compelling. There is a practical reason for including the protagonist in a high percentage of the scenes – you will be better able to attract an actor of a high caliber. Screen time is very important to an actor.

Consider 2006's *DEVIL WEARS PRADA*. The character of Andy (portrayed by Anne Hathaway) is in over 90% of the scenes. The film feels unbalanced because Andy is a voyeur in many of the scenes and not the most interesting character. Amanda Priestly (portrayed by Meryl Streep) and Nigel (portrayed by Stanley Tucci) have bigger and clearer goals and are more invested in the outcome of the plot.

Consider the story problems in 2006's *DREAMGIRLS*. The commitment to the focus of the story is missing. The main character, Curtis Taylor Jr. (portrayed by Jamie Foxx) is in approximately 50% of the scenes, a very low percentage. Curtis is the protagonist because he propels the action of the story, goes through a character change and because his actions affect all the other characters in the film. This lack of commitment to the protagonist is one of the reasons why the screen story is unbalanced and ultimately unsatisfying. The various performers with their personal dreams would be better as subplots that illuminate Curtis' story, however they exist separately and veer off in an episodic, soap opera style. The fabric of the film loses its tightness. *DREAMGIRLS* is a clear example of how a film story could be stronger by putting the primary protagonist in more scenes in the film.

Check the balance of your antagonist's presence

All characters should, in some way, impede the protagonist's journey towards his goal – even friends, loved ones and those who act as the protagonist's cheerleaders. However, in most cases, your story's main antagonist needs to take precedence. He or she needs to be focused on stopping the protagonist from achieving his goal and be the major nemesis of the film.

MISS POTTER: Beatrix's mother (portrayed by Barbara Flynn) is in approximately 35% of the scenes, but her presence is felt in the guise of Beatrix's constant chaperone, the old woman in black, who seems omnipresent in the initial three quarters of the film.

THE DEPARTED: Frank Costello (portrayed by Jack Nicholson) appears in approximately 65% of the film's scenes; another 5% he is the focus of discussion as his picture flashes on the screen in police department meetings. In another 10% of the film, people are acting on his instructions. Costello serves as an antagonist to both the protagonists, Colin Sullivan (portrayed by Matt Damon) and Billy Costigan (portrayed by Leonardo DiCaprio), as well as to his direct nemesis, Captain Queenan (portrayed by Martin Sheen). Thus Costello is a strong and constant antagonistic presence adding to the satisfying balance of this film.

BATMAN BEGINS: Antagonist Henri Ducard (portrayed by Liam Neeson) is in low percentage of this unbalanced film – approximately 35%. The audience is distrustful of him at first, then is led to believe he is a Bruce Wayne's ally, and then is shown his true colors near the midpoint of the story. Ducard is not present in the latter half of Act Two and does not reappear until moments before the climax in Act Three. The presence of the antagonist is out of balance and that is why Act Two feels episodic and lacks a strong driving force.

DEVIL WEARS PRADA: Miranda Priestly is in approximately 60% of the film. Her presence is felt at an even higher percentage because Andy's actions are at the behest of Miranda and because conversations with other supporting characters often revolve around Miranda. The film feels out of balance because Miranda's story is of more consequence than the story of the protagonist, Andy. Miranda is more complex and interesting. Be aware of the balance of your characters. In most cases, the protagonist needs to be prominent and a writer should be careful to not let the antagonist take over the story.

Exercise:

The way you tell your story will inform the percentage of scenes featuring your protagonist. Which of the above films do you think is <u>most</u> like your story in storytelling style? What other films do you think are closest to your script in structure? Because stories come in all shapes and sizes, find a few that are close in style to your own. Study the percentage of time the main characters are on screen – the protagonist and antagonist. Study the balance of the "B" and "C" stories. Decide, for yourself, if you feel the balance aids in the story you want to tell. If a trusted reader points out areas where the story seems to lag, take a look at the percentages of "A," "B" and "C" stories in those areas. Perhaps you need to adjust the balance.

Balance of pacing

Some film stories will move along at a leisurely pace, laying out elements in a way that feels very novelistic. Consider 2004's *THE NOTEBOOK*. The audience sits back and lets the story unfold. In 1994's *PULP FICTION*, author Tarantino never lets the audience sit back; there is constant motion and fast story telling.

Consider 1974's *CHINATOWN*. Its slow pace allows the audience to invest in the growing relationship between Jake and Evelyn Mulwray. The pace also allows the audience to understand the peeling of the layers of the mystery and note how each new clue brings Jake closer to the truth. Alfred Hitchcock worked with scripts that relished the slow development of character and the building of suspense; take a look at 1940's and 1950's films such as *VERTIGO, NORTH BY NORTHWEST, NOTORIOUS, REBECCA*.

Consider the pacing of 2007's period piece, *THERE WILL BE BLOOD.* Nearly 100% of the scenes feature the main character, Daniel Plainview (portrayed by Daniel Day Lewis) and concentrate on his journey to purchase and control land, drill for oil and become a wealthy man. He is a man who feels that wealth will ensure control and dissolve the necessity of having to deal with other people. Most of the scenes are long but the tension remains high because of the intensity and ambition of the main character and the mysterious emotional demons of his past. As he succeeds in one area of his life (business), he fails in another (emotional connections) – and though the pacing is slow, the audience constantly feels off guard because of the mercurial, self-destructive nature of the protagonist.

Consider the pacing of 2007's *SUPERBAD*. The scenes are, for the most part, short and packed with fast-paced dialogue and action. The audience jumps into the story and is taken on a wild ride as situations and emotions get more and more absurd.

Comedies often use quick juxtapositions of scenes to bring out humor. Even in longer scenes, the pace of the dialogue or visuals in comedies may be fast-paced.

Find the right pace for your film. Vary it at places, but find a balance, a sense of consistency. Classically, as the film story moves towards its conclusion, the pace quickens, the sense of urgency in the story increases.

Definition:
A *"ticking clock"* is a story element that sets up a sense of time running out for the protagonist. This is used to accelerate tension and excitement, usually in Act Three.

Adding the element of the ticking clock to your script

Not every script benefits from "a ticking clock." However, this added element can help drive your story – especially in Act Three.

A few classic "ticking clock" examples.

CINDERELLA: Cinderella must leave the ball before the clock strikes midnight.

SLEEPING BEAUTY: An evil curse is put on Aurora when she is a baby. The curse says she will prick her finger on her 16th birthday and fall into a deep sleep, only to be awakened by true love's kiss. When her 16th birthday approaches, worry and fear escalate and only the passing of the last stroke of midnight will alleviate the tension.

1942's *CASABLANCA:* Rick must get Ilsa and Laszlo on the plane heading to Portugal before the German soldiers arrive.

1963's *THE GREAT ESCAPE:* The complicated escape from the POW camp has to take place before the Germans find out about the tunnels. When the plan goes into execution, it has to happen in one night, under the cover of darkness.

1967's *THE GRADUATE:* Benjamin must make it to the church to stop Elaine's wedding.

1973's *THE STING:* The con must be executed with split-second timing – in the slim moments after the actual horse race is run and before the fake bets are taken. Films based on cons and heists work best with a ticking clock.

1985's ***BACK TO THE FUTURE:*** Marty McFly must get to the right place at the exact time the lightning will strike. He must have all the proper elements and relationships in place in order to get back to the present-day.

2006's ***CHILDREN OF MEN:*** Theo has to get pregnant Joy to the Tomorrow Ship before he dies. If he doesn't, the future of mankind may be over.

Adding a ticking clock element – something that must be accomplished before the full moon, or before someone else gets the job, or before someone sets off the bomb, or before the iceberg hits the ship – can help you keep the pace (especially in Act Three) moving at an energized clip.

Does every story need a ticking clock?

No. Some stories span a period of time – hours, days or years. Your story and your characters' journeys will dictate – but it is important to know <u>why</u> time is going by.

In most cases, the shorter the time period, the higher the tension. The need to accomplish the goal in a set period of time can strengthen the sense of action in a story. If you have fashioned a story that takes place over a summer, ask yourself by what <u>specific moment at the end of the summer</u> does the goal need to be reached? At a contest or a sporting event or during an eclipse? What is the specific moment?

If you are working in the romance genre, is there a specific and resonant moment in time that requires a declaration of love? New Year's Eve? Before a wedding? Before someone gets on a plane?

If you have written an action/adventure, does the goal need to be attained before a specific moment? Before the treasure turns to dust? Before the invading army conquers?

Exercise:

Take a look at your script. If you do not have a ticking clock element that helps drive the pace of Act Three, is there one that could be added? It can be small or large. Look at other areas of your script. Adding small ticking clocks along the way (someone has to arrive at a certain point at a certain time to make a meeting or delivery or deadline) can help add pace to your script. Are there any ticking clock elements that might add texture to your script?

A question of balance in the final moments of the film

No one wants to be able to predict the end of a story. It is the writer's job to find the unexpected, an ending that surprises – yet satisfies. Consider the beginning and end of your script; how do they relate to one another?

Do the final moments of your script resonate with its beginning elements? Is there symmetry? **BATMAN BEGINS** opens in the gardens of the Wayne mansion, near the dry well. This is the dry well young Bruce Wayne falls into and first encounters bats. As a young boy, Bruce is terrified of bats and his fear contributes to setting up the circumstances for his parents' murder. The film uses the same location for its conclusion. However, the dry well now has a new meaning for Bruce – it's no longer the place of his greatest fear – it is a place that symbolizes his greatest moments of bravery. 2000's **GLADIATOR** opens with an image of war hero Maximus walking through the peaceful wheat fields that symbolize his desire to go home, far away from battle and his great desire for peace. The film ends with Maximus' dead body <u>floating</u> over the same wheat fields, clearly symbolizing that he is headed to a place of peace in the afterlife.

THE GODFATHER begins in the home office of the godfather (Vito Corleone) and ends with the new godfather (Michael Corleone) officially taking over that office.

You want to find the right balance for all your story elements

Here are some guidelines to consider: If the percentage of story time <u>away</u> from the protagonist is too high, you may want to re-think the balance of your script. If you have too many themes, too many diverse "B" and "C" stories that do not reflect on the protagonist's overall want, you may want to adjust your story.

This is not only practical (to attract a lead actor, one must give him or her lots of screen time) but also good for your story. The more time you take to explore your main character's journey, the main theme and your own point of view, the richer your story will become.

Sometimes we wish there was a definite and successful formula for perfect script balance. But there is not. There is no formula. Screenwriting is a craft <u>and an art.</u> Knowing the craft can guide you (and don't be lazy about doing the hard work demanded of a good craftsman) but <u>never</u> deny your artistic vision.

CHAPTER SUMMARY

- Achieving balance in the various elements of your film story can raise your script to a higher level.

- A balance of various genres can fill out your screen story.

- Achieving a balance of tone is important in your film story.

- Creating a proper balance among the characters in your film will help focus the story.

- Each story is different and each script will demand different story balances.

Chapter Six

CHARACTER IS EVERYTHING

Most successful films focus on examinations of its main characters in emotionally or physically heightened situations because audiences enjoy coming to the movie theatre to either live vicariously or witness others cope in difficult situations. Audiences want to meet, get to know and grow to understand the characters.

LET THE AUDIENCE UNDERSTAND YOUR CHARACTERS

As you rewrite and polish your script, it's time to make sure your characters' motivations and desires are crystal clear. Make sure you allow your audience go through the process of getting to know your characters. Make sure you have "peeled back all the necessary layers" that will reveal character quirks, secrets and agendas.

In most cases, at the initial meeting of a person in a social situation, we take in their outward elements – age, gender, clothes, hair, demeanor and other visible attributes; the layer they present to the world every day. If we get a chance to talk to the person and peel back another layer of his persona, we may ask relatively safe questions to further our knowledge – questions about work or schools or friends or hobbies, questions about where he resides, what sports team he supports, what books he's read lately, political or religious bents and other topics. If the relationship goes deeper, we may peel back the next layer and find out about dreams, aspirations, passions or sense of morality. The next layer could reveal a secret or an obsession. As each layer of the character is revealed, the audience comes to a better understanding of the character. In most cases, understanding produces empathy. Once the audience empathizes with your character, you have them hooked. The audience wants to find out how your character will face the problems you create in your film story – they will wonder if your character will win or lose his fight or if he will accomplish his goals.

Make sure you peel back the layers – you want to get to the core of your characters.

Exercise:

Go through the latest draft of your script. Check to see if you have thoroughly explored your protagonist. Does each scene bring us to a deeper understanding of motivations, deep desires or needs? Have you revealed a deep concern or secret? Does the content of each scene shed new light on the character? Ask yourself: How can the character surprise the audience – and remain consistent?

2002's *ADAPTATION,* written by Charlie Kaufman, is a close examination of the character, Charlie (portrayed by Nicolas Cage). The Act One set-up focuses on character: Charlie is an insecure screenwriter who is afraid to set free his passionate feelings while struggling to adapt a book that exudes extraordinary passion – passion even in a description of a flower. Charlie's professional life is balanced with his desire for love (he fails to connect with the woman he desires because he is unable to commit to passion), his desire for authenticity (he passionately searches for a truth in his writing), his desire for acceptance (he desperately wants to feel accepted by people) and his desire for self-growth and understanding (he constantly analyzes himself and finally seeks help from a screenwriting guru). The "B" story that explores the character of Susan (portrayed by Meryl Streep) is also an examination of character. Susan is a woman who feels she does not understand true passion – or at least has lost touch with her passionate side. She goes in search of passion. Note how both stories are about a desire for passion; Charlie learns how to connect to it so he can build a new life and Susan's pursuit of passion destroys her.

ADAPTATION is a good example of Aristotle's most important maxim of story telling: <u>A story should be about one thing.</u> The characters, Charlie and Susan, take different paths as they pursue passion and the plot takes them in various directions, but the <u>cores</u> of their stories remain about <u>one thing</u>.

Explore the different facets of your characters' lives

There is a reason why most film stories deal with people in crisis. Crisis situations tend to bring out the worst in people – and the best in people. Crises challenge our cores, our moral centers, and our beliefs. All facets of our characters can come into play.

ADAPTATION (2002)   Nicolas Cage, Meryl Streep
- *photo courtesy of Globe Photos*

Question: How can a writer deepen the audience's understanding of his characters?

Answer: Showing characters in various areas of their lives, such as at work and at home, in relationships and alone, with friends and with antagonists, in stressful or non-stressful situations (and so on) can help aid in the audience's understanding of your characters.

Ask yourself if the character you are examining in your latest draft is faceted enough to warrant an audience's attention for two hours. This does not mean that your character has to do something extraordinary or live in an extraordinary world, but it does mean that the character needs to want something in a strong or obsessive way and choose to face the obstacles (or not) that could destroy or make the attainment of his goal impossible. The audience needs enough information about the characters' hopes, dreams, goals, relationships and conflicts and then, when we follow the characters to the crisis point of the film story, they have enough information and empathy to root for the characters to make the right choices.

Consider 2007's **THE SAVAGES**, written by Tamara Jenkins. The main characters of this drama are brother and sister Wendy Savage (portrayed by Laura Linney) and Jon Savage (portrayed by Phillip Seymour Hoffman). We see both of them in their work situations – Wendy does temporary work in New York City while she writes plays, Jon teaches drama at a university in Buffalo, New York and is writing a book on Bertolt Brecht. We are introduced to the romances in their lives – Wendy is in an unhealthy relationship with a married man and Jon cannot commit to his loving girlfriend. We see them in their time alone – Wendy manically exercises and indulges in fantasies of a better and more successful life, Jon tries to make his work all-important but does not feel at peace. We see them both interact with their father – a man who did not raise them with love or affection. We see them deal with (and make mistakes with) the employees at their father's nursing home. Most importantly we see them deal with each other – call each other on lies and fears and support each other with love. This small, powerful film brings the audience in because the characters are richly explored in all the important facets of their lives.

Exercise:

Have a few trusted readers read your latest draft. Ask them when they began to truly care about the protagonist. Ask them to pinpoint a moment or a few moments where they took the side of the protagonist (or the main character you intend them to root for) – ask them when they got emotionally invested. You want your audience to move beyond their curiosity concerning how the plot may play out and get emotionally invested in characters.

Consider 2005's **SIDEWAYS**. The canvas of this Academy Award winning story revolves around a man, Miles, who cannot move forward in his life. Why? Because he cannot be honest with himself about his situations or feelings. Many facets of Miles' life – love (ex-wife and new love), work (his "day" job as a teacher and his hopes of becoming a published author), friendships (his best friend), family (his mother), his passion and knowledge of wine, and his inability to face the truth are all explored. The audience comes to understand Miles and his problem by seeing him deal with the various facets of his life. In each area of his life he is not truthful. Miles' story explores one thing, his inability to move forward because he is unable to face and accept the truth.

Exercise:

View 2005's **SIDEWAYS**. Note how the different facets of Miles' life create constant conflict because of one thing – Miles' inability to accept the truths in his life. Miles is dishonest with himself – and because he cannot face the truth and move forward – this dishonesty creates problems. Take a look at the film again and note how almost every scene illuminates Miles' dilemma. Here's the beginning of a list you could make...

1.   Miles oversleeps and then, on the phone, lies about why he is late to pick up his friend, Jack, for Jack's final bachelor weekend in the Central California wine country.

2.   Miles lies to his landlord about how Miles parked his car.

3.   Miles lies to Jack when he tells him he will get on the highway quickly in order to pick Jack up for the weekend.

4.   Miles allows Jack to lie to his future in-laws about their plans for the weekend.

5.   Miles lies to his mother about the state of his life.

6.   Miles steals money from his mother.

7.   Miles lies when he denies he harbors desires to get back with his ex-wife.

8.   Miles lies about the publication of his newly completed novel.

9.   Miles allows Jack to lie about the reason for their bachelor weekend when Jack wants to bed Stephanie, the wine bartender.

10.   Miles lies when he denies that he made a telephone call to his ex-wife.

11.   Miles lies to Jack's fiancé about Jack's whereabouts.

12.   Miles allows Maya (the woman he desires) to believe he is a successful novelist.

> *Continue the list. Note how each of the lies that Miles tells or allows to be told causes more conflict. Note how Miles' life takes a drastic turn at the end of Act Two when he confronts Jack about Jack's dishonest behavior and inadvertently <u>tells the truth</u> to Maya about Jack's lies. It is only when Miles finally tells the <u>truth</u> and <u>accepts the truth</u> about his life that he can move forward and pursue love and new happiness.*

Why did this film capture the audience's attention? Miles' dilemma – not being able to move forward in his life – is <u>relatable</u>. Most people can point to their own lives and note moments of falling into passivity, moments of not facing the truth, moments of feeling like a failure, moments of not being able to act on desires, moments of lying to those they love or lying to themselves about personal desires. The character, Miles, is an exaggeration. His character is pushed to absurd levels to fulfill the comedy genre – to remove him just enough from our own reality so we can laugh at him – but he still feels real and <u>relatable.</u>

SIDEWAYS (2004) Paul Giamatti, Thomas Haden-Church
- photo courtesy of Globe Photos

Characters with major flaws still need to be understood

Your protagonist can be a "good" person or a "bad" person. The classic hero does the "right thing for the right reason." The classic anti-hero does the "wrong thing for the right reason." Whether your protagonist is an angel or a whistle-blower or a murderer or a drug dealer, one thing is of paramount importance – the audience must understand <u>why</u> he is doing what he is doing. If there is no empathy, you are in danger of losing your audience.

Director Martin Scorsese is attracted to material that examines tough characters – characters that do not always "do the right thing." He has worked with writers such as Paul Schrader (1976's *TAXI DRIVER,* 1980's *RAGING BULL*), Nicolas Pileggi *(1990's GOODFELLAS)* William Monahan (adaptor of 2006's *THE DEPARTED),* writers who have created characters that are not, in all aspects, upstanding solid citizens or people one might desire to have as best friends. The characters are complex – many are edgy or selfish or troubled or violent or duplicitous or unstable or egotistical or not-too-bright or overly ambitious. However, these characters are benchmarks in the lexicon of film because the audience is able to <u>understand</u> them and <u>understand</u> (not necessarily approve of) their actions. <u>Plus, there is at least one redeeming quality about the protagonist in each film.</u> Travis Bickle (portrayed by Robert DeNiro) in *TAXI DRIVER* is an unstable, violent, envious loner with no social skills. However, there are a few elements of his character that allow the audience to "like" or "respect" or "empathize." What are Bickle's redeeming traits? Bickle is a Viet Nam veteran <u>and</u> he tries to persuade a child prostitute to leave her pimp and her life on the streets and return to family and school. The <u>reason</u> he becomes a lone gunman intent on assassination is very clear; he sees the world as debauched and decadent, he wants to cleanse it. The audience is not meant to see Travis Bickle as a Dudley-Do-Right hero – this is a study of a disturbed man on the wrong path. However, the audience is drawn into the story and the film is successful because the audience comes to <u>understand</u> the protagonist. Note how the protagonist in *RAGING BULL*, Jake LaMotta (portrayed by Robert DeNiro), has good and bad traits. He has charisma and talent and works tirelessly to become a boxing champion. He's a man who needs to be loved and appreciated. These are traits an audience can appreciate. However, Jake is also jealous and paranoid and allows the violence that he brings to the ring seep into his friendships and family life. His violent actions eventually destroy the family he so desperately wants around him. This film is an amazing character study – the writers have created moments where the audience <u>understands</u> the needs and <u>understands</u> the flaws that keep LaMotta from achieving a successful, well-rounded life. *GOODFELLAS*: Henry Hill (portrayed by Ray Liotta) tells the audience in the beginning moments of the film of his overwhelming desire "to be somebody." This desire drives all of Henry's actions and , at the end of the film, when Henry (who has murdered and cheated and dealt drugs but lived the rich, pampered life of a "somebody") is in the witness protection program eating spaghetti with ketchup sauce, realizing for the rest of his life he will be a "nobody" – the audience empathizes – and sympathizes – with him. Why? Because his desire "to be someone" is <u>relatable</u>, as is his desire for affirmation from his peers, as is his love for his wife and family. The audience <u>understands</u> Henry. *THE DEPARTED:* Colin Sullivan (portrayed by Matt Damon) is the pawn of the Irish mob boss, a dirty cop, plays people, manipulates people, and is smart and crafty and ambitious. The audience also knows that Colin lost both parents when he was a young child, that the mob boss became a surrogate father to him and that the mob boss even bought groceries for Colin and his grandmother when money was tight. The audience also knows that Colin wants out from under the mob boss' control and that he has political ambitions. The audience also sees Colin fall in love with a "good" woman and sees him hope that she will never find out that he is not the man she thinks he is. The audience may not <u>like</u> Colin, but they <u>understand</u> him.

Check your script. There is no reason for your character to be "all good" or "all bad." A character who makes wrong choices, says the wrong thing at the wrong time, makes mistakes – reveals human foibles – is more interesting than a character who is constantly in the "wrong" or constantly in the "right" column. Let the audience <u>understand</u> your character. 2006's ***EL CANTATE***, starring Marc Anthony as salsa singer Hector Lavoe, is an example of a film that does not allow the audience to <u>understand</u> the character. Hector, against his father's wishes, travels from Puerto Rico to New York City to make it as a singer and performer. He gains success quickly and begins using drugs. He marries. He has a child. He alienates his band members because he is unreliable, showing up late for gigs. He contracts AIDS. This film is based on facts of Hector Lavoe's life, facts seen through the eyes of his wife (portrayed by Jennifer Lopez). What is missing in the film is the <u>understanding</u> of the character. The <u>why.</u> Although you, the writer, may think that it's clear why anyone would want to be a star performer, that it's clear that drugs can seduce, that it's clear that a man may fall in love with a woman who is full of life and beautiful – you must be <u>specific</u> about the <u>why</u> of each element. Why does this particular person desire fame? Why does he need fame? Why is he irresponsible, what does he consciously or unconsciously hope to gain from acting in an irresponsible manner? Why does he want to escape into a drugged state? Let the character speak from his or her heart and <u>explain</u> or <u>try to make sense of</u> or <u>examine</u> the reasons for certain actions. It's not enough to set out the facts – the great movies allow for a full <u>understanding</u> of characters.

Exercise:

If readers or friends express that they find it hard to <u>care</u> about your protagonist, go back and look at the different areas of his or her life; work, relationships, dreams, how he treats his family, how she still hurts from a tormented relationship, how he may be dishonest at work but a good friend and honest on the soccer field. Find one or two things that show your protagonist has one or two redeeming areas in his or her life.

Don't forget your antagonist

A "villain" is an antagonist that is all bad. Comic books and fairy tales feature villains as antagonists. In most well-developed stories and scripts, the antagonist needs to be as interesting and multi-dimensional as the protagonist – have "good" and "bad" elements to his character.

> ### Exercise:
>
> Unless your script falls into the "all good" versus "all evil area" of storytelling, check the construction of your main antagonist. What is redeeming about him? Why do we empathize with her? If a character's life is too narrowly portrayed and you aren't getting the reaction or understanding of that character that you expected – consider adding another dimension to his or her life.

Check your script. Does each scene contain elements of conflict for the characters in the scene? Is each scene centered on a character <u>wanting</u> something and, in most cases, <u>not</u> being able to feel satisfied?

2006's ***DEPARTED*** (based on the Hong Kong film ***INFERNAL AFFAIRS***), a well-constructed and complex film, features parallel stories of two protagonists. One, Billy Costigan, is a cop out to prove his dedication to law and order and the other, Colin Sullivan, is a corrupt cop. Below is a list of their character conflicts in Act One.

Billy Costigan (portrayed by Leonardo DiCaprio)

1. Billy is called in to interview with Police Captain Queenan and Queenan's right hand man, Dignam. Billy's honesty, moral integrity and trustworthiness are immediately questioned. Billy is pushed to his emotional limits as they attack his family, his intelligence and his loyalty.

2. Billy agrees to go undercover in a violent Irish mob to prove his loyalty to the police force. This action introduces the main conflicts that will continue through the rest of the film story. Billy is understandably on edge because his life is now in danger; he has to be on his toes at all times.

3. Billy's mother is dying and he is estranged from his stepfather.

4. Billy is drawn into the world of a charismatic criminal, Frank

Costello. Billy is a young man who responds to a strong father figure and thus has to fight against being drawn in by Costello.

5. Billy is lonely and his undercover role makes him feel more isolated.

6. Billy, while undercover, is faced with having to commit violent acts that are against his nature.

7. Billy is ordered to show up for sessions with the police force's female therapist. Billy becomes attracted to her but cannot tell her the truth about his situation.

Colin Sullivan (portrayed by Matt Damon)

Colin is a corrupt cop, essentially undercover in the police force for the Irish mob boss and his surrogate father, Frank Costello. Colin's conflicts about his role are evident when his overall want becomes clear – he wants respect and legitimate power in Boston (remember he rents a certain apartment because it has a view of the dome of the Government building).

1. Colin rises in the police force fast, due to inside knowledge given to him by Costello. Colin has to deal with the resentment of his peers as well as make sure his true allegiances (to Costello) are never suspected.

2. Colin does not like to be under powerful Costello's thumb but does not know how to get out of his situation.

3. Colin falls in love with the police force's female therapist and cannot tell her the truth about his criminal connections.

4. Colin suspects there is a police officer working undercover in Costello's gang. He fears he will be revealed to be a bad cop. This puts his career aspirations – and his life – in danger.

Note how the two major characters in this film are in constant conflict. Conflict creates interest and tension. You want the audience to be wondering; what will happen next?

Every action should reverberate and cause more conflict for the protagonist.

THE DEPARTED (2006) Matt Damon, Leonardo DiCaprio
- photo courtesy of Globe Photos

The antagonist creates conflict and has his own conflicts

Make sure your antagonist is working at capacity. Does he have his own strong overall want? Does she have her own point of view?

The main antagonist in **THE DEPARTED** stands in the way of the two main characters reaching their goals. Irish mob boss Frank Costello (portrayed by Jack Nicholson) controls dirty cop Colin Sullivan and thwarts Colin's desire for legitimate power. Costello also stands in good cop Billy Costigan's way of getting what he wants – respect. Billy has to bring down Costello and expose his latest crimes to prove he is a loyal member of the police force. Frank Costello is a well-drawn character. The audience is privy to many areas of his life; most of them contain continual conflict. Some of these conflicts include:

1. Costello, head of the Irish mob, is trying to stay ahead of the Italian Mafia to ensure his own power.

2. Costello is suspect of anyone who might infiltrate his gang; he finds trust nearly impossible.

3. Costello has to continually assert his power to keep the community as well as the members of his gang in line.

4. Costello's girlfriend challenges him.

5. Costello uses drugs and this makes him vulnerable. The audience

wonders if this vulnerability will cause his downfall.

6. Costello's paranoia is aggravated.

7. The Boston police force has dedicated a group of officers to bring Costello down.

8. Costello is trying to play many sides; the FBI, the Boston police force, his criminal gang.

Each supporting character should create conflict for the protagonist

Not only is the antagonist meant to create conflict, but also <u>every supporting character</u> should cause conflict for the protagonist. Everyone who has taken a simple science class understands that friction causes heat; and heat is what you want to add to your story – when things are going well and there is no conflict or friction, you are in danger of your story lagging and you are in danger of losing your audience.

Each supporting character must add conflict to the protagonist's life.

Consider some of the other supporting characters in 2006's *THE DEPARTED* and how they add conflict to Billy Costigan's story.

1. Captain Queenan (portrayed by Martin Sheen) is the man Billy wants to impress.

   a. Queenan withholds his trust and confidence and in doing so, causes Billy to take the dangerous undercover job in the Irish mob.

   b. Even when Queenan accepts that Billy is an honest cop and is doing his job well, Queenan cannot openly accept or help Billy because the investigation is not yet over – Billy's cover cannot be blown.

   c. When Queenan is killed, Billy is forced into his greatest conflict; does he continue his charade or try to escape to safety?

2. Dignam (portrayed by Mark Wahlberg) is Billy's aggressively antagonistic superior in the police force and likes to push Billy's buttons.

   a. Dignam openly criticizes and belittles Billy.

b. Dignam questions Billy's loyalties.

c. Dignam openly questions Billy's courage.

d. Dignam physically challenges Billy.

3. Frank Costello, the main antagonist, is the head of the Irish mob that demands loyalty.

a. Frank's suspicions of a "rat" in his outfit are always prominent and Billy can never let his guard down.

b. Frank physically challenges Billy.

c. Frank takes a liking to Billy; he has paternal tendencies to which Billy responds.

d. Frank expects Billy to commit violent acts.

e. Billy has to be clever to maintain contact with Queenan while in Costello's gang.

4. Mr. French (portrayed by Ray Winstone) is Costello's trusted lieutenant. He puts himself on the line for Billy and therefore is watchful.

a. Billy has to continually prove to Mr. French that he is a worthy criminal.

b. It is clear that Mr. French's first loyalty is to Costello.

5. Madolyn (portrayed by Vera Farmiga), the police force's therapist serves two purposes in the film. She asks questions the audience wants to know the answers to – and she serves as the love interest/safe haven for Billy in the story.

a. Madolyn starts as a therapist that Billy resents

b. Madolyn is attractive to Billy and this is not the time he should be seeking out an intimate relationship

c. Madolyn is not available to Billy; she makes it clear she is involved in a relationship with someone else.

d. Madolyn tells Billy she cannot be his therapist anymore

e. Billy is falling in love with Madolyn / she is falling in love with him

6. Colin Sullivan, the "rat" inside the police department and the film's other major character. He is a constant threat to Billy.

a. Colin eludes Billy's attempts to identify him

b. Colin makes it possible for Costello to carry out the crimes that Billy is supposed to stop

c. Although Billy does not know it, Colin is engaged to be married to Billy's love interest

Even the smaller roles in the film story are designed to create conflict. Billy's mother is in a coma and dying and she cannot emotionally support him. Billy's stepfather does not approve of him. Billy's father's history does not help him in the police force or with Costello. Billy's cousin is not sure if he can trust Billy. Officer Brown (portrayed by Anthony Anderson), Billy's friend on the police force, is not sure he can trust Billy.

Exercise:

View 2006's **THE DEPARTED.** List other conflicts in Colin Sullivan's relationships and Billy Costigan's relationships in the film. Do the same for the character of Frank Costello. Then take a look at your latest draft. Have you made foes and friends and lovers and members of family and other characters add to the conflict for your main protagonist? Remember, even best friends should question and create conflict for the protagonist.

Again, compare two films in the same franchise: 2001's *OCEAN'S ELEVEN* and 2007's *OCEAN'S THIRTEEN.* The first features conflict driven by character. Danny Ocean (portrayed by George Clooney) wants to get the love of his life back. Danny uses his friends to make that possible; he engages their services to carry out a heist at a top Las Vegas casino. The story unfolds; each character is drawn and has an arc (large or small). Character desires clearly drive the plot – Danny's good friend, Rusty (portrayed by Brad Pitt) signs on for the job because he is bored running gambling parties for rich Hollywood celebrities. Reuben Tishkoff (portrayed by Elliot Gould) wants in because he resents the fact that the main antagonist, Terry Benedict (portrayed by Andy Garcia) took over one of Tishkoff's casinos. Saul Bloom (portrayed by Carl Reiner) is feeling old and wants to feel alive again. Other characters have their reasons for joining the con job. The story takes a turn when Danny's gang finds out Danny's real reason for robbing the casino: To win back the affections of his ex-wife. Conflict arises because the gang fears that Danny's emotional reasons could endanger the con and the fact that he is making the heist "personal" puts them all at risk. There are high physical stakes and pretty high emotional stakes – and the film keeps the audience's interest because the characters' desires drive the film story.

OCEAN'S ELEVEN (2001) George Clooney, Brad Pitt, Matt Damon, Elliot Gould, Don Cheadle
- photo courtesy of Globe Photos

Unfortunately, the plot – and not character conflicts – drive the disappointing *OCEAN'S THIRTEEN*. Nearly 95% of this unbalanced film is dedicated to plot. The set up of "let's do the heist to avenge Reuben's humiliation at the hands of villainous Willie Bank" (portrayed by Al Pacino) does not play out in a satisfying way because the <u>conflict</u> between protagonist and antagonist feels too removed. There is a very small "B" story that flirts with a relationship arc between Linus (portrayed by Matt Damon) and his father (portrayed by Bob Einstein), but this story does not take on much importance. One could argue that the "chatting" scenes between Danny Ocean and Rusty as they stake out locations for the con are relationship scenes but they do not contain anything that contributes to the story or to a beginning, middle or end to a character arc or even a sense of conflict. They clearly do not drive the story or affect the story. Therefore the scenes feel like "filler". Scenes that do not <u>advance</u> the plot or knowledge of character or contribute to any <u>change</u> of character do not enhance a film.

Avoid "filler" scenes. Make sure the character's pursuit of her overall want is driving your story. Make sure every scene is necessary.

EMOTIONAL TRACKING

As you work on your rewrite, make sure the reader can <u>emotionally track</u> your character. It is necessary for the reader to be able to track your main characters' states of mind and feelings.

The job of a screenwriter is to tell a good story that will touch people – in their hearts and minds. Check to see if the emotional life of your character is crystal clear.

It's not productive to hide behind "the character doesn't know how he or she is feeling." You, the writer, <u>has to know</u> how the character is feeling so you can plot the next scenes. One scene must lead to another. Each scene should have consequences. If your character is confused about his emotional state, or in denial of an emotional state – that is a feeling in itself. That feeling or emotional state will color the character's next scene.

It's also not productive to hide behind "the actor will decide" how the character is feeling. Yes, an actor may decide to play a scene in a different way than you intend, but, ultimately, <u>you are the actor's guide</u>. Your script sets out a way for the character to emotionally get from point A to point B to point C and beyond. If the script does not present a clear emotional map, the through-line of the story can be lost. Take a look at 2007's ***DAN IN REAL LIFE.*** The emotions of the two main characters, widower Dan (portrayed by Steve Carell) and unlucky-in-love Marie (portrayed by Juliette Binoche) seem to randomly flip-flop. The characters meet, enjoy each other's company, and then quickly realize Marie is dating Dan's brother. All three are spending a few days with Dan's large family at a country home. The characters express their attraction to one another, then ignore it, then act on it, then ignore it. It is hard for an audience to root for a pair of lovers if the lovers' actions and reactions and feelings confuse the audience.

How your specific characters react to various situations will affect the outcome of the story. You are the storyteller – you need to <u>know</u> and <u>relay</u> the character feelings and <u>states of mind</u> to the reader and audience.

Audiences go to the theatre to witness people acting on their emotions – something we don't often do in "real life" – so we enjoy watching others commit to their emotional lives. You, the writer, <u>know</u> your characters better than anyone and it's desirable to do all you can to make their emotional lives clear.

Easy ways to emotionally track your characters

The importance of emotional tracking of each of your characters cannot be over-emphasized. Simply stating the events and actions in each scene is, in some cases, not enough. Take a look at your script. Is it clear how a character enters each scene? Is it clear the emotional change in the scene?

Of course, many times the scene – or the previous scenes – will make the state of mind or feelings of your character clear. If, however, clarity is needed, emotional tracking can be helpful.

Remember, in most cases, it is not the writer's job to give specific actor directions like "raising an eyebrow" or "pause" or "snarly" or "giddy" et al. Unless it's a plot point, these specifics are unnecessary and unwanted. However, it is the writer's job to make sure the <u>sense</u> and the <u>tone</u> and the <u>emotion</u> of the scene is clear.

> Example: A simple action line could read:
>
> *Susan sets the table.*

This action line does not give us a clue as to Susan's state of mind. If it is important to the dynamic of the scene, add a clue – one or two words or a short phrase – to aid the reader in understanding Susan's state of mind.

> Examples of how to clarify the action line.
>
> *Susan, upset, sets the table.*
>
> *Susan, drunk, sets the table.*
>
> *Susan, dancing happily, sets the table.*
>
> *Susan, feeling her life is over, sets the table.*

With the addition of one or two words or a short phrase, the reader understands the emotional life of the character in the scene. In most cases it is wise to keep your descriptive words to a minimum.

The tracking of the emotions of the characters can be done with the use of an adjective or adverb in the action line. One can also use the parenthetical line that precedes the dialogue.

Example of the barest information that could be given in this scene:

INT. BARBER SHOP – DAY

T-Jay enters. The place is full of customers. Nick is not there.

T-JAY

Where the hell is he?

Unless a previous scene informs the actor or director (or reader of the script) of T-Jay's state of mind and if it's important to the following of the story, it might be beneficial to add some emotional tracking. See the adjustment below:

INT. BARBER SHOP – DAY

T-Jay, angry and wanting to punch someone, busts in. The customers are startled. Nick is not there.

T-JAY

Where the hell is he?

Or:

INT. BARBER SHOP – DAY

T-Jay, dressed for success and ready to celebrate, peeks in. The customers laugh. Nick is not there.

T-JAY

Where the hell is he?

Another example:

EXT. GOLDEN GATE BRIDGE – NIGHT

Sally has lost her will to live. She approaches the railing…

Or:

EXT. GOLDEN GATE BRIDGE – NIGHT

Sally, horrified, approaches the railing

Leave it to the actress who brings Sally to life off the page to decide how the character embodies a sense of doom or horror.

By putting the emotional tracking in the action line, you are not telling the actor (or director) the specific line read or facial expression you envision in your head but a sense of what is happening in the scene. Remember, filmmaking is a collaborative art. You tell the story and leave the specifics of acting or camera shots to those who are focused on that area of production.

If you want to use the parenthetical line to illuminate the character's state of mind, consider approaching it this way:

INT. BARBER SHOP– DAY

T-Jay busts in, startling the customers. Nick is not there.

> T-JAY
> (angry)
> Where the hell is he?

What is the difference between putting "shouting" in the parenthetical as opposed to "angry"? "Shouting" is a line reading. "Angry" is an emotion and the actor and director can decide, depending on the choices of the actor in building his characterization, if angry means a low growl or a loud shout. <u>Relay the emotion</u> – not the line reading or direction.

Exercise:

Check your script. Is the action of the character letting the reader know <u>how</u> the character feels about carrying out the action? If the dialogue or other elements of the scene do not make the emotion of the character clear, consider adding one or two words or short phrase that will illuminate the emotion under the character action. Remember, no need to overdo the emotional tracking. Use it <u>only</u> when necessary.

Remember, you are very close to your story and characters. They are personal to you. As you wrote each scene you probably envisioned or "felt" each character's emotional state. The reader of the screenplay (and eventually the director or the actor) needs to be able to get inside your head to understand your intentions.

Definition:
***ON-THE-NOSE
DIALOGUE OR VISUALS.***
On-the-nose dialogue
means that a character
is stating the obvious
or baldly making his
intentions clear. On-the-
nose visuals make the
character's intent, feelings
or desires absolutely
obvious.

KEEP YOUR PROTAGONIST'S OVERALL WANT AT THE FOREFRONT OF YOUR STORY

It's important to keep re-examining the overall want of your protagonist. Reset the protagonist's overall want in each act.

ACT ONE: Make sure the protagonist's want/need is clear. Make sure you have illuminated the problem(s) the protagonist will have to face in order to accomplish his overall want/need. Make sure the immediate goals you have set up (the plot) help move your protagonist closer to satisfying his overall want.

Exercise:

Note the page number on which your protagonist's overall want becomes clear. If you feel the set up of the overall want/need is not as clear as it should be, write an "on-the-nose" scene. This can be done using visuals or by writing a dialogue exchange. After you have written the on-the-nose moment or scene, ask: Is there a place for this (perhaps after you polish it or make it less on-the-nose (or not)) somewhere in the first act of your script?

On page one of 2001's **LEGALLY BLONDE**, Elle's first immediate goal is clear; Elle (Reese Witherspoon) wants to marry Warner, her college boyfriend – and in fact, she expects him to propose to her that evening. When Warner tells her that his family expects him to marry "a Jackie," not "a Marilyn," Elle's overall want is quickly made clear – she wants <u>respect</u>. She becomes determined that she will not be considered "just a blonde."

Elle's problems in accomplishing her goal: Warner is off to Harvard Law School. In order to show him she is worthy of his respect, Elle needs to gain acceptance into the very competitive and elite university. She sets out to accomplish her immediate goal. Once Elle accomplishes this and arrives at Harvard, she finds out that Warner is already engaged to a fellow classmate. Her next immediate goal is to prove to Warner that he should reconsider his engagement so she tries to get into his study group … and so on.

Does your protagonist put in words -   or make evident -   her first immediate goal? Does she want to win the soccer game? Take out the alien? Get attention? Get parents re-united? Save a sinking ship? Remember, the immediate goals help make up the plot and plot twists of your story.

1972's ***THE GODFATHER***: Protagonist Michael (Al Pacino), in his first scene, tells his fiancé, Kay, that he wants his work to be outside the family's Mafia business, he wants to forge a <u>legitimate</u> business life, that he loves his family but he is <u>different</u>. This speaks to Michael's overall want; legitimate respect. The audience understands that from Michael's first scene.

Michael's problems in accomplishing his goal are quickly laid out in the story. Most of the Mafia dons want to get into the drug business and because Don Corleone (Michael's powerful father and most powerful don) holds out, his family becomes a target of mob violence. Michael's father is shot. One of Michael's first immediate goals becomes protecting his father...

What if your protagonist is not consciously aware of his overall want? What if it is a subconscious <u>need</u> and the protagonist will realize it <u>as</u> the story progresses? Consider 2006's ***BLOOD DIAMOND***. Danny Archer (Leonardo DiCaprio) and his first immediate goal is very quickly revealed at the opening of the film. Danny's first immediate goal is to get paid for the sale of illegal weapons. This action makes it clear that Danny is unconcerned with the morality of selling illegal weapons – basically he will smuggle anything to make money. This revelation piques the audience's interest; will Danny find anything that matters deeply to him? The audience becomes privy to Danny's life; he's a loner, distrustful, has few friends and no family, lives life on the edge and is, ultimately, lonely. It quickly becomes clear that Danny <u>needs</u> to identify and connect to his own moral center and connect with the world on a deeper level.

REALITY CHECK YOUR SCRIPT

A client of mine was working on a high concept romantic comedy that he wanted to be a love story that would be relatable and touch people's hearts. Initially, the characters were "acting funny and outrageous" in a very exaggerated fashion starting on page one. Actions and reactions were "over the top"; so much so that the sense of reality, the understanding of and the likeability of the characters was in jeopardy. The writer was not giving an opportunity to the audience to connect to any kind of reality about the character – so empathy was not possible. The writer realized that he did not trust that putting <u>real</u> people with relatable, strong desires would keep the audience's interest. He realized he was not trusting that the situations he created for the story were inherently humorous. The *script lacked the level of believability that he wanted to impart. Once the writer pulled back on the overly outrageous Act One behavior and let the reader/audience get to know and understand the characters and the characters' overall wants the script came together. He was able to move into more outrageous and "over-the-top" behavior in Acts Two and Three because he had taken the time to get the audience on board the story train.*

ACT TWO: Remind the audience of your protagonist's overall want/need

As your story progresses into Act Two, make sure your protagonist's overall want does not change. Circumstances may change and immediate goals may change, but the overall want needs to stay consistent. It is a good idea to refocus the audience and remind them of the overall want/need of the protagonist.

Does your protagonist, somewhere in Act Two, re-clarify her overall want? This could be done through dialogue or action.

On page one of **LEGALLY BLONDE,** Elle makes her immediate goal clear; she wants to be Warner's wife. After Warren dumps her, Elle realizes she needs him to respect her, to <u>think</u> that she is perfect wife material. In Act Two, dressed as a Playboy bunny at a snotty, pullovers-and-tweed Harvard Law party, Elle is reminded again that Warner does not take her seriously. She confronts him with the truth, "I'll never be good enough for you, will I?" This knowledge causes her to re-dedicate herself to changing Warner's mind and proving that she is more than just a "blonde." Elle leaves the party and heads to the computer store to begin the <u>serious</u> business of becoming a top student.

In Act Two of **THE GODFATHER,** Michael comes back from Italy. He's older, wiser; he's been married and witnessed his bride's murder. He's committed a violent act and been on the receiving end of many violent acts. But his overall want is the same; legitimate respect. He meets up with his former fiancé, Kay, and he restates his intentions; he is going to make his family's business legitimate. Michael acknowledges this task may take him time, but he has not lost his passion to be a respected American citizen. He sees Kay as the "right" American wife and asks her to marry him.

The crisis at the end of Act Two can also be used to restate your protagonist's overall want

Check your latest draft. Does your protagonist have a decision at the end of Act Two (the crisis point) that relates to his overall want? If your protagonist's overall want is justice, make sure the decision at the crisis point at the end of Act Two, when all seems lost, focuses in and around the topic of justice. If your protagonist's overall want is true love, make sure the decision at the crisis point at the end of Act Two, when all seems lost, focuses in and around the topic of what is true love or how does one identify true love or accept true love or…

At the conclusion of Act Two in *LEGALLY BLONDE,* Elle finds herself at a crisis point. She makes the decision to <u>not</u> let the disrespect of her mentor and peers get her down. She shows up in court to defend her client and puts herself on the line. Will she gain respect or not? At the crisis point at the end of Act Two in *THE GODFATHER,* Michael sets out his terms for setting his family up in a legitimate business in Las Vegas. First he knows he must settle old scores…

ACT THREE: Keep the overall want at the forefront during the climax

Elle, in *LEGALLY BLONDE*, enters the courtroom and has to earn the respect of the judge, the jury, her nemesis and her rival to win the case for her client. When she does win the case, she gains self-respect.

Michael, in *THE GODFATHER*, earns respect by planning a large-scale slaughter of his enemies while, at a church baptismal ceremony, he is being "respected" by family and friends as he stands as godfather to his nephew. Take a look at how the final moments of the film focus again on <u>respect.</u> Visuals feature Michael's hand being kissed – a sign of respect to the new godfather.

Danny, in *BLOOD DIAMOND*, during the crisis and climax of the film, makes decisions that have nothing to do with putting money into his own pocket. His worldview has changed; he now believes in a cause and he is willing to die for it – and for the good of his country.

Consider letting all the supporting characters' stories <u>reflect</u> on your protagonist's overall want

THE GODFATHER is, again, a good example: Michael Corleone begins the film as a man who wants to build a life outside the family's Mafia business, he

---

wants to live a "legitimate" American life, he wants <u>respect</u>. The supporting stories of his siblings help inform Michael's story – alpha brother Sonny wants <u>respect</u>, he wants to lead the family but he is not cool under fire. Weak brother Fredo wants the family's <u>respect</u> but his moral center is weak. Michael's sister Connie wants <u>respect</u> and seeks it by pushing her new husband onto her family; her brothers do not respect her husband. Don Corleone is the most respected of the dons, but <u>respect</u> is not enough against the greed of the other families who want to add drug trafficking to their businesses. Michael's pursuit of his Italian wife is successful because he gains the <u>respect</u> of the girl's father. Michael's American wife, Kay, wants <u>respect</u>; she doesn't want to be kept in the dark about Michael's business.

THE GODFATHER (1972) Diane Keaton, Al Pacino
- *photo courtesy of Globe Photos*

Exercise:

Read through your script. Does every scene inform the life and desires of the protagonist? Do your supporting characters' wants/needs reflect on the protagonist's journey and overall want?

This is the time to stand apart and critically analyze your script. Yes, every scene you have written could have brilliant dialogue, amazing visual elements, deep emotions or great comedy, but does each scene reflect on the want/need of your protagonist? Remember, this is not the <u>only</u> script you will write in your career – there is no need to put everything <u>and</u> the kitchen sink into one script.

Have you built the scenes where the character speaks from his heart?

What can a screenwriter do to create or highlight those moments in the script that will forever brand a character into the audiences' minds? Those moments come from allowing your characters to be emotionally brave and vulnerable and absolutely truthful.

What does your character believe in? What does family or love or children or justice or kindness mean to your character? What makes a character feel small or unimportant? What makes a character feel like he is "king of the world"?

Take a look at 2006's **CATCH A FIRE.** Patrick Chamusso (portrayed by Derek Luke) joins the fight for freedom in South Africa because his wife is falsely arrested and tortured. The writer allows Chamusso's emotions to erupt. The writer finds the words for Chamusso so that he is able to express his feelings to friends – and to his nemesis, Nic Vos (portrayed by Tim Robbins). Chamusso's words illuminate his own emotional state as well as cause Vos to examine his own part in the attempt to control people intent on fighting for their freedoms.

Take another look at the Paddy Chayefsky script of **NETWORK.** Beatrice Straight, playing the protagonist's wife, won the Best Supporting Actress prize at the 1976 Academy Awards because of one scene: Max, the protagonist of the film, has just told his wife he is leaving her for a younger woman. The wife's outrage, citing the injustice of his actions – after all, she has weathered and supported and loved him for years and now will not be on the receiving end of his "winter passion" – is powerful because she does not block her emotional reaction to his betrayal and speaks an emotional truth.

Take another look at 1982's **TOOTSIE.** The screenwriters found just the right words for Michael Dorsey (portrayed by Dustin Hoffman) to express in the final moments of the film – Michael articulated what he learned about himself from his cross-dressing experience. If Michael had not been able to tell Julie, the woman he loves, that he is a changed man, would he have been able to get her to finally accept him?

Character desires and motivations drive the best stories. One of the most important things to do when working on your rewrite is to focus your main character's arc, highlight the beginning, middle and end of their journey of change. Consider adjusting scenes that are not focused on moving the protagonist's story forward.

CHAPTER SUMMARY

- By examining various areas of characters' lives, the writer allows the audience to better understand the story's characters.

- Conflict among the characters helps heighten interest in the story.

- All characters should have internal conflict as well as external conflict.

- When the supporting characters' desires and needs reflect on the main character's journey, the script can feel more focused.

- Allow your main characters to speak or act from their heart and reveal their real selves.

Chapter Seven

PLOT

Plot is important. You want your individual plot points to engage, intrigue and surprise the audience. How do you do that? <u>Let the characters lead.</u> Let the characters' actions and desires <u>cause</u> the plot to unfold in its singular way. Beware of constructing plot points that force your characters to act in a way that is antithetical to the natures you have constructed for them. The audience will feel cheated because a lot of the enjoyment in experiencing stories comes from the audience understanding the temperament and mettle of characters and then seeing <u>how</u> these characters (who have been set up to have certain beliefs and tendencies) deal with various obstacles and adversities. If you have characters react dishonestly and against their core make-up just to enable a plot twist, you will lose your audience.

Your story may have sprung from an idea about a character. Or it may have been inspired by a plot element. The origination of your story makes no difference now – at the rewrite phase of your work. Now you want to make sure <u>character is driving the story.</u>

Exercise:

Go through your script with these questions in mind:

- Have you committed to your protagonist constantly striving to satisfy her overall want/need? If you have veered off that path, does your story feel unfocused and flabby?

- Have you explored the result of your protagonist not achieving her overall want/need? If this want/need is not satisfied, will lives (or world or environment) be in danger? Will the protagonist's world seem meaningless or empty or worse yet – will it be destroyed? Have you made the stakes as high as possible?

Make sure the physical and emotional stakes of the main characters in your story are clear. Make sure all the plot points are fashioned out of characters' plans or desires or actions to accomplish their goals. Make sure some of

Question: What is the most important thing about plotting a screen story?

Answer: A good screen story focuses on a character's journey. Therefore, the most important element to remember is that character arc and plot need to be inter-connected.

Definition:
PLOT is the development of actions and events that move the main characters' stories forward.

PLOT POINTS Plot points are the specific events that shape and shift the story and move the plot elements of the film story forward.

EVENTS are the things that happen in the story.

the obstacles that your main characters face stem from their own foibles or flaws. In the most basic way, make sure character growth or change or challenge is always at the forefront.

Events

Check your script. Is your story moving from event to event? An event can be anything; the first day at work, a graduation, a car accident, buying a first bike for a child, a first kiss, an argument, a promotion, a love-at-first-sight meeting, a reunion, a divorce, realizing a mate is having an affair, a wedding, a trip to the beach, seeing a ghost, a sporting event, a contest, keeping an appointment at the dentist, making the call to start the next World War, walking the dog, killing the alien monster, adopting a child… the list is endless. Some events in your story will loom large. Some events will seem small but may still affect your protagonist in a major way.

Some events will be surprises – think about *THE GODFATHER* – the shooting of Don Corleone at the sidewalk vegetable stand. Think about *SIDEWAYS* and Stephanie's sudden attack with her motorcycle helmet against her lover, Jack when she finds out he lied to her about his plans to be married.

Some events you'll set up and then build up anticipation or trepidation before the actual event occurs – and then let the specifics of the event play out. Consider the final courtroom scenes in 1979's *KRAMER VS. KRAMER* or 1992's *A FEW GOOD MEN* or 1993's *MRS. DOUBTFIRE*. Consider 2005's *THE WEDDING CRASHERS*. When the two wedding scammers (portrayed by Owen Wilson and Vince Vaughn) are invited to spend the weekend at the upscale home of the Treasury Secretary William Cleary (portrayed by Christopher Walken) – the audience begins to anticipate - and enjoys the anticipation - of all the things that could go wrong. Think of the plentitude of films based around sporting events (boxing, baseball, Olympics et al) and the setting up and anticipation of and playing out of the final contest. Consider the westerns or films in the war genre that set up and extend the anticipation of ultimate showdowns.

All events must advance the story

Nothing can be extraneous. Events, in most cases, bring with them a sense of action because you are putting your characters in situations where things happen.

Concentrating on moving your protagonist from <u>event to event</u> will help give a sense of motion to your screen story. Depending on the scope and tone of your script, a very small event can loom extremely large for a character. Think of the films where lovers meet for the first time – some are casual meetings; some are momentous meetings (during battles, arguments, tense situations). Think of the relatively small event in 2006's **LITTLE MISS SUNSHINE:** The family's van breaks down. This event seems small, but is of utmost importance to the family because it jeopardizes their goal (to get to the Beauty Pageant so the youngest member of the family can compete). However, the event serves another purpose; it forces the family to work together as a unit. Think of the event in 2007's **MICHAEL CLAYTON** that causes Clayton (portrayed by George Clooney) to realize the immoral and illegal tactics of a female attorney intent on getting her way; a car bomb explodes and destroys his car. That event turns his suspicion that his co-worker was murdered to <u>believing</u> his suspicions are warranted. The car bomb is an event that forces the protagonist to move to the next step in the story.

> NOTE: If a story is not constructed around events, you run the risk of letting dialogue move the story. In most cases, this will tend to slow down the story. Remember, film is a visual medium. In most cases, you want to take advantage of events, location changes and movement to help you tell your story.

Character makes plot (and events) happen

Consider the 1975 high concept film **JAWS.** Its one liner could be: "A shark attacks Martha's Vineyard and the police chief, *who has just moved to the island and is afraid of the water and has a family trying to adjust to a new home,* has to protect the town." Note that without the distinct characteristics of the protagonist at the center of the plot, the story loses a level of interest. Note that without giving the protagonist a flaw or personal problem that will make the task more difficult, the story can lose a level of inner conflict for its main character. Many of the plot points of **JAWS** are a direct result of the Police Chief Martin Brody (portrayed by Roy Scheider) being <u>new</u> to the island – his recent appointment to the job causes a power struggle between the protagonist and the mayor. Other plot points revolve around Brody's discomfort around water. He has to hire shark experts and rely on them to get rid of the bloodthirsty shark. These supporting characters, ebullient Matt Hooper (portrayed by Richard Dreyfus) and terse and tense

Quint (portrayed by Robert Shaw) also bring about various plot points of the film story: abrasive Quint is a loner who has a personal vendetta against sharks so he tends to be reckless and myopic, Hooper is analytical and pig-headed but friendly and wants to "bond" with people. Their personalities cause conflict and tension for Brody and for the town – and cause the events of the story to unfold in a singular way.

JAWS (1975) Richard Dreyfus, Roy Scheider
- photo courtesy of Globe Photos

Consider the plot of 2007's **SUPERBAD**: Two best friends, Seth (portrayed by Jonah Hill) and Evan (portrayed by Michael Cera) are about to graduate from high school. Seth, *who didn't get into the prestigious college and has always been picked on at school and wants a girl to be interested in him and wants respect*, needs affirmation from Evan that despite the new and different experiences that the future promises – experiences that will lead them away from each other – they will remain best buddies. All of Seth's actions in the film story are motivated by his insecurity (with his physical prowess, his ability to attract a girl, his lack of scholarly acumen, his fear of losing his best friend) and his need for affirmation. The audience goes on the journey with Seth because his choices – which make the plot happen – are all character-driven.

SUPERBAD (2007) Michael Cera, Jonah Hill
- photo courtesy of Globe Photos

Keep the plot simple

Most of us would love to have that high concept idea that will catch the studio's attention and ensure that our screenplay will be produced and find its way to a large audience.

In pursuing that goal, there can be an impulse to over-complicate the plot, thinking that if you throw more twists and turns into the story mix, the plot will seem more original. There can be an impulse to insert a wild back story that is not necessary or attach devious and outrageous motivations that are extraneous to the characters' simple overall wants and immediate goals in the specific film story.

Avoid the impulse. Wall-to-wall plot is <u>not</u> desirable. Trust that your skills as a writer can fill a simple but well-calibrated plot with scenes and sequences where the characters take focus. Audiences are interested in <u>the characters</u>. The best scripts leave room for character illumination. Check to see if you have provided enough room in your story to explore the nuances, ideas, beliefs and dreams of your characters.

Let's look again at the relatively simple plot of 2006's crime drama *THE DEPARTED:* The story centers on two young cops, one corrupt (Colin) and one determined to prove he is not corrupt (Billy). Both want to make a mark in Boston's police department. The head of the local Irish mob is planning to sell contraband to Asian criminals. Colin is aiding the Irish mob boss who is his mentor and surrogate father. Billy is trying to bring that mob boss down and bring a stop to this specific criminal activity. Notice how the plot is centered on <u>one specific criminal activity.</u> Yes, Irish mob boss Frank Costello (portrayed by Jack Nicholson) is a well-known criminal and the police have wanted to get him behind bars for many years, but this film centers on the planning and execution of <u>one</u> crime. The rest of the film story centers on character arcs, the growth and change of the two main characters in which the audience becomes invested, their familial and professional and romantic relationships.

Consider the plot of 2007's comedy, ***KNOCKED UP***. Ben Stone (portrayed by Seth Rogen) is an irresponsible, pot-smoking chlub who goes to a club, meets Alison (portrayed by Katherine Heigl), a single career woman. They get drunk, dance, and sleep together and Alison gets pregnant. Ben has nine months to recognize that he needs to change his life if he wants to embrace a new role of committed lover and father of a child. The events in the film story focus on Ben's inability to leave his comfort zone and his inability to commit to adulthood. His slacker friends make it easy (and fun) for him to remain a slacker. His growing closeness to the dysfunctional family of Alison's sister, Debbie (portrayed by Leslie Mann), makes him wonder if embracing adulthood is desirable. Ben's <u>character traits</u> cause the problems in the rather simple plot that asks this dramatic question: Will Ben and Alison become a couple? The <u>plot is simple,</u> the plot points are all focused on the dramatic question, and the <u>scenes are focused on the illumination and change of character.</u>

KNOCKED UP (2007) Katherine Heigl, Seth Rogen
- photo courtesy of Globe Photos

Exercise:

If you are working in the romantic comedy genre, take a look at the Act One events of the 1994 comedy FOUR WEDDINGS AND A FUNERAL. This is a good example of how to use <u>events</u> to move the story along. If your script is in the horror genre, take a look at 1996's SCREAM. If you are working in a crime/police/thriller genre, take a look at 2001's TRAINING DAY. If you are working on a drama, take a look at 2001's A BEAUTIFUL MIND and list the events that move the story along. Or choose a film that you think is very successful and in the genre you are working in – and list the events that move the story forward.

Definition:
DRAMATIC QUESTION is the main question presented by the character and plot in the story. Examples: Will the protagonist find redemption without putting himself at risk? Will the heroine find love while not believing in its existence?

IMPORTANT EVENTS NOT TO BE MISSED

The inciting incident – a very important event

The inciting incident is the event (word or look or action) near the beginning of your script that takes your protagonist out of his normal life.

Examples of inciting incidents:

THE SAVAGES (2007) Wendy gets a phone call that her estranged father has had a mental breakdown.

JUNO (2007) Teenage Juno realizes she is, indeed, pregnant.

RATATOUILLE (2007) Cute rat, Remy, learns to appreciate great garden grub and his culinary dreams begin.

SUPERBAD (2007) Seth is asked to bring alcohol to a party being given by a girl on whom he has a crush.

THE DEPARTED (2006) Policeman Billy Costigan agrees to go undercover in the Irish Mob.

THE GLADIATOR (2000) Emperor Marcus Aurelius is killed by his son and this causes Maximus to be forced into slavery.

SHAKESPEARE IN LOVE (1998) Viola, dressed as a male, auditions for Shakespeare's play.

MOONSTRUCK (1987) Loretta's longtime mama's boy boyfriend, Johnny, proposes marriage.

RAIDERS OF THE LOST ARK (1981) Jones is offered the job to track down the Ark of the Covenant.

THE WILD BUNCH (1969) The botched robbery of the railroad offices puts Pike Bishop and his gang on the run from the only man who could take them down.

CASABLANCA (1942) Rick agrees to hide the letters of transit in his nightclub.

THE WIZARD OF OZ (1939) Dorothy's dog is taken by the mean Miss Gulch.

The inciting incident sets the story in motion. In most cases, you want to start your screen story as close to the inciting incident as possible – but in most cases – <u>not before the audience gets a good grasp on the essence of the protagonist by showing his normal life.</u> Note how in ***THE SAVAGES,*** the writer lets us in on Wendy's job, her aspirations as a playwright, the fact that she lives alone in a studio apartment, the affair she is having with a married neighbor, her need to make her life more dramatic by making up physical problems – all these character clues before she gets the phone call that her father has had a mental breakdown. It's the phone call that puts her on her journey of change in the story. Note how the lives of the rats in the countryside in ***RATATOUILLE*** are set up before Remy's fine sense of smell and sophisticated palate are recognized by his fellow rats. Note how Seth and his friends in ***SUPERBAD*** are set up as losers and wannabes in life and at high school before Seth is asked to bring alcohol to the "cool" party. Note how Billy Costigan in ***THE DEPARTED*** is shown as a top police cadet with a strong moral sense before he is asked to go undercover. Note how the protagonist, Maximus, in ***THE GLADIATOR*** is set up as a top general and loyal soldier and surrogate son to the Emperor before he is taken into slavery.

Exercise:

Check your script. Have you created an event for your inciting incident that marks a clear need for a change for your protagonist? Could the event be a bigger event? If it works better as a small event, does it clearly affect a change in the protagonist's normal life? Have you taken the time to set up the normal life before the inciting incident occurs? If you are telling your story in a non-linear fashion, have you found a way to make the normal life of your protagonist – before the event that jumpstarts the story – clear through flashback or exposition?

Character introductions

The "cute meet" is a term used in romantic comedies. It refers to <u>how</u> potential lovers cross paths for the first time. Does one fall down a manhole cover and the other rescues him (or not)? Do their bicycles collide? Perhaps the potential lovers meet in law court where one faces a disturbing-the-peace charge or a divorce or a murder charge. Consider 1989's *WHEN HARRY MET SALLY;* Sally (portrayed by Meg Ryan) meets Harry (portrayed by Billy Crystal) while he's in a deep kissing session with his latest girlfriend. Sally is waiting for Harry to join her in a cross-country car trip; she gets impatient and leans on the car horn. It's clear Sally is uptight and wants to stick to her schedule and that Harry is loose and doesn't like his romancing interrupted. From the moment they meet, friction is evident. Consider 1982's *TOOTSIE;* Michael (portrayed by Dustin Hoffman), pretending to be a woman, is working as an actor on a daytime soap opera. Michael had noticed actress Julie (portrayed by Jessica Lange) at his audition, but now they exchange words for the first time. Flustered, he drops his script pages and she helps him pick them up. He desperately wants to flirt (as a man) but can't (because Julie needs to believe that he is a woman).

Consider 1994's *FOUR WEDDINGS AND A FUNERAL;* Charles (portrayed by Hugh Grant) meets Carrie (portrayed by Andie McDowell) at a wedding where Charles gives a hilarious and off-color toast. Carrie asks him to come to her hotel that night. When Charles finally arrives (a series of events almost keep him from getting there) Carrie is stuck in the lobby talking to a very boring but lecherous man. Charles has to cleverly come up with a ruse to free Carrie and finally they get together in her hotel room.

Dramas that feature "B" stories (subplots or supporting stories) based in the romance genre will often feature an interesting "meet." Consider 2002's drama/thriller *BOURNE IDENTITY.* Jason Bourne meets the woman he is to fall in love with under very tense circumstances; he is on the run from people who want to kill him, he needs to get to Paris. Marie, the woman Bourne notices at the American Embassy, is in need of money – and she also has a car. Bourne asks her to drive him to Paris. She is taken aback by the request, Bourne is a stranger to Marie, she also realizes the police are looking for him. Marie says no. When Bourne tosses her ten thousand dollars in cash (payment for the ride to Paris), Marie (desperate for money) decides to take the chance. The <u>event</u> is constructed so that the potential lovers meet in a situation full of conflict and tension.

Consider 1999's **BEAUTY AND THE BEAST.** Belle meets the Beast for the first time while she is in an emotionally charged state; the Beast has imprisoned her father and she hates the Beast for his cruelty. Consider 1942's **CASABLANCA.** Rick and Ilsa were lovers in war-torn Paris and then separated. Rick believes Ilsa deserted him and harbors great anger and hurt. When their lives intersect again they are in a public place (Rick's Café) – representatives of the local police force and the German generals and Ilsa's husband are watching. The level of tension and emotion are heightened by the location and the event and the characters included in the sequence. Consider the event in 2006's **THE DEPARTED** when undercover cop Billy is introduced to the mob boss, Frank Costello. Billy has broken his wrist in a previous event – he now wears a cast. Frank, always suspicious of hidden wires or listening devices, smashes Billy's cast and re-breaks his wrist to make sure Billy isn't wired. The initial meet of these two characters is fraught with tension, violence and emotion.

The Second Opportunity can be an important event

The Second Opportunity (Step #4 of the Eleven Steps) is the opening of your second act. This event will, in most cases, lead your protagonist into a new and/or uncomfortable world where she will be tested in new ways.

Examples of second opportunity events that move the protagonist into the second act:

> **THE SAVAGES** (2007) Wendy and her brother Jon bring their father (who suffers from dementia) from Arizona to New York and put him in a nursing home. They begin to dedicate their time, emotions and energies into being a part of his care-giving team.

> **JUNO** (2007) Juno meets the couple that hopes to adopt her baby.

> **RATATOUILLE** (2007) Remy finds himself in Paris and soon becomes the silent talent guiding young chef Linguini to stardom.

> **SUPERBAD** (2007) Seth begins his quest to find alcohol to bring to the "cool" party, a quest that takes him to places he never expected to go and puts him in situations that test his friendships.

> **THE DEPARTED** (2006) Billy (now undercover) is accepted into Costello's violent gang.

> **THE GLADIATOR** (2000) Maximus, now a slave, is chosen to be a gladiator.

SHAKESPEARE IN LOVE (1998) Shakespeare casts Viola as Romeo in his play.

MOONSTRUCK (1987) Loretta goes to the opera with Ronny, her fiancé's brother.

RAIDERS OF THE LOST ARK (1981) Jones obtains the Staff of Ra. This will help locate the Ark of the Covenant.

THE WILD BUNCH (1969) Pike Bishop and his gang agree to steal guns for the Mexican Army.

CASABLANCA (1942) Ilsa (the love of Rick's life) walks into Rick's Café and opens up old emotional wounds.

THE WIZARD OF OZ (1939) Dorothy's house lands in Oz – on top of the Wicked Witch of the East.

What event have you constructed to move your protagonist into the new world and challenges of Act Two? Has it been preceded by an event that has shut down most (or all) other opportunities that could help the protagonist achieve his or her goals?

Events that highlight the midpoint, crisis and climax

Near the midpoint of your story, halfway through your script (approximately page 50) you want to, in most cases, raise the stakes or shift the story in some way. What event have you constructed? Does it need to be bigger? Can you invest it with more emotional consequences?

Consider the midpoint of **THE GLADIATOR.** Maximus (portrayed by Russell Crowe) has risen in the ranks of the gladiators and has achieved a goal – he is set to fight in Rome before his nemesis, the cruel and evil Emperor Commodus. This is a major shift in story. Now Maximus is close to the political intrigue, closer to being able to get the revenge he desires, closer to a woman who loves him. The stakes are raised, the elements are coming together and the story becomes more complex.

Consider the midpoint of **JUNO.** Juno (portrayed by Ellen Page) is absolutely in love with Paulie Bleeker (portrayed by Michael Cera), the high school classmate who impregnated her. But at the middle of Act Two, Juno pushes Paulie to date another girl – and when he does ask that girl to the Prom, Juno's life begins to fall apart.

The Crisis Event

Consider Step #9 of the Eleven Steps; the Crisis (the decision) your protagonist faces at the end of Act Two. What event or reaction to an event forces your protagonist to make a decision to enter the climax (or not)?

Consider the crisis event in *BEAUTY AND THE BEAST*. The Beast is aware that the last petals of the rose under his glass jar are about to fall off. This signifies that his time is nearly up – he hopes that Beauty will fall in love with him before the petals fall so that he won't have to live as a Beast forever. However, through the Beast's magic mirror, Belle sees her lost and ill father and knows he needs her help. She asks the Beast to let her go to her father – and because the Beast loves Belle and wants her to be happy, he sacrifices his chances for happiness and lets her go. (There are more breakdowns of films at the end of this book and you will be able to look at other crisis points).

Events in the Climax

Most climaxes (Step #10 of the Eleven Steps) will be a <u>series</u> of events or actions. The climax, in most cases, takes up most of Act Three. Each event or action <u>must continue to reveal character.</u> A wild chase or elongated battle scenes will not satisfy if they do not continue to move the protagonist's story forward. The audience must continue to deepen their understanding of character. Make sure your climax is still <u>answering questions, allowing the audience to fill in the final puzzle pieces of story.</u> Take a look at the beautifully constructed climax of 2001's *TRAINING DAY* written by David Ayer. Good cop Jake (portrayed by Ethan Hawke) and dirty cop Alonso (portrayed by Denzel Washington) face off in a violent confrontation. It is much more than a shoot-out; it is a battle of minds and a test of wills. Their characters are still forming, changing, moving forward.

Remember, all events should increase conflicts in the main character's journey.

Events move the story and character arc forward

Consider the events in the drama/horror film, 1968's *ROSEMARY'S BABY.*

- Rosemary and her husband, Guy, are apartment hunting. Rosemary falls in love with an apartment in an old, historic building. It's clear during this event that Rosemary's overall want is love and family. Her immediate goal is to get pregnant and start their family soon.

- Rosemary and Guy rent the apartment. *(This is the inciting incident.)*

- The first night in their new apartment, Rosemary and Guy make love.

- Rosemary meets her a friend who warns her about the building and its inhabitants and Rosemary dismisses the idea that Satan worshippers live in the building.

- Rosemary and Guy meet an odd, elderly couple, the Castavets, who are also tenants in the building.

- Rosemary meets a young woman, Terry, in the laundry room who is staying with the odd Castavets.

- Guy wants a part in a Broadway play. He doesn't get it. He is frustrated with his career.

- Terry, the young woman Rosemary met in the laundry room, commits suicide.

- Rosemary and Guy are asked over to the Castavet's apartment for dinner.

- Rosemary is surprised and a bit pleased that Guy seems interested in becoming friends with the Castavets.

- Rosemary's friend, who initially warned her about the building and its inhabitants, mysteriously dies.

- Guy encourages Rosemary to eat the bitter-tasting pudding the Castevets brought over to them as a "gift."

- Rosemary, nearly comatose from the drug-laced pudding, is raped. (Rosemary thinks her husband initiated rough sex with her and resents him taking advantage of her when she was nearly unconscious.)

- Guy's luck begins to turn. He gets the part in the Broadway play that he desired because the already-cast actor has suddenly become blind.

- Rosemary finds out she is pregnant.

- Mrs. Castavet gives her a potion to drink in the morning to help her have a healthy pregnancy. Guy encourages Rosemary to take the drink despite Rosemary's trepidation.

- Rosemary begins to look ill--

The events continue. Each scene or sequence is built around events. There is a constant feel of movement and forward progress in the story.

ROSEMARY'S BABY (1968) Ruth Gordon, Mia Farrow
- photo courtesy of Globe Photos

Exercise:

Check your script. Are events or consequences of events pushing the story forward? Can you identify any scene where dialogue alone (long scenes of talking with no action or event attached to the scene) causes the plot to move forward? Can you think of an event or action that could be happening <u>while</u> this dialogue exchange is taking place? Explore the possibility of cutting some of the dialogue because the action or event relays some of the emotion or intent of the scene.

Stories can falter if events, circumstances, problems, relationships are not pushed far enough. Think big. Big emotions, big character arcs, big character reactions. Think of the worst possible things that could face your protagonist. Most humiliating. Most dangerous. Most confusing. Most hilarious. Most embarrassing. What event will test your protagonist the most? What event will push every emotional button? If you find that you want to add more events to your script, consider using your protagonist's fears or phobias to construct events filled with conflict.

Exercise:

Take a look at <u>one area</u> of your film story. Perhaps you choose to look at the SECOND OPPORTUNITY (Step #4) – the beginning of the second act. This is the scene/sequence where your protagonist finds himself facing an alternate route – one he did not expect to face – a route that brings with it new and unfamiliar (possibly dangerous) challenges but one that could possibly help him accomplish his goal and achieve his overall want. How can you explore building out that scene or sequence so <u>character and events</u> drive the story?

Example: A student of mine was working on a script where the female protagonist, Rita, a young woman who had come to Los Angeles to pursue an acting career, falls on hard times; she can't get an acting job, she loses her "day" job, she gets evicted from her apartment and decides to head back to her hometown in Montana (despite the ridicule she knows she will face from friends and family because of her failure to become "a star"). The student built up to this point by the end of his Act One and his character is facing denials (Step #3) in all areas of her life. Act Two begins and Rita, trying to pick up her suitcases that her bully landlord had tossed over the apartment building's railings, literally runs into a young man wearing a sandwich board (Dennis). Dennis is handing out flyers that announce auditions for a new show in Las Vegas. Not only is Dennis cute and funny, Rita thinks the flyer is an omen – her last chance to make good. However, she's low on funds – but – Dennis tells her there is a low-priced Vegas bus leaving Union Station in downtown Los Angeles in thirty minutes. Rita knows she has to be on this bus (and be able to buy a low-priced ticket) or she'll miss this opportunity.

My student then cut to Rita on the bus, on her way to Vegas. He missed a great opportunity to let the audience enjoy the obstacles Rita could face as she tried to <u>get to the bus station and purchase her ticket in thirty minutes in Los Angeles.</u>

I suggested that he explore <u>how</u> Rita goes from the idea to go to Vegas to actually making it onto the bus to Vegas. The student built this sequence: Rita, with little time to spare, races to the subway with her heavy suitcases, she gets mugged and loses one suitcase. She has to make a decision — go after the mugger and her suitcase or continue to Union Station to take advantage of her SECOND OPPORTUNITY (Step #4). She decides to forget the suitcase and leaps onto the subway car at the last moment. The clock is ticking but making it to Union Station on time is still a possibility. Suddenly the subway screeches to a stop, a sewer pipe has broken and water is gushing into the subway car and drenches Rita. Rita has to push her way out of the subway station's emergency exit and hail a cab (which causes her to spend a few more dollars of her already low funds.) Finally, Rita (now wet and smelly with one soggy suitcase) gets to Union Station, the cheapest tickets for the bus (all she can afford) are about to be sold out and she's at the end of the line and must find a way to get to the front of the line. So she pretends she knows the person next in line to buy a ticket. She uses her acting skills to talk her way to the ticket window and gets the last cheap ticket. She finally gets on the bus and the cute sandwich board guy, Dennis, shows up as the "tour guide." By creating (or elongating) events, Rita is forced to face more obstacles. The events help show her personality and <u>character</u> traits. Audiences stay interested in the plot if they care about and understand the character. Audiences enjoy seeing the character rise above challenges that seem insurmountable.

Exercise:

Take a look at your script. Can you create more events that will serve as obstacles for your character? Remember, <u>nothing</u> can be easy. Have you gotten everything you can out of every moment, scene or sequence? Now is the time to explore and see if you can add texture and tension to your script.

Simple plot; interesting complex characters

Check your script. Is the plot clear? Remember Aristotle's maxim: A story should be about <u>one thing</u>. Aristotle's advice still rings true today.

Consider films that have an excess of plot and the damage this excess can cause. Consider the poorly reviewed 2007 film, **PIRATES OF THE CARIBBEAN III, AT WORLD'S END**. The excess of plots keeps the audience from connecting with any one character's story. The audience is confused: Is the rescue of Jack Sparrow (portrayed by Johnny Depp) the main plot?? Or does it revolve around Davey Jones (portrayed by Bill Nighy) ? Is the romance between Will (portrayed by Orlando Bloom) and Elizabeth (portrayed by Keira Knightley)the main plot? Or is the main plot centered on the understanding gained by Will and his father? Because the film does not have a strong and focused through-line, it feels muddled and top heavy with special effects. Special effects cannot save a film that lacks focus on a strong character's journey of change. Another poorly reviewed film that suffers from too many plots is another sequel, **SPIDER-MAN 3**. The plethora of villains and the lack of clear character arc for Peter Parker tried the audience's patience and caused a lack of interest.

A writer must be confident that a good story that focuses on a character's journey of change will interest and intrigue an audience. There is no need to fill a story with wall-to-wall plot.

Plot must be filled with conflict

Conflict is necessary in all drama. We have already explored ways to bring conflict into characters and character relationships. Your plot should also be driven by conflict.

Conflict should always be rearing its head in your story. Your protagonist must face conflict <u>at all times;</u> physical conflicts and/or emotional conflicts.

Initial plot conflicts in Act One of 2001's **LEGALLY BLONDE**

1. Elle wants to marry her college boyfriend Warner. Warner does not want to marry her.

2. Warner tells Elle she is not "good enough" to be the wife of a man with political aspirations. Elle faces the conflict of re-examining herself.

3. Elle decides to apply to Harvard Law School to become good enough for Warner.

Question: My story has a couple of important plot lines. How many plots are too many plots for one film?

Answer: There are no rules. The way a screenwriter chooses to express his story and theme will always be singular. It's your story to tell and you must decide what is the best structure to embrace. However, in most cases, it is wise to have a strong "A" story (one that focuses on the protagonist's journey to accomplish his overall want). The "A" story can become even stronger by creating supporting "B" stories that reflect on the protagonist's wants/needs or problems. Remember, you have only 90 to 120 minutes to get your character arcs and theme across. You are not writing a novel. Choose <u>one</u> story you want to tell, the <u>one</u> theme you want to explore and let all supporting stories <u>support</u>, not compete for primacy.

*Question: What about film stories like 2004's **CRASH** or the films of Robert Altman such as 1975's **NASHVILLE** or 2001's **GOSFORD PARK**?*

Answer: These films feature strong stories for multiple characters but are connected through theme. If you are working on an episodic or ensemble script, consider connecting the stories through theme. Ask yourself if the individual stories can (or should) overlap or touch on each other at some time. Ask yourself if one character can (or should) connect the stories. Each film story will be told in its own way – however – your goal is to present a <u>single</u> 90-120 minute piece of thought-provoking or just plain enjoyable entertainment. In most cases, you want to connect disparate stories in some fashion.

a. Elle's college advisor tells her that she doesn't have the credentials or the brains to be a successful candidate for Harvard Law School.

b. Her parents tell Elle that she is not law school material.

c. Elle studies for the LSAT and does not do well on the practice tests. Frustrated, she has to study harder and her friends tell her to forget about it, it's time to shop and party.

4. Elle gets accepted into Harvard Law School.

5. After her acceptance, Elle arrives on the Harvard Campus. Elle is naïve about how people perceive her Southern California pink and perky personality, but conflict is still evident– she is clearly not intellectually on par with her classmates.

6. Elle meets up with Warner in the halls of the University. Elle does not get the welcome she was expecting.

7. Elle goes to her first class. She in unprepared and is asked to leave the class. Elle is humiliated.

8. Elle meets up with Warner and finds out he is engaged – to a woman who clearly thinks Elle is a joke. This creates even more conflict.

Note how every event is imbued with conflict and – in most cases – causes an emotional reaction.

Use all your supporting characters to create obstacles and conflict for your protagonist. It's likely you have built your main antagonist to cause the most conflict for your protagonist. Now is the time to see if you've explored a level of antagonism in all your other characters. Even friends can (and should) disagree and have falling-outs with the protagonist. Parents do not need to be supportive. Teachers may have agendas that do not benefit students. Bosses can be nasty. Find ways for <u>every</u> character to create conflict for your protagonist.

Use environment to create obstacles and conflict: Claustrophobic or unwelcome homes. Unending forests or jungles. Vagaries of a big city. Lack of privacy in a small town. Crowded streets. Empty warehouses. Let the environments you are using help create conflict.

Use weather to create obstacles and conflict: Rain. Wind. Snow. Hot sun. Fires. Storms. Tsunamis. Falling leaves. Heat waves. Tornadoes. Hurricanes.

Flooding. Let weather affect your characters – deepen their anxieties or perhaps cause them to let down their guards.

Check your script. Make sure every scene or sequence has large or small elements of conflict.

BALANCE OF SUBPLOTS
"B" and "C" stories

Subplots (supporting stories) are fantastic story telling tools, they can help advance character and story. Subplots can help reveal theme. Subplots can carry the "message." They can add humor or pathos. Subplots can lighten or darken a mood. They can help clarify a point of view. They can help raise the stakes of the story. In the best screenplays, subplots help round out the main character by showing different sides of his or her life. Friends. Family. Work. Play. Hobbies. Enemies. Debts. Dreams.

The "A" story deals with the dramatic question

The way to pinpoint the "A" story in a script is simple. Ask yourself: What is the dramatic question of my script? Remember, the dramatic question relates to the primary plot. Your dramatic question could be: Will Susan be able to identify true love and get past her prejudices? Or it could be: Will Hank solve the murder and get his promotion to detective? Or it could be: Will Judy be able to identify the supernatural forces and save the world?

Your "A" story consists of scenes or sequences focused on your protagonist's journey of change and the <u>answering</u> the dramatic question.

You may have written a screenplay that has a very important and prominent "B" story. If it is taking up more time (pages) than your "A" story, you have a few options: You can go back into your script and add or readjust scenes or sequences that will pump up your "A" story – or you can re-think elements of your script and consider making the "B" story the "A" story. Or, of course, you can decide that you like your script as it is. Remember, it is your story. However, be aware that some reader may feel (and like or dislike) an imbalance in the storytelling.

Exercise:

Check the balance of "A" and "B" stories in your script.

There is no magic formula but – for now – while you are in rewrite mode – check to see if your "A" story takes up <u>at least</u> 60% of your pages. If it doesn't, ask yourself if your protagonist and his journey to accomplish his overall want is getting the attention it deserves. Remember, there are no rules and your story should play out as you see it, but writers can sometimes think the "A" story is dominating and crystal clear (because it is in their heads) but the actual pages do not support the belief. Counting pages can sometimes illuminate a problem that can be technically addressed.

What "B" and "C" stories have you fashioned in your screenplay? It's time to put them through a checklist; do they have a clear beginning, middle and end?

Consider how 2007's **FRACTURE** could have risen above a thinly plotted crime drama, but didn't. Why? The protagonist Willy (portrayed by Ryan Gosling) wants respect. He thinks he can get it by being a smart, winning assistant district attorney and getting the attention of a large, pricey law firm. The antagonist is Ted Crawford (portrayed by Anthony Hopkins), an aeronautics genius who thinks he's smarter than everyone. Crawford shoots and kills his wife because she is having an affair. Crawford takes a perverted joy is assuming he has planned the perfect crime and will not have to pay for his actions. The "A" story revolves around these two characters. The dramatic question of the film is: Who will be smarter? The "A" story is a good one, the characters are pitted against one another, and they are worthy adversaries. However, I would argue that the "B" stories fail to support the characters or plot. The romance "B" story does not satisfy because the events that make up this "B" story are weak; Willy meets Nikki, (portrayed by Rosamund Pike). She has been assigned to be Willy's mentor at the corporate law film where he has been hired. Nikki is beautiful and smart and enjoys her position and power. There is an attraction that stays at the level of lust (they meet at business parties and she demands that he "call" her later – clearly it is a code understood by both of them that they will sleep together). The romance "B" story never goes through any of the necessary romance genre steps (see the chapter on Genre), does not contain a strong character arc of change and thus cannot engage the audience emotionally. What are the consequences of this romantic relationship?

None. Therefore the "A" story is not really affected by this miscalculated "B" story. Nikki is, essentially, a mis-used character because she does not directly affect the events or climax of the film. A smaller **FRACTURE** "B" story examines Willy's work life. Again, I would argue that this supporting story is also unsatisfying because it is constructed to serve the plot, not the character. District Attorney Joe Lobruto (portrayed by David Straitharn) is angry and disappointed his star assistant district attorney, Willy, has decided to quit the D.A.'s Office for a larger paycheck at a corporate law firm. When Willy fails at his first attempt to prosecute murderer Crawford (his last task for the district attorney's office), Lobruto takes Willy off the case to save the D.A.'s office's reputation. Willy's ego is bruised and he is determined to not let Crawford outsmart him. Willy begs Lobruto for another chance to outsmart Crawford and Lobruto, for reasons that seem to serve only the plot, agrees. Willy fails again and Lobruto is not pleased. Willy is now jobless because the corporate law firm does not want a loser in their midst and he has bungled his job at the D.A.'s office. With no prospects, Willy packs to leave Los Angeles. Lobruto shows up at Willy's house with a sudden and complete reversal of intention; he asks Willy to stay in the district attorney's office. Why? Who knows? Lobruto (who has been set up as a character worried <u>only</u> about the D.A.'s office's reputation and nothing else) is now acting "out of character." This "B" story is only serving plot – not character. Thus, the final scene of reconciliation rings false – and that is why the film leaves the audience unsatisfied.

Supporting characters in supporting stories deserve their own story arcs. Well-thought out "B" stories, especially in crime dramas, can lift film stories above standard television fare. "B" stories can add complexity to the protagonist's problems and goals, help the theme resonate and add surprising elements to the film story.

Exercise:

Check to see if your supporting stories (subplots) are in complimentary genres to your "A" stories. List your "B" stories and "C" stories on a sheet of paper. Do you have a love story in an action movie? Do you have a best friend's romance in a romantic comedy? Is there a subplot with a sibling, parent or boss? Do you have a thriller subplot in your crime drama? Is there a fish-out-of-water "B" story in your sci-fi comedy? Once you have the list of your "B" and "C" stories, check to see if each has a complete beginning, middle and end. Check to see that each affects the "A" story, especially in Act Three.

Letting "B" and "C" stories drop out and remain incomplete can harm your story. For example, I would argue that the plotting of 2006's ***KING KONG*** could have been enhanced if each of the "B" stories had been fully played out. The attachment Ann (portrayed by Naomi Watts) has with the older gentleman in New York City is introduced and then dropped. There is a love affair begun between Ann and Jack (portrayed by Adrien Brody) but the emotional arc of that relationship is never fully played out (take another look at the Romance section of the Genre Chapter.) The I'll-show-'em-I'll-make-good story focusing on filmmaker Carl Denham (portrayed by Jack Black) does not a complete arc. For all ***KING KONG's*** wonderful elements, the film story is unbalanced because the "B" stories are not fully realized.

Exercise:

> Take a look at your script. Are your "B" and "C" stories complete? Do their have arcs (large or small) of their own? How do they affect the "A" story? Will they have a place in the climax of the story? If not, why? If not, do you need different "B" stories? Ask yourself, if you could think of one more "B" or "C" story to add to your script, what might it be?

Subplots should add tension to the protagonist's journey, especially as the story moves towards its conclusion. At some point (usually near the Crisis (Step #8) or Climax (Step #9) <u>all subplots should affect the main story</u>, making the main character's attempt to reach his goal more intense and difficult.

Remember, subplots should have arcs of their own. A clear beginning, middle and end. By making sure your subplots have a clear story arc, you can increase the power of your screenplay.

Some subplots will emerge naturally, some will not...

Some subplots will be so integral to the main plot of the film that they will emerge naturally. In fact, the story will not be able to be fully told without the supporting stories taking stage almost immediately.

There are other times when you may look at your script or story and feel it is too slim in its scope. This is a technical assessment of the state of your story and you may want to consider adding "B" stories or "C" stories.

Where do you find them? Search the world of your protagonist. Who would you say is your protagonist's primary relationship? Is there a friend who has something going on in her life? A sibling or family member going through a life change? A love interest? A work problem? A family conflict? Is there a bully in his world? Is there a desire to lose weight? Is there a desire to get in shape? Is there a hobby? Is there a house to be built? Is there a series of crimes in the neighborhood? In most cases, no matter what crisis is happening in a person's life, everyday chores (work, grocery shopping, taking the kids to school, dealing with crazy neighbors, friends' problems…) still need to be handled. These everyday events could be the source of "B" or "C" stories that reflect on your main characters and enrich your story.

Check your script. Are you supporting stories working to capacity?

CHAPTER SUMMARY

- Plot and the characters' arcs need to be inter-connected.

- Characters make the plot happen

- Plot should be simple, the characters complex

- The audience needs to know the character in order to care when things happen to him.

- The "A" story of the script is based around the plot's dramatic question.

- Subplots (supporting stories) are called "B" and "C" stories. Subplots should support the "A" story.

- "B" and "C" stories can illuminate character and theme and raise the level of your script.

CHAPTER EIGHT

DIALOGUE

If you have polished and adjusted elements of character and plot, it's time to go through your script and examine each character's dialogue. Put a checkmark next to any line that does not accomplish one of the five aims listed below. The lines of dialogue you checkmark are the ones you need to carefully look at to make sure they are not merely "chatter" or repeating information or slowing down your story.

Check each line of dialogue:

1. Does the line of dialogue help illuminate character?

2. Does the line of dialogue help illuminate motivation or a desire of a character?

3. Does the line of dialogue cause a reaction?

4. Does the dialogue increase the conflict in a scene?

5. Does the line of dialogue help move the story or character arc forward?

Remember, in most cases, brevity in dialogue is desired.

If the visual can carry the intent of the character without dialogue, consider trimming or cutting the dialogue. If the visual is not enough and dialogue is needed, ask yourself if you have chosen the words that will create the greatest impact?

Dialogue that <u>only</u> shows off the writer's ability to turn a phrase or tell a joke or wax philosophical will slow the pace of your story. Remember, this is not the only script you will write. Save the dialogue gems that are <u>unnecessary</u> in this script and use them in your next screenplay.

There are no hard and fast rules when it comes to the execution of dialogue. However, there are things you can consider as you look at the dialogue in your screenplay.

Answer: Good characters in a good story will always be the most important aspects of your script, but dialogue that is very character specific can raise a script to a new level – and get you attention in the professional world.

Definition:
A **monologue** is a prolonged discourse given by one person. This person is monopolizing the conversation for an extended period of time and gives no one a chance to express his or her point of view.

Dialogue is a give and take between two or more people – a true conversation. Dialogue can be an exchange of ideas or information; it can be used to give exposition, to express an emotion or an opinion.

Monologue versus dialogue

In most cases, dialogue is the preferred way to get across information (information that cannot be given visually) to an audience. Monologues tend to slow the pace of the film down because the conflict (as only one person speaks) does not feel immediate.

You will create more conflict if you have two or more people debating, arguing, disagreeing or coming up with a plan <u>together</u> than if you have one person stating only his point of view or giving orders.

Example:

EXT. SHOE STORE – DAY

Madeline, upset and not looking where she is going, bumps into a man carrying a large wrapped present.

Madeline

Oh, I'm sorry. I was –
(recognizes Sam)
What are you doing here? I thought you were in Los Angeles – you told me you were going to Los Angeles to meet that agent. Well thanks a lot, now you make me feel real stupid and small. Look, I'm crying. No, I won't give you that satisfaction. You lied to me and now you're – who is that present for? Is it for Holly? Everyone told me you two were together the other night but I told them you wouldn't do that to me… (Etc.)

Madeline's verbal outpour may fit her character. If so, then Madeline should speak the way you, the writer, want her to speak. But if Madeline is not a character that talks indiscriminately and never lets a person get a word in, consider how the next scene handles the same situation with a cleaner sense of dialogue.

EXT. SHOE STORE – DAY

Madeline, upset and not looking where she is going, bumps into a man carrying a large wrapped present.

Madeline

Oh, I'm sorry. I was –
(recognizes Sam)

What are you doing here?

                    Sam
Ahhh - hey. How are ya?

                    Madeline
I thought you were in Los Angeles – you
told me you were gonna meet that agent –

                    Sam
          (awkward)
I guess my plans changed –
Madeline, hurt and humiliated, wipes away tears –

                    Madeline
Oh no, you're not gonna make me do this –

                    Sam
Yeah… ahhh… sorry.

                    Madeline
So – is it true? You and Holly?
          (notices wrapped present in his hands)
That for her?

Leave room for the actor to "act"

Take a look at your script. Ask yourself if you are "over-writing." Are you stating the obvious? Are there areas where you can trim out expositional dialogue because the action or emotion or location gets across elements of the scene and makes some dialogue extraneous? Be aware that the camera can pick up extremely small nuances in the facial expressions and the body movements that an actor may bring to the role. In most cases there is no need to write dialogue to describe reactive feelings that can be made evident through camera close-up or other directorial choices.

Question: If I want my character to take charge and monopolize the conversation and not let anyone force him into a debate or conversation – how can I keep the scene from slowing down?

Answer: Is the person monopolizing the dialogue in the scene <u>doing</u> something? A monologue that takes place while a character is engaged in an action will not slow the pace of the script as much as a monologue from a stationary character. Also consider the reactions of those listening. Are the speaker's words causing reactions? If your character is addressing the troops, is there an underlying tension or story points being played out among the soldiers? If she is giving a sermon, is there something happening among the parishioners? Can you insert action lines that point to peoples' reactions to what the character is saying? Are the words moving the story forward? Will the monologue bring about consequences? Have you trimmed it down to its essentials? You will have your own style, your own way of telling your story. Just keep in mind that, in most cases, the story will be more interesting if there is action, conflict and movement caused by scenes that highlight dialogue over monologue.

Definition: **Over-writing** is a term often used to describe dialogue that is unnecessary to the telling of the story or the illumination of the character. Being facile with dialogue can aid the writer – however, not knowing when to trim out unnecessary words or phrases can also be a hindrance.

On-the-nose dialogue

On-the-nose dialogue means that a character is stating the obvious or baldly making his intentions clear. There is no cover, there is no subterfuge or manipulation or talking around a subject. Bald exposition (exposition that stands out like a sore thumb) can fall into the on-the-nose category. There are times when you want your characters to say exactly what is on their minds – other times, you want to use subtext.

Subtext

Subtext refers to dialogue that "says one thing but means another" or dialogue that covers the real intent or emotion. Subtext is used so your character doesn't have to say what he really thinks or feels and possibly sound unnatural.

People, in real life, have many ways to hide their true emotions. Not many people are willing to be vulnerable. The character in your film story may try to hide a true emotion or desire – but still try to get what he wants using subtext.

Example: Sue wants to invite Joe to the office party, but she doesn't want to take the chance of being rejected because she thinks that Joe may be seeing someone else in the office. Sue mentions to Joe that she lives in his neighborhood and if he doesn't have other plans, it would be easy to pick him up the night of the party. In this exchange, it can become clear that Sue is interested in Joe without her saying, "Let's go to the party together because I really like you and hope we can have a relationship unless you are in love with that girl in accounting."

Another example: Sam loves Kathy, but cannot tell her because of complications in his life because he works as a government spy. Sam tells Kathy that the relationship will never work. However the audience knows (and perhaps Kathy will too) that Sam is really protecting Kathy from danger and he "doth protest too much" because of his deep feelings for her.

Another example: A mother, Gina, throws a Sweet Sixteen party for her daughter, Becky. Gina's ex-husband (and father of the birthday girl) shows up at the party. Gina does not want him there, but he reminds her "Money has its privileges." Without coming out and saying that he is footing the bill for this party and that Gina's dependence on him makes him feel entitled and that he will use the give and take of money as a weapon, we understand the situation and a bit about the relationship of the divorced couple.

Consider these various ways of saying, through subtext, "I love you." In 1982's **TOOTSIE**, Michael lets Julie know his feelings: *"I thought we could start over."* Wesley says to Buttercup in 1987's **PRINCESS BRIDE**: *"As you wish."* In 1989's **WHEN HARRY MET SALLY**, Sally tells Harry that she loves him at the New Year' Eve party by saying *"I hate you."* Stand With A Fist says to Dunbar in 1990's **DANCES WITH WOLVES**: *"My place is with you. I go where you go."* Edward says to Elinor in 1995's **SENSE AND SENSIBILITY:** *"My heart is, and always will be, yours."* Dorothy lets Jerry know she loves him in 1996's **JERRY MAGUIRE** with these words: *"You had me at hello."* Mark says to Bridget in 2001's **BRIDGET JONES' DIARY** *"No, I like you very much. Just as you are."*

Use your dialogue to reveal character

Remember, a writer can help reveal character in many way – among them are:

1. What the character says about self.

2. What others say about the character.

3. What the character does.

What the character says about self

Some characters will have insight into themselves, others will not. Others will lie about their intentions and lie to themselves about their true natures. A character could say he is, at heart, a kind and generous man while his company bilks the elderly out of their life savings. The audience reacts to this lie or sense of self-delusion. A character could say she is cold and unfeeling and incapable of love while her heart breaks because she is hurting someone she really <u>does</u> adore. The audience will realize she isn't in touch with her emotions. There are many ways for the screenwriter to

Question: What if my character is someone who talks a lot? What if I want to portray someone who never stops talking? What if the character is someone who expounds ideas all the time? What if the character likes to hold stage and dominate?

Answers: Of course there are characters like that. An audience can relate, most of us know people who need to talk a lot or who love the sound of their own voice or simply have a lot of information to impart. First, check to make sure that you haven't peopled your script with a <u>series of character</u>s with the same style and rhythm. Then check to see if you have created conflict in the scenes that feature the verbose character. Is there someone <u>not</u> listening? Is there someone <u>questioning</u>? Is someone trying to stop the information from getting out? What does the person want to accomplish? Does she want to change someone's mind? Does he want to encourage an action? Make sure each line of dialogue, even if the character seems to be rambling, serves a purpose, creates conflict and helps move the story forward.

get a character to reveal, through dialogue, information and truths about themselves.

Consider the words written by screenwriters Hubert Selby Jr. and Darren Aronofsky for pill-addicted, TV-addicted 60-ish Sara Goldfarb's (portrayed by Ellen Burstyn) evaluation of herself (to her son) in 2000's **REQUIEM FOR A DREAM:** *"Soon, millions of people will see me and they'll all like me. I'll tell them about you, your father, how good he was to us. Remember? It's a reason to get up in the morning. It's a reason to lose weight. To fit in a red dress. It's a reason to smile. It makes tomorrow alright. What have I got, Harry? Hm? Why should I even make the bed or wash the dishes? …? I'm alone. Your father's gone. You're gone. I've no one to care for….I'm lonely. I'm old."*

The dialogue written for Rick to say in 1942's **CASABLANCA:** *"I stick my neck out for nobody…"* lets the audience know that Rick does not have close relationships with people and has not taken sides in the war. The words give the audience a sense of his alone-ness.

The dialogue written for Joanna, the wife and mother who abandons her son in 1979's **KRAMER VS. KRAMER**, *"I'm a terrible mother! I'm an awful mother. I yell at him all the time. I have no patience. He's better off without me…"* lets the audience know Joanna's state of mind and frustration.

The dialogue written for Elle's hapless boyfriend, Warner, as he tells Elle why he can't marry her: *"You have no idea the pressure I'm under. My family has five generations of senators. My brother is in the top three at Yale Law. He just got engaged to a Vanderbilt for crisssakes."* These lines let us know part of Warner's backstory and his reasons for pulling the plug on his relationship with Elle.

The words written for blonde, perky and popular Elle when she can't understand why Warner's family wouldn't approve of her in 2001's **LEGALLY BLONDE:** *"Everybody likes me!"* This line lets us know that Elle is used to being appreciated, adored and emulated.

Give your character a chance for self-assessment. Does he think he's hot date? Does she think she's always right? Does he think he's a good or bad son? Does she think she's smart or does she feel like she can't keep up with intellectuals? Is he being honest in the self-assessment? Is she deluding herself?

What other characters say about each other

An active way to get information out through dialogue is by letting characters assess each other. This can be used to great advantage when the assessment creates emotional conflict or other strong reaction. Consider 1991's **SILENCE OF THE LAMBS**, adapted by Ted Tally from the novel by Thomas Harris. The writer wrote these probing words for Hannibal Lecter (portrayed by Anthony Hopkins) to give the audience a window into the character of Clarice Starling (portrayed by Jodie Foster): *"You're so-o ambitious, aren't you? You know what you look like to me, with your good bag and your cheap shoes? You look like a rube. A well-scrubbed, hustling rube, with a little taste. Good nutrition's given you some length of bone, but you're not more than one generation from poor white trash, are you, Agent Starling? And that accent you've tried so desperately to shed – pure West Virginia. What does your father do? Is he a coal miner? Does he stink of the lamp?"* Lecter's words sting Clarice, they cause a reaction – and fill the audience in on Clarice's backstory.

SILENCE OF THE LAMBS (1991) Jodie Foster
- photo courtesy of Globe Photos

In 1976's **NETWORK**, written by Paddy Chayefsky, protagonist Max (portrayed by William Holden) assesses the ambitious network executive Diana, the young woman with whom he is having an affair. *"I'm not sure she's capable of any real feelings. She's television generation. She learned life from Bugs Bunny. The only reality she knows comes to her from over the TV set..."*

In the early scenes of 1972's **THE GODFATHER**, Sonny (portrayed by James Caan) scoffs when the warm-hearted, youngest son and war hero Michael (portrayed by Al Pacino) asks to be part of the plan to avenge the shooting of his father: *"You, the high class college kid? You never wanted to get mixed up in the family business."* Michael is stung by the truth of these words and realizes he has a lot to prove to his family. The audience also becomes privy to important backstory. Michael goes through a transformation as he experiences violence against his family. Near the end of the film, Michael is called *"cold"* and uncommunicative. Michael's father eventually makes it clear: *"Michael is in charge (of the family) now."* In the final moments of the film, Michael is called *"Don Corleone."* The audience knows he has absolutely embraced the family business – and his change is complete.

When Ted Kramer's wife leaves him in **KRAMER VS KRAMER**, Ted (portrayed by Dustin Hoffman) does not want to shoulder the entire blame for the marriage falling apart. The screenwriter allows Ted to give his perspective on Joanna, *"Did it ever occur to you guys that Joanna Kramer's not the easiest person in the world to live with? Did it? For one thing, she's always thirty minutes late…"*

Take a look at 1994's **FORREST GUMP.** Forrest's mother (portrayed by Sally Field) has these words to say about her son, *"He might be on the slow side, but my boy Forrest is going to get the same opportunity as everyone else."*

What does your protagonist's best friend or his enemy or his lover say about him – to his face or behind his back? Examples: *"Sweet but neurotic."* Or *"You can't trust him."* Or *"He'll always have your back."* The audience wants to know how others assess characters; it helps them form their own opinions and gives them more insight into the character.

Exercise:

Choose at least two supporting characters in your script. Make sure you know what their opinions or assessments are of your protagonist. Write those short assessments or opinions, either as a short monologue or in a dialogue exchange with another character. After you have done the writing assignment, consider whether this is information that is already in your script – or information that should be in your script. If you decide it's interesting content that helps illuminate character and character motivations, find a place to use it in your script.

One character making observations about the other can reveal important character elements. Characters who question the protagonist about his actions force the protagonist to explain himself (or refuse to) and reveal more character elements. A character trying to cut someone down to size, or trying too build someone up are all methods of letting characters reveal elements about one another.

DIALOGUE QUESTIONS TO ASK

Do all your characters live (and speak) in the same genre?

Be clear about your over-riding genre. Is it comedic? Is it dramedy? Is it a serious drama? Is the dialogue of your characters in step with the tone of your film story? Compare the different tones in the dialogue of the crime drama *THE DEPARTED* and the comedy *LEGALLY BLONDE*. The characters in each <u>belong</u> in their respective films; the tone of their aspirations, their plans, their relationships and the way they speak.

Does each character have a singular voice?

Do your disparate characters use various expressions to mean the same thing? Does your protagonist use "no" or "naw" or "no way" or "bugger off" or other words to express a negative response? How do other characters in your story express the negative? Are some of your characters more educated than others? How do their words show that? Are some characters more aggressive? More passive?

Go through your script and check the dialogue rhythms you have built for each character. Concentrate on one character at a time, read aloud only his or her dialogue. Is it consistent? Have you found a favorite word or phrase for each character? Does one character speak in complete sentences? Does another character always struggle for the right words? What about malapropisms – does one of your character use words in the wrong way? Does a shyness show itself through the dialogue? Or the aggressiveness of a bully?

If you have a facility for dialogue (if you naturally write funny, urbane, clever and witty words), have you inadvertently written all characters as urbane and witty? Or do all your characters speak with a good-ol'-boy drawl? Or are all your characters monosyllabic? Remember; let each character have an individual voice.

Have you let the audience know the dreams of your character?

The deep desires, the dreams, the overall wants and the driving forces behind your characters are always important to explore. Let your characters try to find the words to express why they are doing what they are doing. Consider 2004's ***MILLLION DOLLAR BABY***, a screenplay written by Paul Haggis, based on the stories of F.X. Toole. Uneducated and determined Maggie Fitzgerald (portrayed by Hilary Swank) insists to her reluctant coach Frankie Dunn (portrayed by Clint Eastwood) that she can't put off her dream: *"I'm 32, Mr. Dunn, and I'm here celebrating the fact that I spent another year scraping dishes and waitressing which is what I've been doing since 13, and according to you, I'll be 37 before I can even throw a decent punch, which I have to admit, after working on this speed bag for a month may be the God's simple truth. Other truth is, my brother's in prison, my sister cheats on welfare by pretending one of her babies is still alive, my daddy's dead, and my momma weighs 312 pounds. If I was thinking straight, I'd go back home, find a used trailer, buy a deep fryer and some Oreos. Problem is, this is the only thing I ever felt good doing. If I'm too old for this, then I got nothing. That enough truth to suit you?"*

Consider 1934's ***IT HAPPENED ONE NIGHT,*** written by Billy Wilder and I.A.L. Diamond. They wrote these words for Peter (portrayed by Clark

Gable) about his hopes for love and marriage. *"Sure, I've thought about it. Who hasn't? If I could ever meet the right sort of girl. Ahh, where you gonna find her? Somebody that's real, somebody that's alive! They don't come like that way anymore. Have I ever thought about it? Boy, I've even been sucker enough to make plans. You know, I saw an island in the Pacific once, never been able to forget it. That's where I'd like to take her. She'd have to be the sort of a girl who'd jump in the surf with me and love it as much as I did. Nights when you and the moon and the water all become one. You feel you're part of something big and marvelous. That's the only place to live. The stars are so close over your head you feel you could reach up and stir them around. Certainly, I've been thinking about it. Boy, if I could ever find a girl who was hungry for those things..."*

Consider 1990's **GOODFELLAS**, written by Nicholas Pileggi and Martin Scorsese. Gangster Henry Hill (portrayed by Ray Liotta) tells us at the opening, *"As far back as I can remember, I always wanted to be a gangster. To me, being a gangster was better than being President of the United States…To me, it meant being somebody in a neighborhood that was full of nobodies…"* Note how the writers are able to balance this upbeat, hopeful desire of a young man with the older Henry Hill at the end of the film. After serving as an informant for the FBI and entering the witness protection program, Henry laments his life of being a "nobody": *"..Right after I got here I ordered some spaghetti with marinara sauce and I got egg noodles and ketchup. I'm an average nobody. I get to live the rest of my life like a schnook."*

GOODFELLAS (1990) Joe Pesci, Ray Liotta, Robert DeNiro
- photo courtesy of Globe Photos

Check your script. Have you balanced your verbal or visual character statements of goals or desires? Is it clear, either through dialogue or a visual, how your character has changed from the beginning to the end of your film story?

Exercise:

Write a short monologue that reveals the personal dreams and the reasons for those personal dreams for each of your main characters. Once you have written the monologues, imagine how the same content could be transferred to a scene with another character. Write the scene – using a dialogue exchange to get across the same information on personal dreams. Explore using conflict to get the information out – is someone telling your main character that his dream is impossible to attain? Is someone telling your main character that his dream is silly or unworthy or useless? After you have done the writing of the monologues/scenes, ask yourself if there is a place in your script that this information could be added. Ask yourself if this information enhances the stories of your main characters.

Do your characters have opinions?

"There's no crying in baseball!" 1992's **A LEAGUE OF THEIR OWN.** Screenwriters Lowell Ganz and Bubaloo Mandell's memorably funny line clearly states the opinion of the coach in the 1940s All American Pro Girl Baseball League when faced with the emotional weeping of his female team.

Screenwriter Tim Robbins adapted Helen Prejean's novel **DEAD MAN WALKING.** These words were written for murderer Matthew Poncelot (portrayed by Sean Penn) to say before his execution by lethal injection: .".. *I just wanna say I think killin' is wrong, no matter who does it, whether it's me or y'all or your government..."* The film examines other characters' points of view on capital punishment – some characters think it is just, others think capital punishment is barbaric. Others are only concerned with the technical aspects of carrying out their job and do not emotionally connect to the moral question. If all the characters had been on one side or the other, the balance of the film would have been off, the content would have been didactic, and conflict among characters would have been lessened.

In Eric Roth's screenplay for **FORREST GUMP,** based on the book by

Winston Groom, Forrest Gump had a particularly sweet attitude about life, *"My mamma says life is a box of chocolates. You never know what you're gonna get."*

In **BULL DURHAM,** screenwriter Ron Shelton wrote these words for his character to respond to the question, "What do you believe in?" Bull says" *I believe in long slow kisses that last three days."*

Consider the 1993 **ADDAMS FAMILY VALUES** written by Paul Rudnick. Wednesday Addams (portrayed by Christina Ricci) is in a summer camp play about the First Thanksgiving. She plays the role of Pocahontas. The screenwriter wrote her "adlib" lines to the Pilgrims. *"Wait! We cannot break bread with you...You have taken the land which is rightfully ours. Years from now, my people will be forced to live in mobile homes on reservations. Your people will wear cardigans, and drink highballs. We will sell our bracelets by the roadsides. You will play golf, and enjoy hot h'ors d'oeuvres. My people will have pain and degradation. Your people will have stick shifts. The gods of my tribe have spoken. They have said: 'Do not trust the pilgrims, especially Sarah Miller'...And for all of these reasons I have decided to scalp you and burn your village to the ground."*

Do your characters sound authentic?

Your characters need to sound as if they live in their world; their job, their family, their friends, the environment they call home. Characters in the police force have been trained; they know and use a different professional language than a doctor, lawyer, priest or housewife. Teens speak differently than adults. Characters from the southern United States speak in a different cadence than characters from New England. Characters from different countries will have various ways of speaking – and looking at the world. Make sure you have done your research. Your characters need to sound authentic.

Consider Charles Foster Kane's words in 1941's **CITIZEN KANE:** *"Six years ago, I looked at a picture of the world's greatest newspaper men. I felt like a kid in front of a candy store. Well, tonight, six years later, I got my candy – all of it. Welcome, gentlemen, to the Inquirer! Make up an extra copy of that picture and send it to the Chronicle, will you please? It will make you all happy to learn that our circulation this morning was the greatest in New York, 684,000."*

Consider old prospector Howard (portrayed by Walter Huston) and his knowledge of gold prospecting in 1948's **THE TREASURE OF SIERRA MADRE:** *."..Why is gold worth some twenty bucks an ounce?...A thousand men, say, go searching for gold, after six months, one of 'em's lucky. One out of a thousand – his find represents not only his own labor, but that of 999 others to boot. That's uh, 6,000 months, uh, five hundred years. Scrabblin' over a mountain, going hungry and thirsty. An ounce of gold, Mister, is worth what it is because of the human labor that went into the finding and getting of it...."*

Consider the screenplay for 1993's **THE FUGITIVE**, written by David Twohy and Jeb Stuart. US Marshal Sam Gerard's (portrayed by Tommy Lee Jones) sends his men out to search for escaped fugitive Dr. Richard Kimble (portrayed by Harrison Ford). *"Alright, listen up, people. Our fugitive has been on the run for ninety minutes. Average foot speed over uneven ground barring injuries is 4 miles-per-hour. That gives us a radius of six miles. What I want from each and every one of you is a hard-target search of every gas station, residence, warehouse, farmhouse, henhouse, outhouse and doghouse in that area. Checkpoints go up at fifteen miles. Your fugitive's name is Dr. Richard Kimble. Go get him."* Gerard's dialogue makes it clear to the audience he is knowledgeable and good at his job.

Consider the opening statements in the courtroom made by Joe Miller (portrayed by Denzel Washington) in 1993's **PHILADELPHIA,** written by Ron Nyswaner. Joe is defending a man who has been allegedly fired from his job because he has AIDS. *"Ladies and gentlemen of the jury. Forget everything you've seen on television. There's not going to be any surprise last minute witnesses. Nobody's going to break down on the stand with a tearful confession. You're going to be presented with a simple fact: Andrew Beckett was fired. You'll hear two explanations as to why he was fired. Ours and theirs. It's up to you to sift through layer upon layer of truth until you determine for yourself which version sounds the most true..."* Note how the word "you" pulls the theatre audience into the dilemma. The author is also telling the theatre audience that this may not to be the just, safe or "happy" conclusion and further piques the attention of the audience.

Take a look at 2002's **A BEAUTIFUL MIND.** John Nash (portrayed by Russell Crowe) accepts a 1994 Nobel Prize in Stockholm, Sweden: *"Thank you. I've always believed in numbers and the equations and logics that lead to reason. But after a lifetime of such pursuits, I ask: "What truly is logic?" "Who decides reason?" My quest has taken me through the physical, the metaphysical, the delusional – and back. And I have made the most important* *discovery of my career, the most important discovery of my life: It is only in the mysterious equations of love that any logic or reasons can be found."*

Consider 2002's **GANGS OF NEW YORK.** Butcher and gang leader Bill Cutting (portrayed by Daniel Day-Lewis) shows young Amsterdam Vallon (portrayed by Leonardo DiCaprio) how to knife-fight, using a butchered pig. He stabs the pig in various places: *"You get to know a lot butchering meat. We're made up of the same things – flesh and blood, tissue, organs. I love to work with pigs. The nearest thing in nature to the flesh of a man is the flesh of a pig...This is the liver. The kidneys. The heart."* He stabs the pig carcass. *"This is a wound – the stomach will bleed and bleed."* He stabs the carcass in a more vulnerable area. *"This is a kill."* Another stab. *"This is a kill. Main artery. This is a kill."*

GANGS OF NEW YORK (2002) Daniel Day-Lewis, Leonardo DiCaprio
- photo courtesy of Globe Photos

Take a look at your script. Is there a place to use a character's expertise to get a story point across? Are you characters sounding "of their world"?

Have you explored constructing dialogue that says one thing but means another?

Can you use a metaphor or an analogy to replace on-the-nose dialogue? Are there original ways to get your characters' intentions or desires across?

Consider 1946's **THE BIG SLEEP.** Detective Philip Marlowe (portrayed by

Humphrey Bogart) and Vivian Rutledge (portrayed by Lauren Bacall) are clearly attracted to one another. They are at the racetrack and Vivian tells Marlowe: *"Well, speaking of horses, I like to play them myself. But I like to see them work out a little first, see if they're front-runners or come from behind, find out what their hole-card is. What makes them run."* Marlowe asks if she has found out what makes him run. Vivian replies, *"I think so. I'd say you don't like to be rated. You like to get out in front, open up a lead, take a little breather in the backstretch, and then come home free."* Marlowe asks what makes Vivian run. She replies: *"I'll give you a little hint. Sugar won't work. It's been tried."*

Consider 16-year-old pregnant Juno in 2007's ***JUNO***. Juno likes to shock people with her words. She likes to stand out and enjoys being a non-conformist. She often pushes people away with her glib jokes. She also pushes people away by making negative personal assessments of others' shortcomings. However, underneath her edgy exterior, the audience sees her youth and desire for love and closeness. In a similar fashion, the writer of 2007's ***THE SAVAGES*** creates a protagonist who craves attention. The audience comes to understand that the protagonist, Wendy, as a child, never received enough consideration or sense of being loved by her parents. At the time of the film story, Wendy is now 39 years old and habitually creates scenarios or tells lies to gain attention. The audience understands Wendy's intentions without her using on-the-nose dialogue about feeling ignored as a child.

Does your dialogue attack?

Your character may need to voice his anger or frustration and verbally attack the forces working against him. Don't shy away from letting your character use words to attack. Consider 1946's ***IT'S A WONDERFUL LIFE.*** George Bailey's (portrayed by James Stewart) defends his dead father's name to the powerful and cruel Mr. Potter (portrayed by Lionel Barrymore*): ."..Just remember this, Mr. Potter, that this rabble you're talking about, they do most of the working and paying and living and dying in this community. Well, is it too much to have them work and pay and live and die in a couple of decent rooms and a bath? Anyway, my father didn't think so. People were human beings to him, but to you, a warped, frustrated old man, they're cattle. Well, in my book he died a much richer man than you'll ever be... ."*

IT'S A WONDERFUL LIFE (1946) James Stewart, Donna Reed, Thomas Mitchell
- photo courtesy of Globe Photos

Consider 1954's *ON THE WATERFRONT.* Small-time thug with a conscience Terry Malloy (portrayed by Marlon Brando) finally confronts his gangster brother Charley (portrayed Rod Steiger) in the back seat of a taxicab: *"It wasn't him, Charley! It was you. You remember that night in the Garden, you came down to my dressing room and said: 'Kid, this ain't your night. We're going for the price on Wilson.' You remember that? 'This ain't your night!' My night! I coulda taken Wilson apart! So what happens? He gets the title shot outdoors in the ball park – and whadda I get? A one-way ticket to Palookaville....You was my brother, Charley. You shoulda looked out for me a little bit…. I coulda had class. I coulda been a contender. I coulda been somebody, instead of a bum, which is what I am. Let's face it… It was you, Charley."*

Take a look 2001's *ALI.* Cassius Clay's/Muhammad Ali (portrayed by Will Smith) used these words to explain his refusal to serve in Vietnam: *"I ain't draft dodging. I ain't burning no flag. I ain't running to Canada. I'm staying right here. You want to send me to jail? Fine, you go right ahead. I've been in jail for 400 years. I could be there for 4 or 5 more, but I ain't going no 10,000 miles to help murder and kill other poor people. If I want to die, I'll die right here, right now, fightin' you, if I want to die…You my opposer when I want freedom. You my opposer when I want justice. You my opposer when I want equality. Want me to go somewhere and fight for you? You won't even stand up for me right here in America, for my rights and my religious beliefs. You won't even stand up for my right here at home."*

ALI (2001) Will Smith
- *photo courtesy of Globe Photos*

Have you considered increasing conflict in dialogue exchanges by asking questions?

Putting dialogue in the form of questions can bring more interest and conflict to a scene. The audience becomes engaged because they will want to know the answer. Or they may have answered the question for themselves but they still want to know how the other character will react.

Screenwriter Paddy Chayefsky wrote these words for the wife of the protagonist, Max, in **NETWORK.** He has just told her he is leaving home to move in with his mistress, Diana. *"… this isn't a convention weekend with your secretary, is it? Or – or some broad that you picked up after three belts of booze. This is your great winter romance, isn't it? Your last roar of passion before you settle into your emeritus years. Is that what's left for me? Is that my share? She gets the winter passion, and I get the dotage? What am I supposed to do? Am I supposed to sit at home knitting and purling while you slink back like some penitent drunk? I'm your wife, damn it! And, if you can't work up a winter passion for me, the least I require is respect and allegiance!"* Note how putting her assessment in a series of questions keeps the short monologue from feeling expositional.

NETWORK (1976) Beatrice Straight, William Holden
- photo courtesy of Globe Photos

Contrast two or more points of view

Balance your film with various points of view. Your protagonist may look at the world in one way; your antagonist may see the world in a different way. Another supporting character may have another point of view on a particular subject. By exploring various points of view, the writer can give the audience the chance to examine their own personal feelings on a particular subject.

Screenwriter Aaron Sorkin explored various points of view of honor in 1992's drama *A FEW GOOD MEN;* Lieutenant Daniel Kaffee (portrayed by Tom Cruise) is a lawyer serving in the military. Kaffee believes in the law and the protection for all under the law. In the courtroom, Kaffee interrogates Colonel Nathan R. Jessup's (portrayed by Jack Nicholson), suspected of facilitating harassment of a soldier serving under Jessup's command. This harassed soldier did not live up to Jessup's standards and Jessup made this clear to the rest of his squad, thus opening the door for ridicule and abuse – and eventually physical harm of the harassed soldier. The trial focuses on the reasons for and circumstances of the mysterious death of the harassed solider and the ultimate responsibility for this death. Jessup, a decorated soldier, resents the trial, resents his command being questioned. He is clearly a man who believes the end justifies the means and feels he is above the law. Jessup loses his cool on the witness stand and snaps at Kaffee: *"We use words like "honor," "code," "loyalty." We use these words as the backbone of a life spent defending something. You use them as a punch line. I have neither the time nor the inclination to explain myself to a man who rises and sleeps under the blanket of the very freedom that I provide and then questions the manner in which I provide it."* Jessup's point of view varies greatly from Kaffee and the prosecuting team. Ultimately sides are taken – and the audience enjoys siding with one or the other – and witnessing the outcome.

A FEW GOOD MEN (1992) Jack Nicholson, Tom Cruise
- photo courtesy of Globe Photos

If you are writing a romance, are there characters who believe in love – and others who do not? If you are writing a road trip script, are there characters who act "responsibly" – and others who do not when put in awkward situations? Do all characters get a chance to give their opinions and reasons for their actions? People disagree, so it is wise for the screenwriter to allow his characters to disagree and have strong opinions.

Exercise:

Write a scene where two of your main characters vehemently disagree about a course of action or about personal beliefs. Let them verbally attack each other; bring up the past or present events to support their side of the argument. Let it get personal. After you have written the scene, decide if a version of it belongs in your script (or not).

No need to over-explain or repeat information

Look through your script. Are your characters explaining themselves or explaining their actions, over and over? Are they announcing their plans and then carrying them out? There is no need to announce plans if the audience is going to <u>see</u> them carried out. There is no need for the character to say he is going to the bank if, in the next scene, he is at the bank.

Example:

INT. BAKERY – DAY

Janet pays for her purchases. She glances out the window and sees Donald crossing the street. She turns to Amy behind the counter.

> JANET
> *There's Donald. I bet he's going to the bank. I'm going over there right now and tell him what I think.*

Note the excess in the scene. The audience <u>also</u> sees Donald, therefore Janet doesn't have to say *"There's Donald."* Janet does not have to tell the audience her plan to follow Donald into the bank. It is better to <u>see</u> her follow, enter the bank and find out what she does in the bank – <u>when she does it.</u> Get out of a scene <u>before</u> all the information is given – let the next scene add another piece to the story puzzle. The above scene could have been more economically – and aimed at making the reader read on to find out what happens:

INT. BAKERY – DAY

Janet pays for her purchases. She glances out the window and sees Donald crossing the street. Janet quickly gathers her things – rushes out the door.

INT. BANK – DAY

Donald heads to the bank president's office. Janet rushes in, fuming –

> JANET
> *Donald, you cheat. If you think you're going to get any of my money – you'd better think again.*

Let one scene set up the situation, the next scene give the audience more information, the next scene more or different information. There is no need to tell the audience <u>and</u> show the audience <u>and</u> then tell the audience again – what they already know.

Voiceovers

One of the most important aspects of good storytelling is clarity. If you have decided to use voiceover, there are a few things to consider.

The use of voiceover can be an effective story telling tool <u>as long as it is used properly.</u> Voiceovers should not tell the audience something they already know. Voiceovers should not tell the audience what they are seeing.

Example:

EXT: SUBURBS OF LOS ANGELES – DAY

Small, tightly packed cookie-cutter houses. Mothers are out gardening and gossiping. Kids fill the cul-de-sacs; ride bikes and toss baseballs and play tag. A FOR SALE sign is on the front of one of the houses and a tearful young mother, JANE (age 30) carries out boxes. She puts them into the back of a beat-up pickup. NICK (age 10) super-nerd, exits the house too, he carries his precious science set. Some of the kids jeer at him.

NICK (VOICEOVER)
Yeah, I grew up outside Los Angeles in this place where all the houses were the same and all so close together no one ever had any privacy. The mothers all stayed at home watching their kids and talked about the latest mini-catastrophe. This story starts when my mom decided we had to sell our house and move. I packed by science set, didn't care about much else. Didn't have any friends there.

Note how the voiceover is telling us exactly what we are seeing in the visual. If you are using voiceover, consider using the voiceover to accomplish <u>more</u> than the visual.

Note how the example below informs us about character and even helps start the story.

EXT: SUBURBS OF LOS ANGELES – DAY

Small, tightly packed cookie-cutter houses. Mothers are out gardening and gossiping. Kids fill the cul-de-sacs; ride bikes and toss baseballs and play tag. A FOR SALE sign is on the front of one of the houses and a tearful young mother, JANE (age 30) carries out boxes. She puts them into the back of a beat-up pickup. NICK (age 10) super-nerd, exits the house too, he carries his precious science set. Some of the kids jeer at him.

NICK (VOICEOVER)

No more listenin' to these punks. That's what my dad called 'em – punks. He said that to me – even his last words to me at the hospital – don't worry about the punks. Just think about your design for the fastest rocket to the moon.

Note how this voiceover accomplishes more than the visual. The audience understands Nick's attitude towards his neighborhood, learns that his father is dead, that Nick has aspirations to build a spaceship. The visual gives us information - the voiceover is giving us other information. You are using your screen time to better advantage.

If you are using voiceover, does it help set the world and the tone of your story? Consider 1995's **MALLRATS**, written by Kevin Smith. Brodie (portrayed by Jason Lee) speaks the opening voiceover: *"One time my cousin Walter got this cat stuck up his ass. True story. He bought it at our local mall, so the whole fiasco wound up on the news. It was embarrassing for my relatives and all, but the next week, he did it again. Different cat, same results, complete with another trip to the emergency room. So, I run into him a week later in the mall and he's buying another cat. And I says to him: 'Jesus, Walt! What are you doing? You know you're just gonna get this cat stuck in your ass too. Why don't you knock it off?' And he said to me: 'Brodie, how the hell else am I supposed to get the gerbil out?' My cousin was a weird guy."* Immediately, the audience is introduced into the world. They know it's okay to laugh. They know that Brodie will be their guide through the story.

Take a look at 2006's **THE DEPARTED**. Irish gang leader, Frank Costello's opening voiceover sets the tone and reason for the situations of the story. The voiceover sets up the violence and world that our main characters will inhabit.

he opening voiceover in 1999's **AMERICAN BEAUTY** piques the interest the audience. *"My name is Lester Burnham. This is my neighborhood; is is my street; this is my life. I am 42 years old; in less than a year I will be ad. Of course I don't know that yet, and in a way, I am dead already."* The dience wants to know what circumstances will play out.

Exercise:

Take a look at two films; 1953's **STALAG 17** and 1994's **FORREST GUMP**. Forrest Gump's voiceover is necessary because the film story spans decades of time, a large number of events and features a very singular and quirky character that looks at life in a way that is engaging – and unusual. Note how the voiceover <u>does not tell us what is happening</u> in the scene, but reveals new information. Note how the voiceover in STALAG 17 is not used to advantage; it tends to repeat information already made clear by the situations or visuals. How could the voiceovers in STALAG 17 have been used to better advantage?

Other successful examples of the use of voiceover are Orson Welles' 1948's *LADY FROM SHANGHAI* or Woody Allen's 1977's *ANNIE HALL*. The voiceovers add dimension to each of these scripts.

Character's take on the world – is it yours?

You, the author, have a chance to put your personal stamp on your script. Is there one characters in your script that voices your own beliefs or feelings about the world? Consider how these following lines of dialogue seem to come from the heart.

In1995's *BRAVEHEART*, the character of William Wallace states his belief, *"They may take away our lives, but they'll never take away our freedom!"*

In *CASABLANCA*, Rick lets Ilsa know that he's realized he must rise above personal desires and do his part in the world war. He says, *"Ilsa, I'm not good at being noble, but it doesn't take much to see that the problems of three little people don't amount of a hill of beans in this crazy world."*

In 1979's *APOCALYPSE NOW*, Lt. Colonel Kilgore makes it very clear that he feels alive when at war, *"I love the smell of napalm in the morning."*

In 1989's *DEAD POET'S SOCIETY*, the teacher, John Keating advises his students, *"Carpe diem. Seize the day, boys. Make your lives extraordinary."*

In 1999's **AMERICAN BEAUTY,** Ricky Fitts admits, *"There's so much beauty in the world I feel like I can't take it, like my heart's going to cave in."*

Consider 2003's **LOVE ACTUALLY.** The British Prime Minister's (portrayed by Hugh Grant) voice-over: *"Whenever I get gloomy with the state of the world, I think about the arrivals gate at Heathrow Airport. General opinion's starting to make out that we live in a world of hatred and greed, but I don't see that. It seems to me that love is everywhere. Often it's not particularly dignified or newsworthy, but it's always there – fathers and sons, mothers and daughters, husbands and wives, boyfriends, girlfriends, old friends. When the planes hit the Twin Towers, as far as I know, none of the phone calls from the people on board were messages of hate or revenge – they were all messages of love. If you look for it, I've got a sneaky feeling you'll find that love actually is all around."*

Epiphany

Have you created the "ah ha!" moment for your character? Is there a moment when all the elements and events and conflicts of the story come together for your protagonist and she suddenly <u>understands</u> the world or herself in a new way? Do you have the moment where the audience knows the character is now changed and will, in most probability, be forever changed?

In thinking through the placement of this moment, it's clear that, in most cases, it needs to be near the end of the script. If the character changes too early in the film story – your story could be over.

Consider the Beast in 1991's **BEAUTY AND THE BEAST.** His moment of epiphany comes when, at the end of Act Two, he allows Belle to leave the castle to go help her father. He knows that the last rose petal will soon fall (the film's ticking clock) and that in letting Belle go he will probably be doomed to be a Beast forever. But he finally understands what love is and that is his epiphany. The epiphany can be verbalized (give it a try, don't shy away from it) or it could become evident through a visual.

Question: Is the protagonist's epiphany always wrapped up in the crisis moment – that moment of decision that propels the protagonist into the climax?

Answer: There are no rules dictating the placement of the protagonist's epiphany. It might come at the crisis point at the end of Act Two and be the motivating factor that sends the protagonist into the Act Three climax. The epiphany might come during the climax in the heat of battle or at an emotional moment. The epiphany might come out during the resolution, in the final moments of your film. The epiphany could also be dramatized by showing the "new normal" at the end of the script.

CHAPTER SUMMARY

- Good dialogue illuminates a character and a character's desires and motivations.

- Each character in the film story should have an individual voice.

- Dialogue can manipulate, cajole, attack or express emotion. Using dialogue to heighten the conflict in a scene is a good idea.

- If a visual tells the audience what they need to know, consider cutting dialogue that simply repeats information.

Chapter Nine

THEME

What can raise one script above another? There are many crime stories. Many stories about the mob. Many romances, comedies and dramas. You can make long lists of films in every genre and tone; many have plots that explore similar material. So how can you make yours stand out?

It is the film stories that have committed to a <u>strong theme</u> that truly resonate with the audience. When a studio or production company reader reads a script, he is looking for a compelling story, compelling characters and a reason to recommend the script for production. That reason will be, invariably, <u>theme.</u>

Theme is important. It may have been the impetus that started your film story. Or it may emerge now as you work on your story. If you haven't embraced your theme yet, now is the time to do it. Theme grounds a story. It helps bring resonance to the characters. <u>It helps shape your scenes.</u> Let theme help focus your story.

Identify your most dominant theme

There are a few easy ways to identify the dominant theme in your script. Ask yourself: What does my protagonist learn or realize during the process of the story? How does my protagonist change in the story?

Exercise:

Fill in the blanks with adjectives or descriptive phrases: My main character starts the story as a _____. On this journey of change, the main character becomes (or learns or realizes) _____.

Examples: My main character starts the story as a naïve and trusting college student. On this journey of change, the main character becomes distrustful, hardened and closes herself off from the world. Or: My main character starts the story as nerdy high school student with low self-esteem who can't get a girl. On this journey of change, the main character becomes confident and believes in his abilities – and gets the girl. Or: My main character starts the story as a star soldier in a far-away galaxy – he is well-born, favored, egotistical and confident. On this journey of change he learns to connect with the common man, see the world as corrupt and dedicates himself to poverty and fighting for civil rights.

Another way to try to identify your dominant theme is to explore what the protagonist <u>lacks</u>. Consider Elle in 2001's ***LEGALLY BLONDE.*** Elle (portrayed by Reese Witherspoon) lacks her boyfriend's respect – and the respect of her undergraduate college counselor, her parents and her law school professors and peers. Through her journey in the film story, she realizes that if she doesn't stand up for herself, she is in danger of losing self-respect. Consider 2007's ***KNOCKED UP.*** The protagonist, Ben Stone (portrayed by Seth Rogen), lacks a sense of responsibility and, at an age when most young men are pursuing realistic goals, he is still living with his slacker buddies, getting high and spinning pipe dreams. What Ben Stone lacks is a sense of responsibility– and the <u>desire</u> to be responsible. The protagonist is going to "learn" or "realize" something about himself that relates to the theme during the film story.

Exercise:

Make a list of the one or two most important things your character lacks – what is keeping him from being the person he wants to be? Confidence? Conscience? Empathy? Respect? Love? Self-esteem? Power? Control? Courage? Stick to the emotional or psychological needs – the physical needs like "a new car to impress the girl" or fame or money should not play into your theme. (Those will, in most cases, be immediate goals.) Theme needs to explore the emotional or psychological nature of your protagonist.

Caution: If your protagonist learns or embraces the theme too early, your story may be, essentially, over because the audience will feel like the journey is complete. Make sure you place a series of difficult obstacles in your protagonist's way - make it treacherous (emotionally and physically) to <u>change</u> or to <u>realize</u> or <u>embrace</u> the theme. Nothing can be easy.

Use the "without 'x' there can be no 'y' " template

Every story, whether it's a drama, romance, thriller, comedy or farce needs to have a theme. Consider the theme of 2007's dumber-than-dumb comedy, ***BLADES OF GLORY:*** Without learning to work together, true greatness cannot be achieved. The theme of 2006's action/crime/romance, ***CASINO ROYALE:*** Without trust there can be no love. The theme of 2006's action/adventure/political thriller/coming-of-age ***BLOOD DIAMOND:*** Without believing you can make a difference in the world, there can be no change.

Using the "without 'x' there can be no 'y' template will keep you from being too general – and it will help you hone in on exactly the theme you are exploring. It will help you keep your theme active. It will help you see the anti-theme (the opposite) so that you can explore its ramifications through your antagonist or other characters and events in your story.

Proving your theme

Think of your theme as a scientific experiment. You are out to <u>prove</u> that certain combinations of forces or elements are necessary to bring about a certain conclusion to your story. If your protagonist moves from feeling unloved and unworthy to believing in herself and feeling loved, perhaps your theme is: Without self-esteem, one cannot form a healthy relationship. If you believe the <u>opposite</u> (or are just exploring the opposite – your anti-theme) your theme might be: Without one person being considered the inferior or subservient in a relationship, a marriage (or romantic commitment) will never succeed. By giving yourself a statement that you can prove or disprove (or that people can agree with or not) you will make your theme feel active.

A theme needs to be active and it needs to be able to looked at from various angles.

Exercise:

Think about the change that takes place in your protagonist over the course of your story. Identify what your protagonist lacks – emotionally or psychologically – at the outset of your story. Now fill in the first blank of the next sentence. Without _____ there can be no _____. Put the most compelling "lack" of your protagonist in the first blank. Now fill in the second blank with the word or words that sum up the character's emotional <u>goal</u> or <u>desire</u>.

Examples: Without a sense of family, there can be no sense of home. Or: Without respect, one can never feel worthy. Or: Without a belief in self, one cannot reach his full potential. Or: Without love, one can never feel complete. Or: Without dominance, there can be no order. The theme will be something <u>you</u> are exploring and something that you will want to <u>prove</u> in your script.

Note how most themes are basic explorations of human nature. There is no need to find a "theme that has never been used before." You want to make your theme <u>relatable</u>. You want people to identify with the journey of the character, to identify with what the character learns or realizes or comes to understand.

I mentioned in my first book on screenwriting that a good way to think about exploring the theme in your script is to consider how a music composer approaches a musical composition. Music often features a <u>theme</u> throughout a musical piece. The theme is repeated, turned around and upside down, used in different variations and in different rhythms. Think of your film story as a piece of music, one that explores one theme that resonates in the protagonist's story <u>and</u> in the antagonist's story <u>and</u> in the stories of the supporting characters <u>and</u> in the plot. Make sure you are using <u>one</u> theme, that you are exploring the <u>pros and cons</u> of it. Make sure you have explored the actions of characters that believe in the tenets of the theme <u>and</u> the actions of characters that do not believe in the tenets of the theme.

Let's say your theme is: Without learning to take responsibility, one cannot truly grow up. How do you go about illuminating that in your story? Is your protagonist irresponsible and loses his job? Or loses his wife? Or loses his children? Does a character suffer humiliation because he shows irresponsibility? Do irresponsible characters look attractive or "cool" to the protagonist? Is your protagonist aware (or unaware) that he is irresponsible? Finally, does learning responsibility bring positive results? Consider the protagonists of these classically structured films: 1993's **MRS. DOUBTFIRE**, or the protagonist of 1950's **SUNSET BOULEVARD**, or 1940's **PHILADELPHIA STORY.** All these characters inhabit the theme: Without learning to take responsibility, one cannot truly grow up.

There are also characters that are <u>too</u> responsible. And that super sense of responsibility can cause a character to be too uptight and too unimaginative. There are many stories revolving around characters that "need to let their hair down and really enjoy life." Consider Captain Von Trapp in 1965's **THE SOUND OF MUSIC** or the protagonist in 1954's **SABRINA** or 2005's **40-YEAR-OLD VIRGIN.** What could be the theme? Without opening up oneself to new experiences, one may miss the best things in life.

Bury your theme in a great character story

Audiences don't want to be hit over the head with theme. In most cases, theme should feel almost invisible. If someone asks filmgoers to say what a film is about, most people will rattle off plot points. However, the savvy viewer will recognize theme. The savvy viewer will see that 2007's ***KNOCKED UP*** is about a person who needs to accept responsibility in order to earn the love of the mother of his child. Remember that theme is always in the eye of the beholder. Depending on the age, inclination, experience, state of mind of the film viewer, various themes may emerge from the same story. Another viewer of ***KNOCKED UP*** might relate to another theme in the film: Without giving a loved one space to be themselves, one can never truly know the other person. This theme also resonates throughout the film – and both thematic observations are correct. Each member of the audience will relate to different stories (A or B or C stories) in a screenplay. This might depend on what the reader or viewer is experiencing in his life, or in his day, or in his relationships on any particular day. The "B" story of ***KNOCKED UP*** revolves around pregnant Alison's sister, Debbie (portrayed by Leslie Mann) and Debbie's husband (portrayed by Paul Rudd) and their realization that each must have time to follow personal interests outside the marriage. This "B" story theme folds into the main "A" story because it deals with the idea of responsibility and truth in a marriage.

Question: What if I have more than one theme in my film story?

Answer: Allow yourself to dig into <u>one dominant theme,</u> the one that most resonates for you. If you try to explore too many ideas or themes, your script may get confusing and lack clarity. If someone identifies another theme from your story – that's fine. But know the <u>one</u> dominant theme <u>you</u> are trying to explore.

Examples of well-used themes

Here are some themes that are explored over and over in film stories. Remember, theme explores your perceptions or feelings about the human condition. Humans share common emotional needs; therefore your theme <u>does not have to be</u> "different" or "out there." The originality of your story comes from the characters you create and the way your plot unfolds as you explore a relatable theme from your own <u>personal point of view</u>.

A FEW THEMES THAT EXPLORE THE NEED OR DESIRE FOR LOVE

Without love, there can be no true happiness.

Without knowing one is loved, there can be no sense of peace.

Without learning how to truly love, one cannot be loved.

Without realizing that love (passion) can blind, one can lose sight of true purpose.

Without knowing oneself, one cannot find true love.

A FEW THEMES THAT EXPLORE THE DESIRE FOR FORGIVENESS

Without learning to forgive, one cannot move on in life.

Without demanding justice, one cannot find peace.

Without forgiveness, the heart can never heal.

Without a true apology, forgiveness cannot be felt.

Without admitting a wrong, one cannot embrace forgiveness.

Without admitting to one's own frailties, an understanding of the need for forgiveness is impossible.

A FEW THEMES THAT EXPLORE THE NEED OR DESIRE FOR VIOLENCE

Without violence, the world cannot change.

Without wiping out violence, the world cannot truly change.

Without retribution, one cannot feel at peace.

A FEW THEMES THAT EXPLORE THE NEED OR DESIRE FOR SELF REALIZATION

Without believing in oneself, one can never achieve one's goals.

Without learning to accept help from others, one cannot feel happiness.

Without knowing oneself, one cannot act on personal conviction.

A FEW THEMES THAT EXPLORE THE NEED OR DESIRE TO MOVE ON IN ONE'S LIFE

Without accepting the past, one cannot move into the future.

Without understanding the past, one cannot move into the future.

Without righting the wrongs of the past (revenge), one cannot move forward.

Your theme might be a variation of any of those listed above – or it might be something different. Whatever it is, commit to exploring it fully.

Here are some examples of the themes in a wide variety of films. Remember, you may identify a different dominant theme in these films because each person will take away a different "lesson." However, keep in mind that if you do identify a different theme – you are still recognizing the author's work on his thematic through line.

DR. ZHIVAGO (1965) Without following one's heart, one may never know great passion. This film is sweeping romance set against the Bolshevik Revolution in Russia.

FARGO (1996) Without patience and persistence, one may never find success. This film is a dark crime comedy about misguided ambition and greed and how the best laid plans can get out of hand.

BEST IN SHOW (2000) Without taking a risk, one cannot find great rewards. This film is a satirical comedy that explores the personalities of eccentric people who enter dog shows.

THE INCREDIBLES (2004) Without being true to oneself, one will never feel fulfilled. This is an animated adventure comedy about superheroes reclaiming their place in the world.

BROKEBACK MOUNTAIN (2005) Without taking risks, one may never succeed in love. This is a romance drama about two cowboys who fall in love in a prejudiced world. The theme listed above for **DR. ZHIVAGO** could also be identified as a dominant theme in this film. Remember – theme is in the eye of the beholder.

CRASH (2005) Without connecting to people, one will feel isolated and unhappy. This is an episodic drama that takes a look at various individuals who feel emotionally isolated in their lives.

ONCE (2006) Without taking risks, dreams may never be accomplished. This is a coming-of-age drama about a musician who gains confidence in his art.

THE DEPARTED (2006) Without truth there can be no peace. This is a crime drama focusing on two policemen who want the respect of their superiors.

NOTES ON A SCANDAL (2006) Without truth, relationships

cannot flourish. This is a drama that explores the emotional destruction caused by obsessions and lies.

BORAT (2006) Without trying to understand others, there can be no acceptance. This is a satirical comedy about a man from Kazakhstan who travels across America to meet sex symbol Pamela Anderson.

3:10 TO YUMA (2007) Without respect, one cannot feel worthy. This is a western drama about a man's need to look heroic to his son.

JUNO (2007) Without giving up the need to control, one could miss out on real connections. This is a story of a pregnant teen that tries to control all areas of her life.

Is there a scene in your script that allows you to voice your theme?

Take a look at 2006's ***PURSUIT OF HAPPYNESS***. The theme is evident in the first scene: Without believing in yourself, you can never achieve great things. Down-on-his-luck and unable to make his business plans pan out, Chris (portrayed by Will Smith) reminds himself of his promise; no matter what happens, he will be an active participant in his son's life. He believes he can be a great father. Chris' belief in his sales abilities is also clear. The audience learns he has bet the last of the family money on his own sales skills – that he can sell a high-tech bone x-ray machine to doctors and hospitals. Chris <u>believes</u> he will be a success. When his wife doubts him, he does not capitulate, he <u>believes</u>. When his wife leaves him, he continues to believe he can become a business success <u>and</u> be a great single father. When he is arrested for not paying parking tickets and has to spend the night in jail, he goes to the important job interview at Dean Witter in paint-spattered jeans and t-shirt. He believes (hopes) that being honest about the situation will work to his advantage; he believes he can sway people with words. Chris' belief in his abilities gets him through every adversity he faces. <u>What is the scene that encapsulates the theme with words?</u> Take a look at the scene with his son on the basketball court. His young son has a dream of being a professional basketball player, Chris tells him that it's an impossible dream because his son is small in stature and may not grow tall enough to properly compete. When Chris sees his son's spirits flag, Chris realizes his mistake – that he has planted a seed of self-doubt in his son. Chris re-groups and finds the words to convey the importance of goals and belief in self to his son. In this scene, the theme of the film story is spoken.

PURSUIT OF HAPPYNESS (2006) Will Smith, Jaden Smith
- photo courtesy of Globe Photos

Find a few places to state your theme

Most writers are afraid to write "on-the-nose." However, in your rewrite, find <u>three</u> events in your plot where a character finds a way to baldly state the theme or anti-theme. Of course your character is going to use his own singular verbiage, his own personality to express the theme or question the theme's veracity. Perhaps it's a vehement denial, " I don't believe in love. It's for suckers." Perhaps it's a question, " Do you really believe in love? Do you really think it exists and can make a difference? " Perhaps it's a statement of desire, "I'll never fall in love. Not that I wouldn't like to – I think. I mean, my best friend thinks it was love that changed her life – but well – I think it was the promotion. She's making more money and money makes a person happier. She says it's love but – I guess I'd like to find out but…" Perhaps it's in anger, " Don't you dare say you love me. Like it would make a difference!"

Take a look at your script. Have you explored chances to voice your theme? Is this voicing buried in a scene so it doesn't call attention to itself? Or have you decided you want to boldly state your theme? Whichever way you choose, make sure your theme is evident.

Is the theme (or anti-theme) of your film evident in the actions of the protagonist in the film? Remember, this is the character that the audience follows most closely. The audience will, most likely, be identifying with this character. If the protagonist is not revealing the theme, is there a good reason for that? If your theme is: Without giving love, one cannot be truly loved in return – and your protagonist is already in a stellar, giving relationship and is only <u>watching</u> other characters learn the consequences of not being able to give love, is your protagonist's story as active and compelling as it could be? Make every effort to put the theme in your protagonist's story – let him <u>learn</u> the validity of the theme as the film story progresses.

Let the theme resonate in all your characters

A theme in 1942's *CASABLANCA*: Without commitment, one feels disconnected. How does this resonate with the major characters in the film story? The protagonist Rick (portrayed by Humphrey Bogart) is a man at loose ends. He has not taken a side in the war effort; his nightclub is open to Germans, French, and Americans – anyone who can pay the price. Rick does not connect with patrons of his nightclub; he refuses to care about the fate of the war refugees. At the beginning of the film, in the nightclub, he makes it clear to a woman at the bar that he is not interested in committing to a romantic relationship. All these elements of Rick's character are set up in the first ten minutes of the film. The supporting characters reflect Rick's theme. Ilsa (portrayed by Ingrid Bergman) is a woman who broke Rick's heart in Paris. She cannot commit to following her heart; she is torn between affection/respect/sense of duty for her husband, Laszlo, and her deep, passionate love for Rick. She cannot commit to making her own decision and asks Rick to make the decision for her. Laszlo (portrayed by Paul Heinreid) is a man who is sure of himself and his commitments. He is committed to his wife. He is committed to his cause (to fight the Germans) and he will face torture and possible death because of his commitments. Captain Renault (portrayed by Claude Rains) is a man who changes his commitments daily so that he can always ally himself with the most powerful group of the moment. Other supporting characters show various levels of commitment to various elements in their lives. Note how all the characters and stories are focused in and around the theme.

Consider 1962's *THE MUSIC MAN* (based on a musical play by Meredith Wilson and Franklin Lacey). This story explores truth and confidence. The main character, Harold Hill (portrayed by Robert Preston), is a con artist and – with great confidence – spouts untruths at every turn. He falls in love with a woman, Marian (portrayed by Shirley Jones), who always tells the truth, no matter who it may hurt. Marian's aunt likes to bend the truth to make people feel better. Marian's young nephew, Winthrop (portrayed by Ron Howard), believes in a lie so much that it <u>becomes</u> the truth. The rich ladies in town are set up as gossipers who enjoy passing along untruths about Marian and other people in town. When Harold Hill charms them, they begin to believe untruths about their talents and charms. Finally, at the end of the film, they face real truths. The theme of the film could be: Without believing what your heart tells you, you may never see the <u>real truth</u>. All the characters in the story support this theme – and that's why the film story holds up and still resonates.

Exercise:

Find the dominant theme that resonates for the protagonist. Check all the scenes in your screenplay. Do you need to adjust some of the scenes so they reflect or support the dominant theme? Check all your characters – the antagonist and the supporting characters – are they reflecting or supporting the theme? This does not mean adding "on-the-nose" dialogue. Consider the <u>actions</u>, the <u>plot</u>; the <u>reason</u> people are acting as they are acting. In most cases, the exploration of the theme will be subtle – but it should be there.

Let your plot reflect the theme

Check each sequence in your script. Is each sequence supporting or reflecting the theme? If your story is about a main character learning to believe in her abilities, do we see events where she does <u>not</u> believe in herself? Or events where she tries to believe in her abilities and fails? Or an event where another character is so sure of his cleverness or toughness that it's clear his confidence is making him stronger? Or is someone so over-confident he is making mistakes that will come back to haunt him?

If your story is about a main character learning to believe in love, are there sequences that show him <u>not</u> believing in love and making a mess of things? Are there sequences that show others taking a risk in love and winning or losing? Are there sequences that show the pros and cons of love?

You want to illuminate the positives <u>and</u> the negatives of your theme in your plot.

AUTHOR'S POINT OF VIEW

Your script will be original if you have used your own voice, your own ideas, explored your own "take" on your characters and built the world of the story as you perceive it. Your script is a reflection of you. Never sit on the fence. If your script is dealing with the vagaries of illegal drug trading, are you painting this world as good and beneficial or as a scourge to society? If your script focuses on the drilling of oil in national parks, do you think it's more important to provide oil or save nature? Who are your good guys? Who are your bad guys? Who wins? Does your story champion hope or caution or a sense of bleakness?

Each writer should have an opinion. And remember, every opinion is valid. Be passionate about your ideas. This does not mean adding long monologues for your characters. There is no need to state your point of view in "on-the-nose" dialogue – let the characters and the story reveal your point of view.

Take another look at 1976's **NETWORK**, a brilliant film written by Paddy Chayefsky. Think about how the author's point of view becomes clear. This is a film about the business of network news and the various factions that control it. Some characters champion the journalist integrity of hard news, news that informs and educates. Some characters believe network news should be entertaining and others believe that profits are of most importance. Chayefsky uses the protagonist Max (portrayed by William Holden) as the reasonable voice. At the beginning of his career, Max was excited about investigative journalism and network news and believed his job was important because it revealed truths to the television audience. Whether or not the news created profits for the network was not of primary importance to him. Chayefsky uses Max's friend, aging on-air news commentator Howard Beale (portrayed by Peter Finch), as the wronged man fired by those in network management who put profits before all else. Howard becomes the film's truthsayer. Howard, in the midst of a nervous breakdown, calls it as he sees it and tells the television audiences that greedy corporate forces, through television programming, are trying to shape the mind of the populace. The two most sympathetic men in the story, Max and Howard, are painted to have strong bonds of friendship and strong moral codes – both have an inner integrity. Chayefsky chooses less attractive traits for the other characters – characters that want to take down the time-honored journalistic traditions, characters only interested in profit. Chayefsky paints these characters as cold and flawed and incapable of emotional depth. It's clear what side Chayefsky sees as more life affirming and "right." But Chayefsky did not let the good guys win in his story. Howard is killed and Max's life is in ruins at the end of the film. It's clear that Chayefsky doesn't expect "the better side of human nature" to win on the capitalistic corporate battlefield.

What raised 2006's **LITTLE MISS SUNSHINE,** written by Mike Arndt, above its simple story? It revolves around a dysfunctional family who takes its youngest member from New Mexico to California so she can compete in a beauty contest. The author's focus in the story? Family. The author's point of view? That family stands together – that family will always have your back no matter how much you, at times, may disagree or dislike each other – or become uncommunicative or suicidal. A theme of **LITTLE MISS SUNSHINE**: Without the emotional support of a family, one can let personal disappointments (or disasters) loom too large and become destructive.

Know the reason why you wrote your story

Screenwriting is not journalist writing, there is no need to give "just the facts, ma'am." A screenwriter needs to find a theme, or a reason, or an understanding of the human condition in a story. Screenwriters look for the reasons a crime took place or the reasons a marriage failed or the reasons a father/son relationship went sour. Ultimately, it is the screenwriter's take on character the character's actions and story that is the most interesting part of film stories. It's a good idea to check through your script to see if all areas support your theme.

You may not have clued into the reason you wrote your story as you worked on your first draft. You may have gotten intrigued, obsessed, engaged or challenged by exploring a character or by the task of getting from plot point to plot point. That's fine. But the first draft (the craftsman's work) is done and now it's time to bring your script to a new level. Commit to your theme. Commit to bringing out the author point of view – your point of view,

CHAPTER SUMMARY

– A writer gains respect and attention when his thematic vision is clear.

– Let all the characters support your one, dominating theme.

– Let all the storylines support your one, dominating theme.

– Character and storyline serve as window to the author's point of view.

Chapter Ten

THOSE FINAL TRIMS

A screenwriter's first draft may be overwritten. That's natural because as you write, you're exploring your story's world and its characters. You've been trying to find the emotion in your characters' lives – reactions, assessments of events and other characters. You've wanted to make sure everything is clear. Images have popped into your head and you have tried to describe those images in full and complete ways.

That's all good.

Now, in your rewrite, is the time to try to trim out the excesses. It is time to trim down action lines. You want clarity and succinctness. You want to choose words that evoke an emotional response or, in the shortest possible way, make a visual clear. You want to trim down dialogue exchanges to make sure every word spoken has purpose and/or illuminates character.

Let's concentrate, first, on action lines.

How to trim action lines

It's always a good idea to trim down action lines so that they give necessary information but do not bog the reader down in too many details. Leave in hints of your personality, your point of view – but sparingly. A little bit of excess goes a long way.

For example, an over-written first draft action line may read something like this:

INT. REBECCA'S APARTMENT – DAY

Cluttered with remnants of childhood – teddy bears, dolls, worn dolls, unfinished embroidery projects, bronzed shoes and dream catchers – there is no clear path through to the open doorways festooned with tired balloons and feathers. The furniture is vintage IKEA, most of it broken and painted bright colors – the cheap paint now peeling. Sixties fashion clothes are strewn on the floor and chairs, seventies wedges hang from a rafter. Worn wigs sit atop lamps. Photographs of drunken parties

Question: What if, after doing all the rewrite and polish work on my script, it is over 115 pages? What if it still feels a bit flabby? What if a person in whose opinion I trust has read it and feels it reads too slowly?

Answer: Learning to properly trim your script is a very important screenwriting skill. You want to cut out at least 95% of the fat (leave some room for you own personality and style) and leave your script lean and mean.

are tacked to the walls. REBECCA, 23, passed out and snoring on the floor, clearly didn't make it to the couch last night. She's thin with dark stringy hair. She wears a pink camisole and mini-skirt, her stockings are ripped and one sneaker remains on her left foot. Her hoop earrings catch the morning sunlight that has found a spot to shine through the dirty window. Her lips are parched, her mascara smudged. Bubbles of saliva form in the corner of her mouth.

The doorbell RINGS. Rebecca groans, slowly wakes. She manages to rise to her knees, uses her hands to push up from the floor, tries to shake the fog from her brain. Doorbell RINGS again. Rebecca straightens the straps on her camisole, looks in the mirror. She groans again and grabs a wig and pulls it over her hair. She stumbles to the door and realizes she wears only one shoe.

Naturally, when writing the first draft, the screenwriter imagines a scene, imagines what the director might highlight, how the cinematographer might light the scene, how the actress might look and how she might play the scene. However, most of the above description is unnecessary for the understanding of the <u>story</u> and it is the screenwriter's job to tell the <u>story.</u> Remember, making a film is collaboration – and unless you plan to finance, produce and direct, cast, light and shoot, edit and market your film, you will be working with other talented people who fill various roles in filmmaking. The set designer and props master will fill a space, the actress will bring to life a poor girl who drinks too much, clings to childish memories and loves to wear costumes. The director will block any movement that does not come from the actress. That means you can be more spare in your setting and character descriptions.

So how could the above action line be trimmed down?

INT. REBECCA'S APARTMENT – DAY

Cluttered with vintage clothes, photographs of drunken parties and toys from childhood – teddy bears, dolls and dreamcatchers. The cheap furniture has been painted in attempt to make it stylish. Wild-colored wigs sit atop lamps. REBECCA, 23, thin, passed out from late-party hangover, snores on the floor.

The doorbell RINGS. Rebecca groans. The doorbell RINGS again, insistent. Rebecca finally gets up and stumbles to the door.

The desire is to make your script a "fast read." You can accomplish this by moving the story along and not getting bogged down in description.

One word is better than two

Use simple adjectives or adverbs. It's not necessary or advisable to use a "novelistic" way of describing your character's state of being.

Example of novelistic description:

EXT. DOCKS – NIGHT

Another huge explosion. Sam, remembering the night of bombing on the African village and feeling that hopelessness once more, stands rooted to the spot. And then it's near-dark again. He sees members of Gray's gang searching the area. His hands slide to his jacket pocket, feeling for the knife that he thinks will protect him, forgetting he left it on the kitchen counter. His mind moves to Jenny, the woman he loves. If he dies now, he will never be able to tell her he's sorry. Suddenly another explosion rocks the earth. Sam forces himself to move. He races for cover.

Think of what an actor can play. An actor cannot let the audience know what he is remembering. An actor cannot let an audience know that he is suddenly thinking of a lost love. An actor can only act and react – and deal with the action of the story.

Example of trimmed-down (non-novelistic) action line.

EXT. DOCKS – NIGHT

Another EXPLOSION. Sam, stunned, is riveted. Finally he notices members of Gray's gang search the area. He grabs for his knife. It's not there; damn. Another EXPLOSION. Sam races for cover.

The shortened action line imparts the necessary information. There is no way an actor can silently get across "*… remembering the night of bombing on the African village*" or "*His mind moves to Jenny, the woman he loves. If he dies now, he can never tell her he's sorry…*" so those phrases can quickly be trimmed. There is no need to tell the reader that Sam left the knife on the kitchen counter. If it is important, this information can be imparted in a previous scene and the reader/audience will know why he does not have his knife.

Keep your action lines to a minimum. Work for clarity and a sense of movement.

Technical things you can do to make your script a "faster read"

Here are a few technical tips to consider. Go through your script and consider trimming action line elements mentioned below:

1.   Take out all camera directions. Remove all references to camera angles, zooms, pans, dissolves, tilts, aerial views and any other technical terms that will pull the reader out of the story. Remember, it's your job to simply <u>tell the story.</u> Once your script is chosen for production, and you sit with the director and she wants you to add camera directions (so that the crew will know what technical things to have on the set that day or to remind her of her ideas of how she wants to shoot the scene) – that is the time to do it. There is no need for you to impress the reader with a knowledge of special effects or camera movement or editing know-how. Simply tell the story.

Example of a script filled with technical direction:

CAMERA TILTS UP to show Rebecca's distraught face. Ben's face is REFLECTED in the mirror in front of her. CAMERA WHIPS as Rebecca jumps up and around to confront Ben.

SMASH CUT TO Rebecca attacking Ben with the heavy bookend. QUICK CUTS as Ben protects his head, falls to his knees, crawls towards the front door trying to escape while Rebecca becomes more unhinged.

These details of camera and editing directions distract the reader from the <u>story.</u> A more reader-friendly version of the above that simply tells the story in a suspenseful way:

Rebecca, distraught, sees Ben's face reflected in the mirror. She grabs the heavy bookend and attacks. Ben tries to protect himself, he falls to his knees, crawls towards the door but Rebecca is unhinged and relentless.

2.   Make sure your action lines are written in the present tense. You want your script to read as if things are happening <u>now.</u> Sometimes the style in which a screenwriter writes is a result of how he verbally tells personal stories to friends – he may relay events that have happened and fall into using the past tense. Screenwriting needs to feel active. Using the present tense can add to the immediacy and suspense in a story.

Example of an action line filled with past tense verbs.

Rebecca has entered the tunnel and seen Toby unconscious. She felt tears spring to her eyes and brushed them away. Toby stirred. Rebecca screamed.

Example of how the action line is written using the present tense.

Rebecca enters the tunnel. She sees Toby unconscious. Tears spring to her eyes – she brushes them away. Suddenly, Toby stirs. Rebecca SCREAMS.

3. Use short sentences. Run-on sentences can be more difficult to read.

Example of an action line that is a run-on sentence.

Rebecca, who is still upset, enters and sees Ben and George who are sitting against the wall and smoking cigarettes and eyeing girls – so Rebecca turns and pushes through the crowd and causes a waitress to spill a tray of drinks as she, screaming, rushes out.

Example of a trimmed down action line using short sentences.

Rebecca, upset, enters. She sees Ben and George smoking and eyeing girls. Rebecca turns suddenly, causes a waitress to spill a tray of drinks. Rebecca SCREAMS and rushes out.

4. Trim out "ing" verbs. Use the most active tense of a verb to make your script a fast read.

Example of an action line that uses "ing" verbs:

Rebecca is racing across the street, weaving in and out of traffic. Taxi drivers are honking their horns, the cops are yelling for her to stop. She is seeing Toby running ahead, pushing the stroller filled with diamonds.

Example of how to use the most active verb:

Rebecca races across the street, weaves in and out of traffic. Taxi drivers honk, cops yell. Rebecca sees Toby run ahead, he's pushing the stroller filled with diamonds.

5. Trim out all the "we see" or "camera sees" handles that you may be using. In an essential way, the screenplay is the blueprint of a story meant to be told through a visual medium. It is not only redundant to add the "we see" or "camera sees" but in using one or both of these handles, the writer allows the reader to stand apart from the script. A screenwriter wants to viscerally engage the reader. Make the reading experience as immediate as possible.

Example:

We see Rebecca enter the tunnel and watch her approach the unconscious Toby.

Example of how to trim out the handle and engage the reader in a more immediate and suspenseful way.

Rebecca enters the tunnel. She approaches the unconscious Toby.

I have read scripts written by a well-known screenwriter who uses this style:

WHAT REBECCA SEES: Toby racing across the street with the baby stroller filled with diamonds.

WHAT TOBY SEES: Toby notices cops on the corner, the road being blocked ahead. He sees Rebecca motioning to him.

It's a personal style used to strongly suggest to the director how to shoot the scene. However, I argue that it keeps the reader from simply getting to the <u>story.</u> If it is <u>truly important to the advancement of the story</u> (a plot point) to highlight what a character is seeing at a particular moment, there are options to use (but not overuse):

REBECCA'S POV: Toby racing off, clearly not caring about her safety.

WHAT REBECCA SEES: Toby racing off, clearly not caring about her safety.

Or you can simply write it as if you are telling a story:

Rebecca sees Toby racing off, clearly not caring about her safety.

Commit to your own style, but it is best not to overdo camera or editing or acting direction in your script. Allow your script to be an easy and clear read and let the reader "see" the film in his head – as the <u>reader</u> imagines it.

6. Find the most visceral way to express the emotion of characters in action lines. Remember, there is no need to use nicely constructed, complete sentences.

Example:

Rebecca notices Toby's roaming hand on Gayle's thigh. Her heart sinks for a moment and then, suddenly, her anger erupts. She kicks and tips the table and grabs the microphone.

Shorter and more visceral:

Rebecca notices Toby's roaming hand on Gayle's thigh. Damn, life sucks. He's a shit. Enraged, Rebecca kicks the table – owww, that hurt. She tips the table. Grabs the microphone.

There is no need to use ten words when five are all that are needed. No need to use five words when three will suffice. No need to use three words when one will suffice. And remember, there is no need for complete sentences – find your style. Let the emotion and excitement of the story be reflected in the action lines.

Exercise:

Take a look at your action lines. Have you included too much detail? Trim out scenic description and excess actor direction; no need to tell an actor when to pause, when to pick up a glass or tie a shoelace <u>unless it changes the motivation of the scene or affects the plot.</u>

Some writers have a natural style that is clear and concise. Other writers overwrite – they don't trust that fewer words can make the scene just as potent (or more so). You want to maintain your own style, but you also want to make sure your script will be a fast, clear read.

Exercise:

Take a technical look at your script. Go through with a pen and cross out every extraneous word in the action lines. Here are a few of the commonly overused words and phrases:

and	*but*
however	*then*
as	*while (fill in name) is (fill in action)*

There is no reason to write something like this: *Sam walks into the room and then he turns on the light. Then he turns and heads to the liquor cabinet and then he pours himself a whiskey – then burps.*

If this is the action, consider writing it more tersely. *Sam walks into the room, turns on the light. Frantic, he pours himself a whiskey. Burps.*

This second example gives the same information <u>plus</u> it helps track the character's emotional state by adding the word *frantic*.

Take a look at novelist Stephen King's book, published in 2000, entitled *ON WRITING*. King advocates using as few words as possible to convey story points and character elements. He also advocates using the first word that comes into your head – ones that can be easily understood by the reader. His advice is – keep it simple. This is an excellent book for screenwriters to have on their shelf.

DON'T REPEAT INFORMATION

Another thing that can slow down a script (and story) is <u>repeating information</u> the audience has already been told or shown. Sometimes writers do this without realizing it – sometimes it is done because we get caught up in the logic of making it clear who knows what when.

Example: If the audience sees one character (Bill) find out about a story point (let's say he finds out about a friend getting fired from his job) and then the audience hears Bill tell another character (Ann) about the friend getting fired and then Ann tells another character (Sam) that the friend got fired – the audience (reader) is going to start skipping pages and/or resent that she has to read <u>again</u> what she already knows.

How can a writer get around the repeating of the information if everyone <u>does</u> need to know about the friend's firing? Consider this: Bill is the first one who gets the news. Start the scene with Ann <u>after</u> Bill has told her the news, cut into the scene on her reaction. Start Anne's scene with Sam <u>after</u> he has heard the news and when he is <u>taking some action because of the news.</u> The audience will fill in the blanks.

Take a look at 2005's ***SIDEWAYS.*** Miles' friend Jack has been carrying on a torrid affair with Stephanie (the wine bartender) while on his last weekend as a bachelor in the wine country. Miles slips and accidentally tells Maya that Jack is getting married in a week. There is no need for the audience to see Maya tell Stephanie the news – the next time we see Stephanie is when she attacks Jack with her motorcycle helmet, angry that he lied to her and led her to believe he loved her. It is very clear that Maya told Stephanie the needed information but the audience didn't need to see that exchange.

Another example: ***BATMAN BEGINS***; Bruce Wayne, after returning from his self-imposed exile to the Far East, returns to Gotham. He is determined to save the city. He discusses his desires with his butler and valet, Albert, and expresses his desire to find a disguise that could become a "symbol" of the fight for right and truth. Bruce climbs into the caverns underneath the Wayne mansion to re-visit the place of his great fear. There, surrounded by bats, Bruce clearly gets the idea for his disguise. He doesn't need to <u>tell</u> Albert – it is enough for us to see a scene with Bruce and Albert working on the Batman mask. It's clear the information has been passed on – off screen – and the audience/reader realizes, in a more interesting way, that Albert knows of Bruce's decision.

Exercise:

Check your script. Mark any scenes that have repeat information in them. Find a way to excise as much repetition as you can.

HAVE YOU WRITTEN TWO (OR THREE OR FOUR OR MORE) SCENES ACCOMPLISHING THE SAME THING?

Let's say that you need a scene to show that your main character, Suzanne, is touchy about the fact that she can't get an internship in a prestigious law firm. You have written a scene where Suzanne, teary, defends herself to her overbearing and judgmental father. That is followed by a scene where Suzanne, again teary, slams into her apartment where her roommate is waiting for Suzanne's part of the rent. Suzanne defends herself, saying her plans have gone up in smoke – but she will pay her share of the rent. That's followed by scene where Suzanne, still teary, has to tell her law professor she didn't get the internship. Each scene is accomplishing the same thing – and you only need one of them. If you want to use that sequence, make sure in each subsequent scene there is character or plot movement. Consider this sequence; Suzanne, teary, defends herself to her father – it's not her fault she can't get the paid internship at the law firm. Suzanne, anger now replacing the tears of self-pity, slams into her apartment to face her roommate. When her roommate insists on the rent money, Suzanne negotiates a one-day reprieve, promises she will have the money by sunset tomorrow. (This heightens Suzanne's stakes and level of tension.) She goes to see her law professor, she is now dry-eyed and determined. She needs a job, any job; can he help her?

Each scene needs to move the story forward. Suzanne's relationship with each of these supporting characters needs to be specific, there also needs to be a specific and varied agenda or desire in each scene. If you have two or three (or more) scenes that accomplish the same thing and you cannot adjust them so they are all advancing story or character, decide which scene you like the best and cut the others.

Be tough on yourself. Each scene may be brilliantly written, but it also must advance the story. Only scenes that advance story or give new illumination to character should remain in your script.

ENTER LATE AND LEAVE EARLY

Take a look at each scene in your script. Note the character element or plot point in the scene that affects the story. Is it in the middle of the scene? Or is it close to the end of the scene? If so, ask yourself if, perhaps, you could start the scene later – enter it mid-scene so that the story point is closer to the top of the scene.

If the character element or plot point is near the top of the scene, and the rest of the scene does not advance the story, consider exiting the scene at an earlier moment.

Leaving questions unanswered

Consider exiting a scene before all questions are answered. This will keep the audience wondering what decisions will be made and what actions will be taken. This will heighten interest in following the story.

Example:

> *The scene focuses on Henry and Judy, they are ex-lovers and used to be bank-robbing partners. Judy is now ill and wants to do one last job so she can pay her medical bills. Henry has given up crime and now lives a straight suburban life and is about to get married. His wife does not want him to see Judy. Judy asks Henry to do her this favor – one more bank robbery – for old time's sake. The scene cuts out before the audience knows Henry's decision.*

By cutting before the audience or reader knows Henry's answer – the writer ensures that the audience will stay with the story until that information becomes clear. (Perhaps the next scene is Henry and June at a used car lot choosing a getaway car and so the audience knows Henry acquiesced. Or perhaps the next scene is Judy sitting in her doctor's office admitting she won't be able to pay for the surgery – and we know that Henry denied Judy's request.)

Certain information – and even answers to important questions – can be left to subsequent scenes.

DIALOGUE

Dialogue trims

Dialogue can tell a great deal about a person – age, education, background, place of origin, religious beliefs, moral character – as well as a character's ability to express opinions, beliefs and intents.

The dialogue in your first draft may be overwritten. That's natural and normal. As you initially set out your story, you are creating the world and characters. You have tried to find the emotion in your characters' lives – reactions, assessments of events and other characters. Now is the time to take a hard look at your dialogue and make sure each word serves a purpose.

> **Exercise:**
>
> Take a look at excellent films in similar genres to your own. As you view the films, try to "see" the dialogue as if it were written on a page. Note how much the actor does <u>without</u> dialogue.

Great dialogue is a wonderful treat for an audience. 2006's ***THE DEPARTED*** features dialogue that illuminates character elements and moves the story along and brings up challenging ideas. Each character has a singular way of speaking: Billy (portrayed by Leonardo DiCaprio) thinks before he speaks, he has deep anger that is palpable yet is able to control his emotions. Colin (portrayed by Matt Damon) has a smart-ass, confident way of speaking. When he is with his criminal mentor, he does show respect and adopts a different tone, but when with his fellow officers, he's glib and arrogant. Dignam (portrayed by Mark Wahlberg) uses verbal abuse to attack and test others. Queenan (portrayed by Martin Sheen) is reasoned and sensitive. Costello (portrayed by Jack Nicholson) is verbose, likes to tell stories and waxes philosophical at times.

The dialogue in 2007's **JUNO** received critical attention because the screenwriter, Diablo Cody, found an original "teen speak" for her lead character.

Exercise:

Reading the scripts for the films you admire or want to study is always important. The serious screenwriter will get more out of the read, in most cases, than in re-watching the film. Especially when you are in the final trim stage with your script, reading screenplays is essential. Find three scripts of well-respected films in the same genre(s) you are writing. Note the dialogue exchanges – the length of each exchange, the cadence of various characters.

Trimming out the parentheticals

A parenthetical is a description of the emotion the character is feeling when he says a line of dialogue – or an insight into the character's state of mind at the time he imparts the dialogue.

Example:

> YOLANDA
> *(sarcastic)*
> *Yeah, sure I love you.*

Or:

> MARTY
> *(lying)*
> *I don't know what you're talking about.*

There is no need to overdo the use of the parenthetical. In most cases, the scene should support the characters' intentions. In most cases, the actor will make choices or how to say a line – and that is the actor's job. However, if it is not clear in the scene, or there is a sudden switch of emotion that is important to the scene – using a parenthetical can be used for clarity. Scripts that feature an overuse of the parenthetical tend to look amateurish. Remember, you need to just <u>tell the story.</u> Don't direct or coach the actor. Only use the parenthetical when it is absolutely necessary.

Exercise:

Trim out the use of the parenthetical; only include those that are necessary to convey an emotion that is not inherent in the scene or in the dialogue.

Let's approach it technically.

Exercise:

Read through your script concentrating on one character at a time. Have a pen or pencil in hand. Start your protagonist.

1. Make a checkmark next to a line or bit of information that is said more than once. Even if the information is said to a different person – and one that needs to be updated – still put a checkmark next to it.

2. Make a checkmark next to any dialogue that explains or tells of an action that we will have seen. Even if it is an emotional telling or told to a person who has not been witness or involved in the action, put a checkmark next to it.

3. Make a checkmark next to an explanation or declaration of a feeling.

4. Make a checkmark next to any explanation of how a supporting character fits into their lives; through work, family, past relationships.

Trim out the excesses, trim out all the unnecessary elements.

Now is the time to be get all the elements of your script in shape. Focus on making your script a lean and mean machine.

CHAPTER SUMMARY

- Trimming your script to its near-bare essentials can make for a "faster read."

- Feel free to leave elements of your own style or personality in your script.

- Action lines should be simple and clear.

- Dialogue should help advance story and illuminate character.

- It's a good idea not to overuse the parenthetical.

- Trim out repetitive information.

Chapter Eleven

REWRITE CHECKLIST

Hopefully you feel good about your rewrite. Hopefully your story's characters are well-defined, your protagonist has gone through a difficult emotional or physical (or both) journey and the outcome of the character's story is satisfying. Hopefully your plot is well-drawn, simple and allows space to focus on character insights and character growth and change. Hopefully you have polished dialogue so that each character has his or her own voice. Hopefully you have trimmed your script so that it is a lean, mean story machine. Hopefully you have identified theme and focused your story in and around that theme.

Use this checklist to go through your script one more time.

Act One

(Steps 1-3 of the Eleven Steps)

1.   You have set up your the world – does your description of place or time evoke a feeling? Can the reader sense genre? If it's a comedy, does the description of the opening visual cause a smile or laugh? The 2004 draft of the horror film *DAWN OF THE DEAD* opens with a murky fog on screen and an image of a skull emerges from the fog. A draft of 2006's *DEVIL WEARS PRADA* begins with fashion icons gathered in a chateau outside Paris, touting their talents and Miranda Priestly's fashion-sense perfection – and then quickly cuts to unfashionable Andy in the dirty, busy streets of NYC. The worlds are clear, the conflict foreshadowed. The 1994 drama *SHAWSHANK REDEMPTION* begins in the dark woods. A lone cabin sits, remote. Right away there's an ominous quality. Then two lovers, not paying attention to their surroundings are revealed. Perfect place and perfect situation for something bad to happen. 2006's *FLAGS OF OUR FATHERS* opens on a woman's hand sewing an American flag. Work on your opening, make sure it draws the reader in, intrigues, has something <u>special</u> to evoke.

2.   Introduce the protagonist in a way that will clarify who he or she

Question: Does a screenwriters ever feel as if their script is as good as it can be?

Answer: Truthfully, the answer would have to be "no." There may be days when you feel your script is perfect, brilliant and should attract top talent. Other days you may doubt your script. Remember, screenwriting is a craft and an <u>art</u> – being in the art category means it's always open to interpretation. And as the world changes (personal and global) the script's resonance will change. The most important thing to do is to get your script in its best possible shape, send it out into the world – and start on a <u>new</u> script. Rewriting the same script over and over will, in most cases, not be productive. Keep creating new material. That being said – it's important to polish each script until it shines.

is at this moment in time. Don't waste words simply describing hair, eye color or build. Those details tell the reader nothing. Mike Arndt, the screenwriter of 2006's ***LITTLE MISS SUNSHINE,*** describes the father, Richard, as having a peppy, upbeat demeanor that masks a seething frustration and insecurity. Nancy Meyers in her script for 2003's ***SOMETHING'S GOTTA GIVE,*** describes protagonist Harry as cool, confident, enviable and over-sixty. Find the right description. Make sure you've put in an age for your protagonist. Get the audience interested in this person right away.

3.   Have you put your protagonist in a <u>place</u> that tells the audience something about his character? Have you put your protagonist in the middle of an <u>action</u> that will help reveal character.

4.   Start your story as close to the <u>inciting incident</u> as possible. Trim out extraneous scenes and dialogue.

5.   Make the protagonist's overall want clear. (The <u>why</u> can come now or later, depending on how you want to tell your story.) Use action or words – the words can come from the protagonist or from a supporting character. In 2002's ***ADAPTATION***, it's clear from Charlie's first interior monologue on page one that he wants to feel good about himself, he wants others to think well of him. In ***LITTLE MISS SUNSHINE,*** each character is introduced and their overall want revealed at the same time. 2000's ***ERIN BROKOVICH*** makes her overall want of respect clear from on the first page as she goes through a series of job hunts.

6.   Have you had your protagonist state or make evident her first immediate goal? On page one of 2001's ***LEGALLY BLONDE***, Elle's first immediate goal is clear; she wants to marry Warner, her college boyfriend – and in fact, she expects him to propose to her that evening. 1972's ***THE GODFATHER***: Protagonist Michael, in his first scene, tells his fiancé, Kay, that he wants his work to be outside the family business, he wants to forge a <u>legitimate</u> business life. Danny Archer's first scenes in 2006's ***BLOOD DIAMOND*** make it clear that Danny is unconcerned with the morality or consequences of his weapon transactions, he will smuggle anything to make money, that he lacks a strong moral code.

7.   Polish the scenes and sequences in Act One. Trim the fat from the action lines. No need to describe the setting in too much detail.

"Dark, empty cabin" is sufficient. "Fancy, expensive restaurant" or "neighborhood diner" is sufficient. Too much scenic description will slow the reader.

8.   Unless it's a character choice, trim out dialogue or information that is repetitive. Ask yourself if an action is making a character's response or desire clear; perhaps there's no need for a line of dialogue.

9.   Make sure each scene/sequence is moving the story forward?

10. Make clear what your antagonist wants and how it relates to the protagonist's overall want. Make it clear why your antagonist wants to stop the protagonist from achieving his goal. Check to make sure your antagonist is actively trying to block your protagonist.

11. Are the supporting characters affecting your protagonist? Are their stories reflecting the theme?

12. Check pace. Are things moving along at the pace you want? Do you feel some scenes are going on too long and yet you don't know what to cut? Consider dividing the scene into two parts, having it take place moving from one location to another. Be brutal in your cuts, it's easy to fall in love with a line or action or thought of a character – but if all elements do not actively move the story forward – consider trimming.

13. Do you need to add a day? Delete a day? Consider how many days (or weeks or months) you need to convey the events in Act One. Are you moving too slowly, too "moment to moment"? Or are you moving too fast?

14. Have you introduced your "B" and "C" stories and do they relate to the protagonist's "A" story?

15. Consider introducing a runner that can be repeated as needed in Act Two and Act Three. This runner can help make time passage clear or it can help support the theme (or both).

16. Let your protagonist hit a major roadblock – the denial. Your protagonist now has to change course in order to achieve his overall want.

Act Two

(Steps 4-9 of the Eleven Steps)

1.   Have you broadened your story's conflict? Is the problem facing your protagonist more far-reaching than he or the audience originally expected? Does the story now affect more people? Does your protagonist's actions/desires/consequences affect a wider world?

2.   Have you challenged your protagonist? Are her known talents/ connections/ resources failing her? Does she have to learn new ways to accomplish her goal?

3.   Check to see if the overall want of your main character is consistent. Example: Jane wants love; she thinks she's in love with Joe so she pursues Joe. But then her estranged father becomes ill and she has to leave Joe's side to nurse her father and hopefully rekindle a lost paternal love. Meanwhile, Joe has cheated on her and she falls out of love. Then her best friend Sam is revealed as her soul mate and despite swearing off romantic love due to her broken heart, she falls for Sam because love is what makes her life feel meaningful. Her original overall want is the same (desire to find love).

4.   Have you made sure your protagonist, somewhere in Act Two, re-clarifies her overall want? Is it done in dialogue or action? It is a good idea to re-focus the audience and remind them of the overall want/desire/goal of the protagonist.

5.   Have you intensified the need to achieve the immediate goals and overall want?

6.   Are you using the flaws of your protagonist and antagonist to add complexity to the story?

7.   Have you introduced all the subplots and secondary characters? If you add plots and characters too late, they will seem like devices inserted to help facilitate the end of the story.

8.   Have you continued to develop your story's subplots ("B" and "C" stories) simultaneously with the main story line? These subplots should relate to the main story line. Have you built strong and complete arcs for your "B" and "C" stories?

9. Have you built a series of obstacles and reversals? Remember, nothing can be easy.

10. Have you emotionally tracked your characters? Plot is necessary, but character growth is most important.

11. Have you fashioned a midpoint of your film that raises the stakes for the character and/or twists or shifts the plot?

12. Have you found an opportunity to give your protagonist a taste of success? Have you let things go well for a short while, tease the protagonist with a sense of victory? Then have you reversed the circumstances?

13. Are your "B" and "C" stories contributing to the downward spiral of your protagonist's story?

14. Have you checked to see if you are starting scenes as late as possible and leaving them before the tension dissipates?

15. Have you made sure you are not repeating information?

16. At the end of Act Two, at the crisis moment, have you put your protagonist in a position to make a decision? Does he go forward or give up? What path does he choose?

17. Have you connected the crisis moment (decision moment) of your protagonist with the overall want that has been driving him throughout the story?

Act Three Checklist

(Steps 10-11 of the Eleven Steps)

1. Have you made sure the main character's overall want remains the same?

2. Have you made sure all stories – "B" and "C" stories – come together and add difficulty and complexity to the final act?

3. Have you made sure all the major characters are affected by the outcome of the story? How has the world changed (in a large or small way)?

4. Have you set up that your main character is in danger of <u>losing it all?</u>

5. Have you tested your protagonist's moral and physical and emotional strength like no other place in your story?

6. Are the stakes as high as you can make them? Is your character in her biggest battle? Facing his biggest problem? Her biggest fear? Will all defenses crack?

7. Have you accelerated the action?

8. Have you found a way to surprise the audience, keep the character's journey continuing and avoid predictability?

9. Have you allowed the antagonist and protagonist to really confront each other? Face to face. No messengers or go-betweens. Never take the easy way out.

10. Have you avoided tying up everything in a bow?

11. Have you created a surprising but satisfying ending? When the truth comes out and the new normal is revealed, is there a sense of the future?

Chapter Twelve

BEFORE THE SCRIPT
HITS THE MARKETPLACE

When you have completed your rewrite, it's time to print out another hard copy of your script. You will want to see how the script lays out on paper, if the margins are correct and other formatting issues are working properly. Printing a hard copy will also allow you to read your script "with fresh eyes" – so you can identify typos or other errors.

Format

It's important. Proper format is very very important.

Don't kid yourself that the content of your story and excellent character work and dialogue will shine through despite formatting errors. It won't. Chances are the script won't even be read. The business is too competitive. A script that is not pristine in its format will not be received well – it says "I don't know what I'm doing, I don't know the business and I haven't take the time to find out about it."

Go through this hard copy of your script for any formatting errors. Here are a few places you can go to obtain proper formatting: Cole and Haag's *The Complete Guide to Standard Script Formats* and Christopher Riley's *The Hollywood Standard: The Complete and Authoritative Guide to Script Style and Format* and Joan Erskine's *Screenwriter's Initial Draft Pad: With Formatting Rules* and Rick Reichman's *Formatting Your Screenplay*.

Spelling and grammar

Go through your script, one more time, and check for spelling errors or typos. Many readers at studios and production companies have literary backgrounds and they will find misspelled words annoying. You do not want to annoy the readers; you want them on your side. Many production executives will stop reading if the spelling and grammar mistakes are too numerous. There are many other scripts to read where the writer has taken the time to spell-check and correct grammatical errors. After you have gone through your script, have a friend or an editor do another read – and circle any errors that may remain. Invariably, a few words or punctuation errors will slip past the best intentions of multiple readers. Don't stress about it if you catch a <u>few</u> errors after your script has gone out – but go ahead and correct them on the master copy for subsequent submissions. Computer spell-check and grammar-check programs are great assets, but we all know they will not catch everything.

Length

A professional screenplay is between 95 to 110 pages. Some writers may push to 120 pages. Does it really matter if the length of your script is over 120 pages? What if it is 130 pages? Or 140 pages?

First of all, the length of the script does matter. The reader will pick up your script and note the page count. If your script falls on the long side, the reader knows his workday has just been elongated. If your script is on the long side and you don't grab your reader in the first five to ten pages, the desire of the reader to finish the script may diminish greatly. And most importantly, if your script is on the long side, the reader may think you are an amateur – that you don't know the business or that fact that most films do not surpass the two-hour mark.

Make sure your script is lean. Trim out all the excess. Make every effort to get your script below 110 pages. (See Chapter __).

Cover sheet

Keep it simple. Use a standard card stock, you can find it at an office supply store. Fancy colors or graphics are, for the most part, considered a sign of an amateur. You can use a different color of card stock (most screenwriting advisors will suggest neutral tones) if you want something other than white – however white is the standard.

Make sure your cover sheet includes all the necessary information: Title of your film story. Written by (your name). The title (usually done is all capital letters) is centered on the page, and placed about a third of the way down from the top of the page. The "written by" credit is usually centered under the title.

SCREENPLAY TITLE

by

Screenwriter Name

Contact information
Agent (or Manager) and Agency or Screenwriter name
Phone number
Email

Registered with WGA
(or Library of Congress)

COVER SHEET

Answer: In my opinion – nothing – if the graphic or picture is well done and does not put a visual into the reader's head that could affect the reading of the script. However, individual tastes vary and the reaction of the reader is hard to predict, so consider what kind of visual you want to put in the reader's head. Stay away from standard clip art. In the long run, in most cases, plain and simple is best. Let the script speak for itself.

As for using a bright or colorful card stock for the cover of your script – the accepted wisdom in the industry is to keep it neutral because individual executives may have an aversion to one color or another. Yes, I know, that seems a bit overboard – but follow your gut.

On the bottom left hand side of the cover sheet, make sure you have your contact information; this can be your phone number and email address or it can be your mailing address and email address. Or it can be the contact information of your agent or manager. Be sure an email address is included – it is the easiest way to communicate for most people and helps avoid the "phone-tag" syndrome (someone calls you, you're not home, he leaves a message, you call back, he's not home, you leave a message and so on and so on…).

Include the date of the draft on the cover sheet. This can be below or above your contact information.

Most script readers will assume the script is registered or copyrighted, but it is acceptable to add "WGA Registered" or "Copyrighted material" under the contact information on the bottom left hand side of the cover.

Use a header on every page of your script

When submitting your script to an agent, manager or production entity, consider using a header on each page of the script. This should include the title of the film story and your name. *Example: Deadly Vacation/John Smith.* This will give the reader a quick reminder of the title of the story, imbed it in his brain – and also imbed your name. On the practical side – if the script comes loose from its brads, it can be easily re-assembled.

If you are submitting to a contest, the people who run the contest may be sending the script to readers without the authors' names attached to avoid any personal biases. If this is the case, make sure you delete the header for the submission.

Page numbers

Make sure your script includes page numbers. This will help orient the reader – remember a page of script is thought of as a minute of screen time. Over the length of a hundred-page script, this approximation holds pretty true.

Another reason to include page numbers is clear: If, for some reason, your script becomes loose and pages are scattered, the reader will be able to put the pages back in order.

Use brads of the proper length to bind your script

Professional screenplays are three-hole punched and then bound with brads. Brads (brass fasteners) can be bought at most office supplies stores. In the Los Angeles area, the proper size brads (Acco #5 are considered to be the best, they are ¼" thick and can service a 110 page screenplay) can be hard to come by because knowing screenwriters scoop up the boxes when they see them on the shelves. The brads need to be strong enough and long enough to properly hold the screenplay pages together through an entire read of the script. Brads that are too thin and too short will not support the weight of the pages as they are turned, the script will fall apart – and this will annoy the reader. Remember, you do not want to annoy the reader.

Why brads? The brass fasteners allow the assistant in the production company to easily take the script apart so it can be photo-copied for multiple executive reads. Once the script is copied, the assistant can easily re-assemble the script. When a script is in production and rewrites come in, only the re-written pages will be copied. These new pages need to be inserted into the script and brads help make this process easy.

The standard screenplay is three-hole punched – but the screenwriter will only use two brads to hold it together – one in the top hole and one in the bottom. Why? It's traditional – but it also has a practical aspect. Try it out. This configuration does make page turning easier – which does help make the script a faster read.

Copyright your script or register it with the WGA

Before you send your work into the marketplace, <u>always register your script</u>. You have put in countless hours, days, weeks – or perhaps years – creating your film story and writing your screenplay. You want to protect your literary work before you send it out into the marketplace.

You can copyright your literary work with the Library of Congress in Washington, D.C. on Independence Avenue. Check out the website: <u>www.copyright.gov/register/literary.html</u>

The Writers Guild of America will also register your script. You do not need to be a member. There is the WGA West (based in Los Angeles) and the WGA East (based in New York City). For a relatively small fee, the WGA will keep a copy of your script on file with its registration date in case there is ever a dispute of authorship. Check out the website: <u>www.wga.org</u>

Question: Is there a plus to registering my screenplay with the WGA as opposed to the Library of Congress?

Answer: Not really. However, you may look a bit more savvy or professional if you have "Registered with the WGA" on the cover of your screenplay. Professional screenwriters register their work with the WGA and the reader will be used to seeing that on the cover of the script. WGA members who are writing for studios or production companies are also required to send the WGA copies of their contracts. The WGA keeps copies of scripts and contracts in case there are disputes of authorship or payment.

Question: If I do another rewrite and do minor changes (some dialogue, a few scenes), do I need to re-register my script or copyright my script again?

Answer: No. If the changes only make the <u>same</u> story with the <u>same</u> characters better, then there is no need. You have the core of the story and characters protected. However, if you do major changes such as changing locale, changing characters and their motivations or change the story elements significantly, it is a good idea to protect this new work through registering it or copyrighting it.

There is also the Writers Guild of Great Britain: www.writersguild.org.uk

There is also the Canadian Writers Guild: www.writersguildofcanada.com

And, there is the Australian Writers Guild: www.awg.com.au

All of these Writers Guilds (depending on your location) will register your screenplay.

Your script will not be read by either of the Library of Congress or the Guilds. It will simply be registered with the date it was received. If there is any dispute that rises over your script, the WGA or Library of Congress will have a copy of your script and the date it was received. If you think you are a victim of plagiarism or literary theft of any kind, is up to you to defend your position – and the date of your registration might become very important.

Online registration of literary work is available through the WGA.

Some contests want work submitted via email

Enter writing contests. One of my agents told me he is more inclined to read a script that has won (or received honorable mention) in a screenplay contest.

Many contests request scripts via email. Enter your script in a PDF file. This safeguards your work because the receiver cannot alter the content of a PDF file. Make sure your screenplay has *"Registered with the WGA"* on its cover or *"Copyrighted Material"* on its cover. Ask for a dated confirmation from the contest that they have received your screenplay and keep this confirmation information. If there is ever any dispute concerning literary theft of any kind, the date of the confirmation of receipt will be important.

Most contests will have an entrance fee. This covers the time of readers, any prizes a contest may offer and the cost of publicizing the contest.

Many contests are well run and get the attention of the film industry. Find the ones that enjoy a good reputation. If you are new to the screenwriting profession, entering contests is a <u>very important thing to do.</u>

Writers Guild of America

The Writers Guild of America (WGA) is a labor union composed of writers of feature films, television series, news programs, documentaries, animation and content for new media technologies. The most important duty of the WGA is to represent the member writers in negotiations with film and television producers. The WGA has constructed a collective bargaining contract that sets pay scales, health coverage contributions, credits and residuals.

The WGA contract sets minimum salaries for writing services. If a producer hires a writer, negotiations will start at the set minimum salary. In the feature arena, there is a scale of minimums that correspond to the expected budget of the film. In the television arena, there are different minimums for network and cable productions.

Employers who are signatories of the WGA (those producers who have agreed to abide by the most recent WGA collective bargaining contract) pay a small percentage, on top of the writer's salary, into the healthcare program set up by the WGA.

The WGA is responsible for determining writing credits for films and television programs. This is an important issue and the WGA takes it very seriously. A writer who receives onscreen credit will not only receive artistic recognition but he will participate in the financial rewards that an onscreen credit assures in the WGA writer's contract. The WGA has a system of arbitration; when more than one writer works on a produced project, each writer will prepare a written statement of credit expectations. The WGA has a core of arbitrators, made up of member writers who volunteer to sift through all drafts of the scripts. These arbitrators determine the percentage of work done by each writer involved in the project and thus determine onscreen credits.

The WGA monitors and collects residuals for its members. Residuals are payments for the reuse of films and television programs; if a film written by a WGA member plays on network or cable, the writer will receive a payment for its usage. If a television program is in re-runs – the writer will receive a payment for each re-run. This is a huge job that the WGA takes on – as one can imagine keeping track of what films or television programs are featured in subsequent markets.

The WGA Registry is the world's largest screenplay registration service. The main reason for registering your original work is to establish the completion date. If, at some point in your career, you feel your work has been plagiarized, you will have a registered script at the WGA that is available for any legal action you may take.

There is the WGA West, with its main office in Los Angeles and the WGA East, with an office in New York City. WGA's website is www.wga.org

MORE BUSINESS INFORMATION

The Spec Script

This is a script written on speculation (no one is paying you to write it). Most writers start here and most writers continue to write spec scripts throughout their career. Spec scripts are very important. Put it in your mind that you need to write at least one spec script a year. Even if you are being paid to write, try to squeeze in time to do your original work. Not only will it keep you in touch with your singular point of view, your own voice, your own interests (you are choosing the topic, the characters, the story, the voice – not the producer or production company) but you will also, at the end of the process, own your work.

Always writing on assignment may fill your bank account, but at the end of the process, you don't own your work. Whoever has paid you to write the script – he or she owns it. If the film does not get produced (and a very high percentage do not) you are not in the position to try to sell your work to another studio or production company because it is not your property. A writer should have pieces all her own, that are her brain children, that she can try sell or produce or direct herself.

Taking notes

There are few people who can give notes without bias. Each person has different values and life experiences, different senses of humor, different points of view. It is the writer's job to be strong (not inflexible) and to believe in his or her own vision. Yes, a friend or an agent or peer who reads many scripts might have valid and helpful suggestions and may give fabulous notes that will only enhance your script. But there are also friends, peers and industry professionals who give notes that can take the life out of a story. No one but the writer truly understands how changing one detail of character or story can completely unravel an entire script. Protect your work. Know why you wrote it, know your theme and know what makes it important to you. Let notes give your vision more clarity. Don't rewrite just to please someone else.

Sometimes agents, producers, directors, friends or whoever are giving you notes that will point to a problem in the screen story. You may agree or disagree that the story element is a problem. If you get the same note from multiple sources, it's usually time to consider the note's validity. There may, indeed, be a problem. All of those readers may have different suggestions for how to fix the problem area. Don't get confused. It doesn't matter how you fix it, just that it gets fixed. You will come up with the fix your way. Follow your own path.

Be grateful for all notes. Someone has taken the time to read your work and put some thought into it. Even if you don't take the notes, thank the reader for her time and assure her that all notes will be considered. There is no need to get defensive, just write down all the comments, go home… and sit with your script and consider if the notes are something you want to implement – or not.

> *Note: A writer's original work should always reflect the characters and stories that the writer is passionate about – a writer needs to follow his own muse. Remember, a writer who writes for the existing marketplace could miss the mark. Films take time to write, produce and distribute. If a writer sets out to write a script in the vein of the film she just saw in at the local multi-plex, by the time the script is finished, the vogue may have changed. There's no predicting what will catch an audience's imagination.*

INTERVIEW WITH SCREENWRITER
JONATHAN HALES

Screenwriter Jonathan Hales (*STAR WARS, EPISODE II, ATTACK OF THE CLONES, THE SCORPION KING, THE MIRROR CRACKED* and more) believes that within any successful film story is a presentation of a puzzle. "The function of art is to make sense of things. Our lives are chaotic and unshaped and sometimes painful, bizarre and sad, so we desire art to inform our lives and help us make sense of them. As a piece of art – a film script takes on a shape. And the more perfect the shape, the more satisfied we are – and the most satisfied the film's eventual audience will be."

Hales began his feature film screenwriting career doing an un-credited rewrite on the adaptation of mystery writer Agatha Christie's *DEATH*

ON THE NILE in 1978. "I had done some television plays and my agent recommended me." The producer and director only wanted character work done on the younger people in the script, so that was where Hales concentrated his efforts. He turned in his rewrite, it was well received and he was asked to stay with the project to polish more of the dialogue and events on the rest of the film.

I asked Jonathan Hales a few specific questions about storytelling and screenwriting. First we focused on the spec screenplay and then we talked about how he approaches re-writing on assignment – when hired on to do work on a project that is earmarked for production.

> **Question:** *Jonathan, what is your normal working day?*

> **Hales' response:** *I keep regular office hours – sitting down at my desk by 10 am and work until 1 pm. I stop and eat lunch and by 1:45 I am back at my desk until about 4 pm – sometimes beyond. I don't do a certain number of pages a day – I really think more in the amount of hours I put in – but I average about seven good pages a day. Once I get over that terrible feeling of staring at the stack of empty pages, I feel good. I enjoy it once something is going. At the end of the day – when I feel "I've had enough" – I make sure I know where the elements of the script will be going the next day. It's quite nice if you have finished half down a page because the next morning, your first goal is just to fill the rest of that page…*

> **Question:** *When writing an original screenplay, do you think it is plot or character that gets you started?*

> **Hale's response:** *Most of the screenplays I've written on spec have started with character <u>and</u> plot. Usually a specific person has done whatever – something – and the character causes the plot to begin. Genre is always foremost in my mind. I like thrillers, so I tend to work out plot and character at the same time. I think John Huston's adaptation of Dashiell Hammett's THE MALTESE FALCON is one of the best crime thrillers. THE LADY VANISHES, adapted from the Ethel White novel by Sidney Gilliat and Frank Launder and directed by Alfred Hitchcock, is also one of my favorites. I think all good film stories – in the crime or mystery genre or not – must have suspense – and a series of puzzle pieces that come together – in them.*

Question: *What is most important to you in a film story – plot or theme?*

Hales' response: *Ideally the plot should be working out the theme. Theme should become apparent through the action of the plot – if you can't accomplish it there, there might be something wrong in your script.*

Question: *When finishing a first draft of a spec screenplay, do you take time to let it sit before you decide if there is more work to do?*

Hales' response: *Yes, the time out helps a writer get distance, perspective. A script needs thinking about. Of course, when you finish something you always think it's pretty good – you ride that wave of energy. When the energy wave crests, I read it through again. It's only in taking time away from it that you can then go back and see how much work the draft needs.*

Question: *Do you give your first draft to anyone else to read?*

Hales' response: *Having someone read the first draft of a script helps you to confirm what you already know – the parts that are terrific and the parts that are not. When I give it to someone it's more to confirm the parts I think work and to confirm the parts where I feel it may be going wrong. I never argue with people about their opinions or suggestions – I just listen and take what I like and disregard the rest. I tend not to give it to my agents for their opinions – even though they may be intelligent or clever. They tend to be thinking only of a sale or the immediate marketplace so their opinions will be skewed. I did have an agent, Peggy Ramsay in London, who would tell you exactly what she thought – I did listen to her because she knew how to talk the writers' language. But most agents don't speak the writers' language– so I give my scripts to readers who can recognize good story – whether it's a commercially viable story (at this time and place) or not.*

Question: *Do you find it helpful to have your script read out loud by friends or actors?*

Hales' response: *I don't give it to a group to read aloud – just to trusted readers to read in their own private spaces – people who know good story.*

Question: *How does your writing process change when you are "on assignment" – hired by producers to write a specific script?*

Hales' response: *If producers come to me with a project and they are paying me quite a lot of money, they are the bosses. I consider myself the typewriter that is trying to give them what they want. I write the first draft, listen to their notes and I deal with notes (for the most part, unless they are really stupid) by trying to do what they say. I continue in this vein until I can't agree at all. If I am not fired, I ask my agent to tell them I can't do anymore on it. Of course, if I come to them with an idea for the project and they want to buy my idea and my services – it's different.*

Question: *There's another area where screenwriters work – the rewrite. When a studio hires you to rewrite an existing script, how do you approach the work?*

Hales' response: *When a screenwriter is hired to do a rewrite on someone else's script – he or she can be the first rewriter – or one of the middle rewriters – or the last rewriter who works on the project just before production starts or while production is in progress. <u>Everything gets rewritten.</u> Even the most established writers who get single credit on screen – we know their words and ideas get rewritten and tinkered with…*

Question: *When asked to rewrite another writer's work, how do you begin the process?*

Hales' response: *When you are being considered for hire, the producers will normally send you the latest script and ask you to read it. They may know the specific areas they want rewritten – they may not. You go to a meeting in their office, tell them your ideas of how to approach what they consider to be problem areas. If they like your ideas and points of view, you get hired. Sometimes the producers already know they want <u>you</u> to do the rewrite. So they tell you <u>their</u> ideas and if you agree, and you feel as if you can fulfill their wishes, you take their money and do your best.*

Question: *If you are getting multiple and varying notes from different sources in the production process, how do you approach this situation? Who do you listen to?*

Hales' response: *It happens quite a lot. I deal with it in at least* two ways – depending if I want to stay on the payroll. I try to reconcile the notes and try to satisfy everyone's desires because that's what they are paying me to do. If the notes were utterly conflicting – I would try to talk to the powers and see if they can come to an agreement.

Question: *How do you decide who holds the most power? Many productions have multiple producers, there is the director, there are studio heads and actors and…*

Hales' response: *That power can be in the lead actor or in the producer or in the director. Sometimes it's clear. Sometimes it's not. One may not know until you've made the wrong choice.*

Question: *When doing a production rewrite, how closely have you worked with a director?*

Hales' response: *I have worked closely with directors like John Huston (one of the great directors I worked with early in my career) and more recently, George Lucas – and sometimes I have never met the director. Sometimes I deliver the production rewrite to the producer and he or she will hand it over to the director. Then the director will do his own rewrite on my latest draft. Or he will bring in another writer of his own choice to do the production polish. That's to impose his authority. That's insecurity in the director.*

Question: *What's one of the reasons for your success?*

Hales' response: *I have never have missed a deadline. I deliver my drafts early or absolutely on time.*

Question: *Do you have any advice to screenwriters – young and old, inexperienced or experienced?*

Hales' response: *Learn the rules of the game of the Hollywood business and on each specific project. If you don't like the rules, don't join the game.*

If you join the game, always do your best – like a Boy Scout. Whatever I've done I've tried to do my best. And most importantly, keep your nerve – you are living on your wits and part of living on your wits is committing to keep your nerve. If you can't – go get another kind of job.

On Assignment

When you are hired to write a script for a production company, director, producer or friend or other entity – and there is payment involved – this is called writing "on assignment."

Every screenwriter has stories of doing rewrites and stories of being rewritten. *THE VERDICT*, a film that was made in 1982 and directed by Sidney Lumet has an interesting history. David Mamet wrote a draft (based on a book by Barry Reed). The producers did not respond well to the script, feeling that the lead character was too abrasive and unsympathetic. They hired (and paid for) another writer to do a draft. They weren't happy with that draft. They hired (and paid for) another writer to do another draft. Robert Redford, the actor who had been attached to the product, dropped out because he did not feel positive about any of the drafts. When the project was pitched to director Sidney Lumet (*DOG DAY AFTERNOON, DEATHTRAP, FAMILY BUSINESS* and more), he asked to see all the drafts of the screenplay that had been written so far. The draft that excited him the most was David Mamet's draft – the very first adaptation of the book. Lumet used Mamet's script and Paul Newman signed on to play the lead. The film was nominated for an Academy Award for best picture, Newman was nominated for best actor for his performance, Lumet was nominated for best director and Mamet was nominated for best screenplay adaptation.

INTERVIEW WITH SCREENWRITERS
BOB TZUDIKER AND NONI WHITE

Bob Tzudiker and Noni White make up a screenwriting team whose credits include *NEWSIES* and *102 Dalmatians* as well as Disney's animated *TARZAN* and *HUNCHBACK OF NOTRE DAME* as well as 20th Century Fox's *ANASTASIA* and more. Their writing work has been nominated for two *Annie Awards*. Both have worked as actors and writers and are adept at working in collaboration with studio executives, directors and animators. They have been tapped as the "rewriters" on various other projects – and they have experienced being re-written on their own projects. They approach each job anticipating – and enjoying – the collaboration with executives, directors and actors.

> *Question: You two started your screenwriting career by writing a spec script you titled MRS. FAUST. Would you say that spec script jumpstarted your career?*

Tzudiker and White's response: Yes, MRS. FAUST was about a woman who sells her soul to the devil on a 30-day free trial offer. The script was sent out – and was soon getting great reactions around town. Studio executives and production company executives wanted to meet us. It did not sell then (it sold more than a year later), but we wanted to make the most of these meetings so we decided to find a project we could pitch. Our goal was to sell an original idea and get paid to write a project that we were passionate about…

Question: How did you two land on the idea for NEWSIES?

Answer: We had found a mention in the New York Times Book Review of the New York City newsboy strike. This strike was in 1899 resulting from newspaper publishers Joseph Pulitzer and William Randolph Hearst's desire to obtain more profits by squeezing the lowest worker. The story caught our attention. We decided to research the details and found a story that excited us. We fashioned a pitch we could take out to various producers. Our pitch was for a drama – there was no musical component to it at all.

Question: How did NEWSIES land at Disney?

Tzudiker and White's response: Our agent set up a meeting for us with Marianne Sweeney who was an executive in Mike Finnell's production company. She and Mike got excited about the story and they set up pitches at Disney and at Spielberg's company. Our meeting with Disney executive Donald DeLine came first – he responded to the pitch and bought the project – so we never went to our Spielberg meeting.

Question: How many drafts did you do of NEWSIES?

Tzudiker and White's response: After we handed in our first draft, we got notes from Donald DeLine and went into our second draft. He gave us more notes and we did a third draft – and fourth draft – and fifth draft.

Question: How did the script change from draft to draft?

Tzudiker and White's response: Donald DeLine's notes were all targeted at making the characters' motivations and obstacles more clear. For the most part they were polishing notes, not major *story changes. Donald is the kind of executive who understands the domino effect that one note can have on an entire script; you change one story point and entire motivations, events and sequences might have to change to accommodate that one note. Donald was able to see the larger picture. When we did address a note and he then realized that the note was not helpful to the overall story, he would rescind his idea. The script just got better as we worked with him.*

Question: *When did the musical element get introduced?*

Tzudiker and White response: *Disney had just had great success with THE LITTLE MERMAID. Jeffrey Katzenberg (then one of the top executives at Disney) decided he wanted to do a live action musical – and thought NEWSIES would make a good one. He and Donald DeLine did not agree on this approach to the script – Donald wanted NEWSIES to remain a straight drama. This was happening at the time that different production divisions of Disney were being reorganized and Donald moved on to another division. So at this point, we were given a new executive, David Vogel. David was ready to go with Jeffrey's vision of NEWSIES – so the script morphed into a musical.*

Question: *How did you approach rewriting your drama into a musical?*

Tzudiker and White's response: *We did not envision NEWSIES as a "break-into-song" musical. We revised our final draft so that the music came from natural sources – like singers singing for coins on a street corner or coming out of a club or from a church– we wanted to feature the music of America at the turn of the century. We got very excited about this – we wanted to incorporate the great jazz and other cutting edge music of the era. We did not envision original songs written for the film.*

Question: *How did the "break-into-original-song" draft of the script come about?*

Tzudiker and White's response: *Kenny Ortega was brought on to direct. His background is musicals. Kenny – at first – was on board to create a musical using only "source" music. Meanwhile, Vogel was asking for rewrites to amp up the love story. We did a 5th draft incorporating all these ideas. Once that 5th draft was* *delivered, we were replaced as writers and we were no longer a part of the discussions in shaping the final product.*

Question: So the original "break-into-song" draft was fashioned by other writers?

Tzudiker and White's response: Yes. Fortunately, for us, Kenny Ortega instigated an open door policy for us once the production began. We were able to be on the set and see the project that we originated and nurtured come to life. This is unusual for a director to be so welcoming and we, to this day, appreciate Kenny's making this possible for us.

Question: You two did receive sole screen credit on NEWSIES?

Tzudiker and White's response: Yes. The changes to the story were not substantial enough for the Writers Guild of America's Arbitration Committee to warrant the subsequent writers getting credit.

Question: Did NEWSIES come close to being the film you had envisioned as you wrote the first draft of the script?

Tzudiker and White's response: We feel the final product does not match the original story – or way of telling the story – that we had envisioned from the outset. We still have problems with some of the choices that were made when we were not on board the project. The experience was wonderful at times, frustrating at times. However, we approach every film project as collaboration; a major studio film is not a product that one creates alone. A writer must enjoy working with executives, a director, actors and other creative entities on the team. But we feel, despite our reservations about some elements of the film, the essence and spirit of NEWSIES survived.

The process of writing an animated feature is very different. The time frame is elongated and there are many more creative people involved in the process; executives, the director (there could be more than one), the story board artists, the animators, the voice actors and sometimes lyricists and composers. An animated sequence can be re-drawn and re-focused innumerable amount of times. On **TARZAN**, Tzudiker and White were brought in to work on Tab Murphy's original draft of the script.

Question: How do you start the rewrite process when you are asked to come on to an animated film project as it goes into production?

Tzudiker and White's response: Tab's draft of TARZAN was excellent. The executives brought us in because they and the creative team wanted to take the script in a different direction but were having trouble making the turn. The first thing we did was listen to many creative people who had varying opinions on the focus and direction of the film; the producer, two directors, two studio executives, two heads of the studio, and an animator who was head of making sure the visuals told the story. Many times the notes would address the same areas but the suggested "fixes" were different. Our job was to create a consensus of ideas and then, working closely with the directors, choose the story elements that needed work. They said 'everyone knows it when they see it, the trick is to have everyone see it at the same time.'

Question: So when you got all the input from the various people on the project, what did you do next?

Tzudiker and White's response: We always approach the existing material asking questions – what is the story about? What is the core of the story? We feel if the writer (no matter if he or she is the first writer or the tenth writer) does not approach the whole piece first and understand the theme and character arcs, the job of the writing – and especially the job of rewriting – can go askew. Once we feel we have a handle on the complete piece, we take one sequence at a time – asking – how does this sequence work in the whole story? How can we improve it? How will it help accomplish the end goal?

Question: How do you deal with notes from producers or directors that you may not agree with?

Tzudiker and White's response: If we don't understand or completely agree with a note from a studio executive, we ask ourselves – what caused the executive to <u>stop</u> the flow of his or her reading at this point in the script and feel the need to give a note? Is the actual problem at this specific point where the note came into the executive's head, or have previous story elements or character actions caused this moment not to work as well as it should? Then we address the underlying cause rather than the specific note.

Actors may ask for script approval. Sometimes an actor will allow the producer or studio to attach their names to a project (in order to get financing or to attract other actors) but have an "out clause" if they do not respond positively to the final draft of the script that is slated for production.

A writer must remember that an actor is reading the script from a very different point of view than a director or producer or screenwriter. An actor is looking at <u>the role he or she is being asked to portray</u>. How big is the role? Is it a lead role? Is it a supporting role? Is it a minor but pivotal character? How many lines does the character have? Is the character one that the specific actor wants to have on his resume? If an actress feels more comfortable portraying sympathetic characters, and the role she is offered is that of a demented serial killer, she may turn down the role. Do not take it personally – the role could be wonderfully written and worthy of being the base for an Oscar-winning performance, but the actress may be concerned about her career and her audience base.

Actors have various reasons to take – or not take – a certain role. If the actor you envision as the romantic lead of your film has recently completed a romance and wants a change of pace, he may turn down the role. If the actress doesn't feel comfortable doing action sequences, and your script is full of them, chances are she will turn down the role. An actor is building a career, just as you are, and he (or his agent or manager) has an idea of what kind of roles he should play next, or what studio he should work with next, or what director he should work with next. Your script may be brilliant – but it doesn't fit into the scope of an actor's plans.

Bob Tzudiker and Noni White were hired to do a rewrite on the 2000's Disney's live action film *102 DALMATIONS*. Their first task was to finish a draft in six weeks so the studio could deliver it to Glenn Close *(FATAL ATTRACTION, DANGEROUS LIASIONS* and more) – the actress they wanted to play Cruella De Vil. Tzudiker and White completed their draft, Close was pleased with the draft and agreed to sign on to the project. The film went into serious pre-production. However, Glenn Close had another clause in her contract – she could insist that Disney hire playwright and screenwriter Tom Stoppard (*SHAKESPEARE IN LOVE, EMPIRE OF THE SUN* and more) to do a polish on the script. Ms. Close exercised this clause and Stoppard did another draft of the script. However, when production began, Tzudiker and White were brought back onto the project to be in England and execute any production rewrites that were needed during the actual shooting of the script.

Tzudiker and White are always working on new, original material.

> **Question:** *How do you know when your spec scripts is ready to go out into the marketplace?*

> **Tzudiker and White's response:** *It's a gut feeling. First we give our script to a few friends we consider to be fair readers. We want these friends to be honest, to give us feedback on story, characters, clarity and style. If we receive the same criticisms from a number of readers, we know we must address the problems.*

> **Question:** *Have you ever written a spec script that you have not put into the marketplace?*

> **Tzudiker and White's response:** *We have one script that we have completely rewritten three times. Each draft has its problems. We have not given it to our agent or to anyone because we don't feel it is what we want it to be. It's not a good idea to put a script into the marketplace if you cannot completely stand behind it.*

The Producer

The film producer is the person who, in most cases, has gotten excited about your script and decided to dedicate energy (and sometimes money) to getting your story into production. Some producers are creative, some simply find the money for the project. A good producer will understand the theme and story of your script and work to bring it to life in an authentic way.

INTERVIEW WITH PRODUCER
JON DAVISON

Producer Jon Davison *(SEARCHERS 2.0, STARSHIP TROOPERS, ROBOCOP, TOP SECRET!, TWILIGHT ZONE: THE MOVIE, AIRPLANE!* and more) has worked with many writers at various stages of the script process – first drafts through production drafts. I asked him these questions:

> **Question:** *When you decide to commit to a script as a producer, do you find that a rewrite or polish is usually necessary to get the script ready to go to the studio or financial entity?*

Davison's response: When I see a script that excites me, the last thing I want to do is start mucking about with it. I'd rather take it to a few financers and get their opinion and feedback. If they have some ideas and suggestions that are compatible with the writer's and mine, then I try to pursue it with them.

Question: Do you have "trusted" readers who give you solid thoughts on a script you might be interested in pursuing? How do you determine which suggestions might be of value?

Davison's response: It's probably a good idea to let a person or two read the script to see if they find any portion of the work confusing or unclear in a way not intended by the writer. It is better to have to a few extra lines of exposition in the script than to have the reader scratching their head. One of things that has really changed since I started in the film industry, is that people don't read screenplays as carefully. In fact, it often seems they don't read screenplays at all. It's very hard to get anybody in a position to say 'yes' to a script to read it. The classic William Goldman quote is, "nobody knows anything." This could now be amended to add, "nobody reads anything." One of the reasons American studio pictures are so dreadful is the emphasis on concept over execution. Concept is an easier thing to sell, however – in the <u>execution</u> lies the art.

Question: When you sit down with a writer to give notes on a script, how do you expect (hope) the writer will respond?

Davison's response: All you can hope for is the writer will respond honestly and not take the notes too personally. He should defend what he believes in but be open enough to explore different suggestions to see if he can make them work. Inevitably, most of the suggestions the writer gets are not going to be too brilliant or constructive. They'll be coming from readers, executives, directors, producers and a lot of other people who don't write for a living. Most of these suggestions are going to have to be deflected or ignored if the original work is to survive. As you can imagine, it's a very political process. There's a lot of ego, anxiety and panic involved. Generally, the writer needs to become the spokesman for the screenplay, laying out calmly the virtues and drawbacks of the various suggestions proposed to him.

Question: When a rewrite is necessary, how do you go about *getting your thoughts together for the writer? Do you give written notes? What seems to work best in your experience?*

Davison's response: *The best way for me to get my thoughts together is to type a set of notes. Then I sit down with the writer, talk through the major points and give him or her the notes. Some writers want to discuss their reactions immediately, some want some time to think about them. Most writers do a combination of both.*

Question: *When and why do you feel it might be time to bring another writer onto a project?*

Davison's response: *Personally, I never like to bring in another writer, If the script was good enough to pursue, there's no reason the original writer can't implement any needed changes. Whenever the studio or director has forced me to change writers, I believe it's been a mistake – every single time, no exception. I remember one picture in particular when the director convinced the studio to hire a succession of big name writers on weekly deals for substantial amounts of money. Every one of these "A List" writers made the project worse. The original writer has lived with and thought about the script for many months, sometimes years. These hot shots gave it some thought on the ski slopes, poured out their first instincts and merely exposed problems that the original writer had solved. Directors often want to bring on their pet writers. On a number of occasions, I've seen these new writers turn a "go" project into a development deal. If the original writer doesn't want to continue with the project, that would necessitate a change. But I've never known that to happen.*

Question: *If the studio or production company gives you and the writer notes that you feel do not work, how do you approach the situation?*

Davison's response: *Carefully. I try to determine what the studio executives or production company executives are trying to accomplish dramatically and emotionally. The specific suggestions are often much less important than the goal they are trying to reach. I try to work toward whatever their larger concern is and don't start reacting to their specific suggestions. Often times what they desire is simpler than the notes would imply and boils down to: funnier or scarier or more exciting.*

Question: When a director is brought onto a project, do the director notes get special consideration? In your experience, do directors feel free to do rewrites (themselves or hire another writer) as they see fit?

Davison's response: Once you hire a director, the eight hundred pound gorilla is in the room and you're going to have to deal with him. And you're going have to support him. So before hiring a director it is very important to make sure that you and he want to make the same movie. You need to sit down and discuss the script in considerable detail. It's important for both parties to make sure the marriage they are entering into can work.

Question: Do you feel like it's a good idea to have a writer on during production or do you think the director (or producer) can handle production revisions?

Davison's response: It's definitely a good idea to have the writer around during the pre-production, production and post-production of the picture. He or she is a major creative force on the picture and should stay with the project to the (bitter) end. Personally, I think the writers should be in the casting but most directors are too insecure to allow it. They should be on the set during the early days of shooting and then if they've got something better to do (like make a living), they can go away and come back as needed. They should view early cuts of the film and help with the ADR and loop group work. If the writer hasn't been completely screwed over and demoralized, it seems you get all this for free. What a deal!

The Pitch

The pitch is a verbal presentation of your film story. Development executives and producers hear pitches nearly every day, looking for that story that might make a box-office hit. If the pitch catches the imagination of the producer or executive, a deal would be made and you would be hired to write the screenplay of the story that you "pitched." A good pitch should be no more than ten minutes, should concentrate on the main character's growth and journey, set up the world and major conflicts of the story, sketch in the opposing and aiding forces and be as exciting as you can make it. Be creative, bring in simple visual aids if available, but keep it short.

Using the Eleven Step Story Structure as a guide will ensure that the pitch has a solid beginning, middle and end and includes a series of conflicts and character changes.

Selling a story on a pitch is not easy, especially for a writer with no credits. If you are passionate about the project and are lucky enough to get into a room to pitch your story, go for it because it's a chance to make contacts in the professional arena. Don't be disappointed if the pitch is not bought. Don't stop believing in your story. Just be working on the screenplay as you pitch it around town. Ultimately, a script is more easy to sell than a pitch.

INTERVIEW WITH SCREENWRITER
MATTHEW JACOBS

Matthew Jacobs grew up in Great Britain, attended the National Film and Television School, began his film work at the BBC and moved to California. He has worked as a screenwriter, actor, director and producer. His studio projects include *EMPEROR'S NEW GROOVE, LASSIE, DR. WHO, UGLY* and more. His independently produced projects include *HALLELUJAH ANYHOW, MOTHERTIME* and 2008's *NOWHERE MAN*. Jacobs has an entrepreneurial approach to filmmaking – he is always working on new material – writing or producing or directing – or all three at the same time.

> *Question: Matthew, when you have finished a first draft of an original spec script, do you take time away from it before you decide if any rewriting is necessary?*
>
> *Jacobs' response: Yes, I take as much time as I possibly can – I may even try and write another script.*
>
> *Question: If you decide a rewrite of your own work is necessary, how do you go through the rewrite process?*
>
> *Jacob's response: In the rewrite, I try to regard myself as a "filmmaker" rather than a writer, so that means I'll put on all the hats – director, producer, editor – as I consider my rewrite. For me, the script is the cheapest way of "making" the movie – so during the rewrite phase, I feel free to try out new scenes to see*

how they may fit – or I re-arrange scenes to see if the story comes alive in a new way. That said, I don't really have a process for rewriting – the specific project seems to dictate my approach. I read and re-read and I listen to everyone. Then I make my own notes on every page. I break down structural changes and I launch in from the top again. I want to feel like I'm building a better building and not just redecorating.

Question: *Do you find having the script read out loud by actors or friends to be helpful when you are considering rewrites that may be needed?*

Jacobs' response: *Sometimes, depends on the movie – if it's a comedy, then absolutely. Hearing the dialogue is good, but actors who may make the wrong choices or who are not right for the part, can lead you astray and make you question your work. It's important to keep everything in perspective. You have to be able to tell if the story works.*

Question: *Do you have "trusted" readers who give you solid feedback? How do you determine which suggestions might be of value?*

Jacobs' response: *I like readers who are encouraging, so I tend to use other writers because they know the process, the hardships of writing and the pitfalls. Only suggestions that will make the movie better and are truly positive are considered.*

Question: *If you are planning on directing your own spec script, do you approach the rewrite process differently?*

Jacobs' response: *Sometimes. Trying to do a production rewrite for yourself can be a bit frustrating because you are so close to the material. So you hope you have a producer, an editor, or a cast who you can really bounce stuff off so the script can get better.*

Question: *When do you determine that a script is ready to go into the marketplace?*

Jacobs' response: *Personally I have little idea, even though I may tell everyone that I do. And remember, some great scripts may never be ready for the marketplace because they don't fit into the "commercial" niche. They may be too "particular." The marketplace may reject a well-written and beautiful film script,* *that's why it's good to get your material produced in alternative ways too. Normally I write speculatively with a very definite route to production already in mind.*

Question: *Is it valuable for you to envision a certain actor in a role – does that help you in the rewrite process?*

Jacobs' response: *Yes and no. The character has to live in its own right in my mind. However, if I personally know the actor and I know they'll say yes and I'm involving them in the development process, then obviously, I'll think about the actor. It's a real balancing act. Sometimes saying this is really a specific stars' role will help financiers see where you are going. And then again, many producers will <u>not</u> want any specific talent attached because it might limit the sales possibilities – depending on the "hotness" of an actor's career at a specific moment.*

Question: *What is the page count that you shoot for in a feature script?*

Jacobs' response: *Anything between 105-135 pages (people seem to like 110 for live action, 95 for animation). A good producer doesn't care as long as what you've written is brilliant – those producers are very rare, but normally very successful. They know the script is just a way-station to getting various other stuff done so all that matters is does it work, do you want to see it, can they use it to get the money and get the director and get the cast.*

Question: *If you are writing on assignment for a studio or producer, how do you approach taking their notes?*

Jacobs' response: *Respectfully. I try and assess why they have given me a note rather than what their note is specifically. They're paying me to come up with better ideas than they have. Of course if I think their suggestion works I'll try it.*

Question: *If the studio or producer gives you a note that you cannot make work, how do you approach the situation?*

Jacobs' response: *I tell them I can't quite make their specific notes work but I have a plan to address their notes in a different manner. Then I do something I think works. If they fire me, so be it.*

Question: *If you are getting multiple and varying notes from* *different sources in the production process, how do you approach this situation?*

Jacobs' response: *I tell them their notes seem to conflict a bit, but I have a plan to address their notes in a different manner. Then I do something I think works. If they fire me, so be it.*

Question: *When doing a production rewrite, how closely have you worked with a director?*

Jacobs' response: *Very closely. If the production writing is going well it's like a good love affair. You want to please them and they want to please you. If there's no passion there, then there's no fire. If there's no fire, it may end up being a very boring movie. During production rewrites is when you and your director really learn about the script. The best (if not the only) way to learn about screenwriting is to <u>make</u> your scripts, not to sell them.*

Agents

An agent is the writer's representative in the film business. The writer agrees to pay his or her agent ten percent of each writing assignment or sale.

There are two kinds of agents: Agents who love the written word and have opinions about material and get passionate about your work and are interested in the sale of your material … and agents who rarely read a finished script, rely on coverage of readers and assistants to form their opinions and are <u>only</u> interested in the <u>sale</u>. Both are acceptable, both have pros and cons.

The agent who actually reads your screenplay and has opinions and wants to give you notes can be helpful or harmful. Are the notes of value? Do the notes enhance your vision? Would the notes change your screenplay significantly and in a way that would take a detour from your original impetus? Is the agent trying to fashion your screenplay to fit the current marketplace? Or to fit his version of your story? Is the agent reluctant to put your work into the marketplace for some reason? Does he believe in it or not?

The agent who is not a reader and relies on assistants to form opinions for him can also serve a purpose. If this agent is an incredible salesperson and can sell your screenplay – that can totally be sufficient. The agent has done his job. Some writers depend on mentors or peers or family for feedback on their work and do not need the extra eye of an agent.

Find an agent who approaches your work in a way that makes you feel comfortable.

The most important thing a writer must remember when working with an agent: <u>An agent is a businessperson.</u> An agent needs to pay the rent, keep his or her job, impress the boss. Most want to make a mark on the industry, just as the writer does. Agents can make their mark only through their clients. They want you to be good, they want you to be prolific, they want you to make their job easier.

Agents expect writers to network, make contacts, keep contacts, and be able to work with the various personalities of producers and directors. Once you have an agent, don't sit back and wait for the phone ring.

Agents will focus on clients who are bringing in the most return. That's reality. The writer's job, when not on assignment, is to keep writing on spec so the agent has product to move into the marketplace.

Reputable agents will be signatories of the Writers Guild. This means they have agreed to abide by the rules, regulations and industry standards set by the Guild.

Managers

Managers seek out work possibilities and contacts for their clients. Managers usually work in tandem with agents or attorneys to identify and set up meetings with buyers/producers/directors/executives. They will help identify available jobs and are expected to know the marketplace. Managers usually deal with a smaller client pool and are more readily accessible to the writer than an agent who works in a large company and has a long client list. Managers take another percentage of the writer's paycheck; usually this percentage is negotiated on an individual basis.

Attorneys

Writers would be wise to employ an entertainment attorney to look at any contract or deal memo they are interested in signing. Since it is the studio and production company attorneys' job to write contracts designed to keep as much money and control in their employers' pockets, writers need attorneys who have <u>their</u> best interests in mind.

A studio or production company's attorney keeps his or her job by finding ways of keeping rights, residuals, bonuses, monies, sequel privileges, participation in toys or books or television shows based on the writer's material safely in the studio or production company's control. A writer's attorney's job is to find a way for his or her client to participate in anything that emerges from the writer's material.

An entertainment attorney who is on the writer's side and has a wide knowledge of the industry players, the studio system, and all areas of the film business is a necessary adjunct to the working screenwriter's life.

> **Question:** *What if my friend or brother or uncle or niece is a lawyer in Oklahoma who specializes in tax law? Can I ask him or her to look at my contract?*

> **Answer:** *Yes, of course you can. But you are putting yourself at a disadvantage. First of all, this lawyer will not have the expertise or the knowledge of the film business. He or she may not be able to point out certain areas in the contract that need to be questioned or adjusted. Find an attorney who has specialized in the entertainment business.*

How does a writer get an agent or manager or attorney?

The simple answer is this: By getting a writing job and proving you are a person who will make money as a screenwriter. Remember, agents and managers and attorneys are businesspersons and to them, the making of films is more a business than an art.

This true story exemplifies a road to getting an agent: After I had moved to Los Angeles and landed a few feature film writing jobs as well as worked on staff on a television show, I hoped I had gotten enough work to be able to ask a favor of my agent. I asked if he would consider a recommendation of a talented friend. My friend had a spec half hour comedy script that was hilarious and I knew she could be successful. I asked my agent to read the script. A year went by and he never found the time (yes, this is a 30 page script, double-spaced and could be read in 20 minutes but agents do get busy finding work for their existing clients). My friend did not wait for my agent to tell her she was good. She did not wait for him to agree to help her find work. She continued to make contacts herself. She signed up for a writing seminar at the WGA in New York. There she met the head writer of one of the most successful situation comedies on network television. This head writer responded to her seminar contributions, read her spec script, thought she would be a good addition to his staff and hired her. When I called my agent to tell him the good news, he suddenly had "just read her script last night and had planned to call her today about representing her." He asked me to please call her and tell her that he would be happy to negotiate her new contract for her. What's the "lesson" of the story? Believe in yourself and pursue your goals. Keep getting your product out into the marketplace. A writer needs to be looking for opportunities to use his or her talent.

Bottom line? How to get an agent's attention? Get a job. How to get a manager's attention? Get a job. How to get an attorney's attention? Get a job.

How to find that first job

How does one get a job without an agent or manager or attorney? Write your spec scripts. *Note the <u>plural – scripts.</u>* Having one script does not instill confidence in those who might want to represent you that you have a strong commitment and passion for writing.

Make contacts. Enroll in classes or workshops. You might learn something, but beyond that, you will begin to network with people with similar goals and interests. Once you make a connection, stay in touch. Chances are someone will land a job or an agent or manager and pave the way for friends to take advantage of that contact.

Go to screenings and be open to meeting people. Find an online chat room for screenwriters. Of course, always use your best judgment – find writers as serious as you are and don't get bogged down in critiquing others' work if it takes time from your own writing. Be your own judge, find fellow writers whose work you admire and stay in touch with these writers.

The WGA holds seminars and events; some are open to non-WGA members. The Academy of Television Arts and Sciences in Los Angeles holds regular events where industry professionals answer questions or give presentations; some are open to non-members.

Enter contests

Enter your scripts into screenwriting contests. With a contest win or honorable mention, you can make yourself look more bankable. As I mentioned, one of my agents told me he is more inclined to read a script that has won (or received honorable mention) in a screenplay contest than to read a blind submission – or even one of his client's friend's script. Let literary agents or managers know of your success in contests.

Send out query letters asking agents, managers, producers, development executives to read your work. What does a query letter look like?

Query Letter

A query letter is written in hopes of interesting a buyer or writer's representative in reading your film script. First, let them know who you are – in one sentence. Are you new to Los Angeles? Are you a lawyer or doctor or minister or cowboy who has turned to screenwriting? If you have been referred to them by someone, let them know that. In one sentence.

Fill in the blanks in this letter – and then extrapolate and make it your own.

Your Name
Your Email Address
Your Telephone Number
Your Street Address
Your City and State and Zip

Name of Agent/Manager/Producer/Actor
Name of Their Company or Affiliation
Their Street Address
Their City, State, Zip

Date

Dear Ms. Or Mr. _____,

My name is _____, (add one personal thing about you as a writer). I have recently completed an original screenplay entitled _____ .

TITLE OF YOUR FILM SCRIPT is a (FILL IN GENRE) about a (FILL IN WITH YOUR LOGLINE) . Add one or two <u>short</u> *sentences (not run-on sentences) about plot or character that you think is relevant and will pique their interest.*

What strikes most people as unique about this script, is that my main character is (FILL IN DETAILS WITH JUST A FEW SENTENCES). In my opinion, this script could attract actors like _____ or _____ .

I am hoping you will consider reading my script because I admire your work on (MENTION THE FILM HE OR SHE WAS INVOLVED IN – OR THAT THE AGENCY HAS A GREAT REPUTATION OR….)

I'll give your office a call next week to see if it is possible to send in my script for your perusal – or feel free to contact me. Of course, I am willing to sign a waiver agreement.

I am hoping you will find my script of interest.

Thank you,

Your Name
(Repeat your Email address)

Keep it short, add a bit of personality if you feel the urge. Remember, this is a <u>business</u> and proper business approaches are expected. Check out the websites <u>http://www.breakingin.net</u> or <u>http://www.wga.org</u> for more Query Letter advice.

Screenwriting Groups

There are screenwriter support groups that meet on a regular basis. Some meet in coffee shops, some meet at members' homes. Groups are usually organized like this: Screenwriters meet once a week or once a month to read their work aloud. The screenwriter may read the script, or it may be read aloud by others in the group, each taking a different character. All or parts of the script may be read in one session. The writer is then given feedback on his work thus getting support and suggestions from fellow writers.

Favorite Websites

There are new and useful websites cropping up regularly on the internet. Here are a few of the good ones to check out:

http://www.imdb.com – Internet Movie Database. Include film credits, industry news, filmmaker dialogues and more.

http://www.moviebytes.com – Moviebytes is a good source for contests, industry news, what's selling and what's in production.

http://www.boxofficemojo.com – Online movie production and box office reporting site. Also includes reviews, industry bios and more.

http://www.wordplayer.com – Wonderful site aimed at screenwriters, with articles written by screenwriters

http://www.script-o-rama.com – Drew's Script-o-rama is a great place to start to look for the produced screenplays you want to read or download.

http://www.screenplayguide.com – This site deals with format questions.

http://www.scriptsales.com – This site features Done Deal, a listing of recent sales of books, scripts and pitches. It also includes lists of agents, manages, law firms, production companies and more.

http://johnaugust.com – This site features information about the business of screenwriting as well as the craft. John August is the screenwriter of *CHARLIE AND CHOCOLATE FACTORY, BIG FISH, CHARLIE'S ANGELS: FULL THROTTLE* and more.

http://www.creativescreenwriting.com – This site features screenwriting tips as well as contest information and seminar information.

http://www.writerswrite.com/screenwriting – This site features screenwriting tips as well as contest information and seminar information.

http://www.sydfield.com – This site features screenwriting tips as well as contest information and other links to screenwriting resources.

Use your search engine to seek out other sites that might be of interest to you. Technology has made it easy to get answers to most of your questions. I have had students find writing and production jobs through Craig's List!

CHAPTER SUMMARY

– Knowledge of the business of being a screenwriter is necessary for success.

– The most important think is to continually produce (write) product for the marketplace.

– Agents, managers, attorneys can help the career of a screenwriter.

– Create a network of writers and business associates in the industry.

ELEVEN STEP FILM BREAKDOWNS AND NOTES

Breaking down successful films can illuminate good structure as well as aid the screenwriter in examining various templates in storytelling techniques. All of these films included in these Eleven Step breakdowns are award-winning films. All are various combinations of genres. Note how the breakdowns focus on the protagonist's journey, the person that goes through the most change in the story. Watch these great films again; note how each genre is satisfied, how the genres are mixed and how the protagonists go through very clear character arcs.

JUNO

2007

written by Diablo Cody

GENRE: Dramedy/ Coming-Of-Age/ Teen

DRAMATIC QUESTION: Will Juno ever be able to believe that Paulie really loves her and admit her love of him?

THEME: Without taking a risk, one can never learn to trust.

ACT ONE: The character of Juno (portrayed by Ellen Page) is introduced and her problem is also set up on the first page. Juno, age 16, has just used multiple home-pregnancy tests and now has to finally accept that she is, indeed, pregnant. As Juno comes to this realization, we realize she's funny and quirky but has a way of keeping people at a distance. How does the audience know this? Juno dresses as if she does not care what people think of her and she has developed a verbal repartee that stops people from getting close. She is a loner, save for one good girlfriend, Leah (portrayed by Olivia Thirlby) and the high school boy, Paulie Bleecker (portrayed by Michael Cera) who has captured her affections. However, it's clear that Juno craves attention and acceptance – and love. Juno has a sense of the dramatic; she likes to stage her world to show she is different. Early the next morning, after realizing she is pregnant, Juno drags a cast-off barco-lounger and other set pieces to Paulie's front lawn. When Paulie comes out in the morning to join the track team run, Juno is sitting in the barco-lounger, sucking on a corncob pipe. She tells him she is pregnant. It's clear Juno is hoping for an emotional reaction from Paulie, a sign of his love for her. When Paulie is simply stunned and unable to compute this shocking news as quickly as Juno wants him to – she tells him she was thinking abortion was the best option. Paulie stammers and agrees that Juno needs to make her choice. Juno, disappointed and denied the affirmation of this love that she seeks, acts matter-of-fact - like this is just an everyday, not-a-big-deal problem - and heads off.

ACT TWO: Juno puts herself on a path to her second opportunity by looking into her options. At the planned parenthood clinic, Juno sees a classmate picketing against abortions. Juno decides she cannot go through with an abortion. Juno and Leah scour the local Pennysaver newspaper for couples seeking adoption. It becomes clear that Juno wants to find the perfect home, the perfect parents, she wants to set her child into a stable and loving household (a situation that Juno does not feel she has herself). Juno and Lea happen on a picture of a couple seeking adoption and Juno thinks this couple could provide a home that would be perfect for her baby.

> NOTE: *These underlying emotions of Juno are not stated in a direct manner. It's Juno's actions and interests and sarcasm that make all clear to the audience.*

Juno has a loving father, a stepmother and stepsister. The relationships are supportive and surprising. The attitudes of her immediate family start Juno on her journey to understanding love in a new way. When Juno meets Vanessa and Mark "the perfect couple" (portrayed by Jennifer Garner and Jason Bateman) who wants to adopt Juno's baby, she puts all her energies into feeling good about her baby's chances of being loved and having a perfect life.

The film keeps its focus on Juno's journey with the core characters - Paulie, Juno's father, Juno's stepmother, Juno's best friend and the perfect couple. Juno excludes Paulie from the pregnancy process; she pushes him to date another girl. Paulie eventually calls her on her actions and lets her know how he feels (as best he can in his non-verbally adept way) - that he feels pushed away and hurt that she does not include him in the pregnancy. Juno begins to see how much her father supports her and how his love is unconditional. She begins to realize that she has not given her stepmother the opportunity to be a real mother-figure to Juno, or given her stepmother room in the home to fulfill all her own desires. Juno's best girlfriend always keeps it honest, does not keep anything from Juno and shows true friendship. It's clear that Juno cannot see the love and support and the "perfect" life she has and the audience hopes Juno will eventually learn to accept it.

What Juno experiences as "the perfect couple" is her biggest disappointment. Mark reveals himself to be immature and unready to be a parent and Vanessa is desperate to be a mother – single or not. Juno has a decision to make.

ACT THREE: Juno makes choices that affirm what she has learned on her journey. Life cannot be "perfect". But a person has to take emotional risks to try to get as close to "perfect" as one can.

ELEVEN STEP BREAKDOWN AND NOTES

1. JUNO WANTS to believe in love. **WHY?** Her mother left the family when Juno was very young. She has not been able to trust that love can be lost lasting and one can trust it to be consistent.

2. JUNO LOGICALLY GOES FOR IT

    a. Juno has a longtime crush on Paulie Bleecker and has sex with him

    b. When she realizes she is pregnant, she tells Paulie

3. JUNO IS DENIED

    a. Paulie is too stunned to emotionally connect with her and Juno feels she cannot count on his love and has to take this on her predicament by herself

4. SECOND OPPORTUNITY FOR JUNO TO BELIEVE IN LOVE AND THAT SHE IS LOVABLE

    a. Juno can't go through with the abortion

    b. Juno and girlfriend Leah find an ad in the newspaper for a couple who wants to adopt a baby

c. Juno tells her dad and stepmom and feels their support

5. JUNO'S CONFLICTS ABOUT TAKING ADVANTAGE OF HER SECOND OPPORTUNITY

   a. Juno has to carry the pregnancy to term and still go to high school

   b. Juno does not know if this adoptive couple (Vanessa and Mark) will be good parents

6. JUNO GOES FOR IT

a. Juno and her dad go meet the hopeful adoptive couple, Vanessa and Mark.

7. ALL GOES WELL

   a. Juno thinks Vanessa and Mark are great and would be perfect parents, especially when she finds out Mark is a musician

   b. Paulie invites Juno to go to the movies, she feels he is still there for her. She doesn't go with him because she has to go to her ultrasound appointment.

   c. Juno is bonding with her stepmom because the stepmom is supportive and helpful and accepting and protective of Juno's predicament.

   d. Juno is bonding with Mark over their mutual love of music and horror/gore films

NOTE: Tension enters this area because the audience fears Juno may be bonding with Mark on a deeper, possibly romantic level and this could be dangerous

   e. Juno runs into Vanessa at the mall and sees how good she is with children.

   f. Vanessa is able to feel the baby kick in Juno's womb and Juno sees how much this baby means to Vanessa.

   g. The ultrasounds show Juno's baby to be healthy.

8. ALL FALLS APART

a. Juno finds out that Paulie has asked another girl to prom

b. Juno finds out that Mark wants to divorce Vanessa, he tells her he is not ready to be a father.

c. Juno, driving home, pulls over and cries on the side of the road.

9. CRISIS

a. Juno asks her dad if there is lasting love, if two people can love each other forever? Her dad replies that it is not easy, but one cannot stop trying to make that kind of love work. Juno makes a decision.

10. CLIMAX

a. Juno and Leah fill Paulie's mailbox with his favorite snack: orange-flavored tic-tacs

b. Juno goes to the high school track and finds Paulie at practice. Juno lets him know she loves him and why. It's clear Paulie feels the same about her.

c. Juno goes into labor

d. Juno is at the hospital with all those who love her; stepmom, dad, Leah and step sisters

e. Juno has the baby

f. Paulie rushes to the hospital and comforts Juno

11. TRUTH COMES OUT

a. Juno allows Vanessa to adopt the baby as a single mom. Juno knows Vanessa will be a great mother. Juno realizes that the "perfect family situation" may not exist.

b. Juno's family gets a dog, something Juno's stepmom has always wanted but Juno had, inadvertently, prevented.

c. Juno and Paulie go back to playing music together – and having a solid relationship.

NO COUNTRY FOR OLD MEN

2007

written by Joel Coen and Ethan Coen
adapted from a novel by Cormac McCarthy

GENRE: Drama/Horror

DRAMATIC QUESTION: Will Sheriff Ed Tom Bell find the answer to this question: Can true evil be stopped?

THEME: Without acceptance that evil exists, one cannot survive.

ACT ONE: Sheriff Ed Tom Bell's VOICEOVER at the top of the film sets out the dramatic question of the film. Bell (portrayed by Tommy Lee Jones) gives the audience his background - his father had been a sheriff before him, so had his grandfather. Bell, as sheriff, has apprehended many criminals and wrongdoers, but he is considering the difference between the common criminal and the truly evil element in the world.

Bell's voiceover is provided as Chigurh (portrayed by Javier Bardem) is being arrested by a deputy for stealing a car. At the sheriff's office, the deputy is relaying news of the arrest and Chigurh, showing clever skills at finding a way to be lethal while still in handcuffs, strangles the deputy in a matter-of-fact but very violent manner. Chigurh leaves the deputy for dead, steals the deputy's car and then uses the car's sirens to pull over an innocent driver on a deserted highway. Chigurh coolly kills the driver with his weapon of choice - an air gun - and steals the newly dead man's car and drives off.

In this rather quick opening of the film, the truly evil element is introduced. The audience witnesses Chigurh's modus operandi and the dramatic question of the film is made clear.

The PLOT is now introduced. Llewelyn Moss (portrayed by Josh Brolin) comes across a drug deal gone bad; bodies lie dead. He tracks down the one wounded survivor of the melee (a man Moss is certain must have gotten away with the money). He finds the man, now dead, and takes a suitcase of money, the payment for the drugs. Moss decides to keep the money so he and his wife can have a new and easy life. Moss is doing the <u>wrong</u> thing for what he considers the <u>right</u> reason. Later that night, Chigurh arrives at the drug deal gone bad scene with the head drug dealers. They realize the suitcase of money is gone. Chigurh finds out there is a tracking device in the suitcase. He kills the drug dealers, takes the tracking device and is off on the hunt of Moss. Chigurh is doing the wrong thing for the wrong reason – his ego. He is the devil incarnate, no one will outshine him; no one will take what he aims to have for himself. The audience already knows Chigurh's methods and addiction to the kill; Moss's fate is sealed at this point – how the hunt is carried out (a staple in horror films) is the only thing in question.

Until the sheriff, Ed Tom Bell, is introduced. Bell is on the right hand of good; he has dedicated himself to keep good and bad in balance. Bell is smart and analytical; his good ol' boy drawl belies his understanding of the crime. Bell begins his hunt too – hoping he can get to the naïve Moss before evil (literally) destroys him.

A sense of doom permeates the story from the outset. Bell's question about evil sets it up. Moss' wife "has a bad feeling" about her husband's actions. When Bell gets to Moss' trailer he sees the detritus left by Chigurh's use of the air gun to break into the trailer. Bell intuits that Chigurh has just left the premises because there is still sweat on the milk bottle. Bell, who has already witnessed the drug deal gone bad scene, the kill of his deputy and the kill of the man on the highway, begins to feel the pangs of denial – harnessing this evil may be beyond his capabilities.

ACT TWO is the race between good and evil. Can Bell get to Moss before Chigurh? Will Moss' ego allow him to give up the money to save his life and the life of his wife? Will Moss understand what he is up against? Will Moss lose his soul to the devil because he is too proud? Will Chigurh (evil) prove absolutely indestructible? Evil proves to be relentless and it cannot be brought down. The horror of the story deepens and deepens and finally in ACT THREE, Bell realizes he cannot stop or harness true evil… and he retires from law enforcement.

Evil wins: the essence of the horror genre.

ELEVEN STEP STORY BREAKDOWN AND NOTES

1. SHERIFF ED TOM BELL WANTS peace and justice. WHY?

Bell grew up in a family of law enforcement officials. He wants to keep his town in order, to take out the criminal element so that the community can enjoy home, hearth and a peaceful life.

2. BELL LOGICALLY TRIES TO KEEP PEACE AND JUSTICE

    a. Bell is a sheriff

    b. Bell investigates the killing of his deputy and the victim of the car theft

    c. Bell investigates the drug deal gone bad crime scene

    d. Bell tracks the drug deal money to Moss because Moss' truck is still at crime scene

    e. Bell figures out the air gun is the criminal's weapon of choice

3. BELL IS DENIED

    a. Bell figures out the criminal is one step ahead of Bell in Bell's pursuit of Moss

4. BELL'S SECOND OPPORTUNITY TO TRY TO MAINTAIN PEACE AND JUSTICE

    a. Bell goes to Odessa to talk to Moss' wife. He hopes she will see reason and be able to talk Moss into turning himself (and the money) in.

5. CONFLICTS ABOUT TAKING ADVANTAGE OF SECOND OPPORTUNITY

    a. Bell has to get his secretary to call Bell's wife <u>after</u> he leaves for Odessa because he knows his wife will not want him to pursue this case

NOTE: This is where Bell states his overall want; he says he repeats this to himself twice daily "Truth and justice, we dedicate ourselves daily and new."

6. BELL GOES FOR IT

    a. Bell goes to Odessa and talks to Moss' wife, Carla. He advises Carla to make it clear to Moss that he has some really bad people after him. He tells Carla about the air gun weapon *(it is at this moment we understand that Bell has figured out the weapon, the exposition comes out in this film as it needs to come out, not before).*

NOTE: As Bell's story unfolds, the horror elements build. Chigurh has killed more people – three men in a motel room (the same motel Moss had initially tried to hide the money). Wells (portrayed by Woody Harrelson) is hired to retrieve the money by the businessmen representing the drug dealers. He knows what he is up against in Chigurh, but again, his ego and arrogance lead him to believe that he can outwit Chigurh. Wells visits Moss in a Mexican hospital and cannot convince Moss that Chigurh is a man who kills for "convenience" and that Chigurh is unstoppable. Again, it is Moss' ego that will not allow him to believe that he cannot outwit or outlast evil. Wells does not last long, he is killed by Chigurh – and Chigurh is back on the hunt for Moss.

7. ALL GOES WELL

a. Bell finds out about the three deaths at the motel. Bell hopes the path to Moss will become clearer.

b. Carla, Moss' wife, calls Bell and tells him that Moss has told her to meet him in El Paso.

8. ALL FALLS APART

a. Bell gets to El Paso motel. Moss is dead (along with others).

b. Bell sees Carla's grief

c. Bell meets with local law enforcement and he is unable to help

d. Bell admits to local law enforcement that he feels Chigurh is like a ghost – barely visible but always there.

e. Bell goes back to the El Paso motel to look at Moss' crime scene, sees that a door's lock has been blown open with an air gun

9. CRISIS

a. Bell has to decide whether or not to enter the motel room, knowing he may be entering a place where pure evil could be lurking

10. CLIMAX

    a. Bell enters the room.

    b. Bell sees his own shadow on the wall

    c. Bell sees blood on the floor

    d. Bell opens the door to the bathroom

NOTE: The audience knows that Chigurh is inside this room - the tension is high.

    e. Bell sees the window is locked.

    f. Bell sits on the bed, sees the grate of the air conditioning duct is off (this has been set up as Moss' hiding place of choice for the suitcase of money).

11. TRUTH COMES OUT

    a. Bell is visiting an old man (Ellis) in a wheelchair back in his hometown. Ellis asks why Bell retired from his sheriff's position. Bell says he quit because he felt <u>over-matched.</u> Bell says he expected God to come into his life – and God did not come into his life. Bell feels God does not have a good opinion of him.

    b. Bell is still struggling with his question about why true evil is in the world. Ellis tells Bell that he "can't stop what's coming… that's vanity, thinking you can."

    c. Chigurh kills Carla – it's a point of honor because he had given the Moss a choice: Give me the money and I'll let your wife live. Moss did not give up the money, thinking he could still outsmart Chigurh – therefore Chigurh has to carry out his threat.

    d. Chigurh is hurt in an automobile accident but again, survives and walks away from the scene

    e. Bell is bored being retired, but also haunted by dreams of death.

LEGALLY BLONDE

2001

screenplay by
Karen McCullah Lutz and Kirsten Smith
Based on novel by Amanda Brown

GENRE: Comedy/Coming-of-Age/Fish-Out-Of-Water

DRAMATIC QUESTION: Will Elle find and accept her own self worth and talents?

THEME: Without believing in yourself, nothing can be accomplished.

ACT ONE sets up the normal life of Elle, a graduating senior and sorority president on the campus of a Southern California university. She has two close girlfriends and they are all a-twitter – they are sure Elle will receive a proposal of marriage on her dinner date that night with her long-time boyfriend, preppy Warner. A shopping expedition ensues, the perfect dress must be found. In the exclusive stores, it becomes clear that Elle is a savvy shopper, knowledgeable about quality in clothes and the latest fashions and that she is much smarter than her blonde and perky looks may lead one to think. These scenes set up Elle, her normal life (she is respected by her friends, gains the respect of the showgirl) and Elle's expectations. The scenes also set up the world and the tone of the film story (comedy).

That evening, on her date with Warner, Elle is stunned. She does not receive a proposal of marriage, she is dumped and told that she would not be acceptable as a wife to an East Coast lawyer with political ambitions - she is more a "Marilyn" than a "Jackie". This scene sets up what will be Elle's driving need for the rest of the film; she wants to get the respect from Warner and Warner's family and Warner's world that she thinks she deserves.

The next day Elle allows the hurt and depression to take over, she spends the day crying and watching soap operas and eating chocolates. This is an important emotional moment; it has to be clear just how deeply Elle wants Warner – enough to enter the fish-out-of-water element of the film story.

Most films that feature the fish-out-of-water genre will have a simple and relatively short Act One. The fun of the genre is gained by showing the protagonist in his or her <u>normal life</u> (one which is safe or familiar, where the protagonist is able to function at a high level or familiar level) so that when put in the fish-out-of-water situation, the audience who now knows the character, can anticipate some of the problems the character will face in circumstances that are not-understandable and unfamiliar.

ACT TWO starts with Elle's second opportunity: She decides she will get accepted into Harvard Law School so she can prove to Warner she deserves more respect. The audience sees a few more areas of Elle's life; her college counselor and her rich parents and the mansion in which Elle grew up. This positioning of information is well-placed, we are now interested in Elle and invested in her pursuit, we have seen how much she was hurt by Warner's rejection and assessment.

> NOTE: There is plenty of room for comedy in this film story. The plot is not intricate; it's very very simple, thus giving writers more time for character comedy moments.

Elle again shows her commitment to her love for Warner by pulling out all the stops to gain entry to Harvard Law School. These sequences are designed to be relatively short; the audience wants to see how Elle manages the impossible, but they are also anticipating her success so they can see her enter the fish-out-of-water conflict to "get her man".

Elle arrives at Harvard and meets the <u>core</u> characters that will make the next part of her life difficult and force her to reassess her definition of herself (the coming of age genre really kicks in). In the next 50 minutes, Elle goes from naïve and trusting – she is used to people liking her – to more realistic and wise. She goes from student-light to student-serious. She goes from not caring about the law to realizing the law's importance.

What keeps us engaged with spoiled and rich Elle? Why do we want her to succeed? Despite her background, Elle is kind, generous and not an elitist. She becomes close friends with a blue-collar manicurist. She stands up for the law school nerd. She <u>looks</u> like the typical self-centered socialite, but she does not act like one. In contrast to her Harvard Law peers, she is more humane, vulnerable and caring.

When Elle is faced with her crisis decision – whether or not to continue her law school internship after her mentor makes sexual advances – the audience has seen a transformation in Elle. Her decision could go either way, which decision will gain her the most respect?

ACT THREE is relatively short because the coming-of-age moment is clear when the audience knows of Elle's crisis decision. The fish-out-of-water genre is satisfied, it's clear Elle can now maneuver in her new world. Therefore, the <u>plot</u> is the only thing left to flesh out. Essentially, Elle's character arc is over. Act Three leaves room (but not a lot) to show a new Elle; she has impressed others with her growth, and proved she is very capable and not just "blonde" and has found a new self-respect.

ELEVEN STEP BREAKDOWN AND NOTES

1. ELLE WANTS respect. WHY? She has never felt disrespect; she has always felt good about herself.

2. ELLE LOGICALLY TRIES TO GET RESPECT

    a. Elle is obviously respected on campus in Southern California. She has good friends and she is the president of her sorority.

    b. Elle gains respect of the shop girl when she makes it clear she will not be taken advantage of in the clothing store.

    c. Elle dresses for respect when she goes on the date with Warner where she expects a marriage proposal.

3. ELLE IS DENIED RESPECT

    a. Warner tells her she's not "good enough" to be his wife because he comes from a family that has a history of entering politics and she would not fit into that world because she is "a Marilyn", not a "Jackie".

4. ELLE"S SECOND OPPORTUNITY TO GAIN RESPECT

    a. Elle sees in a magazine that Warner's brother is marrying a law student. She decides to apply to Harvard Law School so she will be "good enough" for Warner and his family.

5. ELLE'S CONFLICT IN TAKING ADVANTAGE OF THIS SECOND OPPORTUNITY

    a. Elle's parents try to talk her out of it

b. Elle's college counselor discourages her

c. Elle would have to leave her West Coast friends

d. Elle has to study hard for the Law School entrance exams, make a video interview and impress the Harvard acceptance committee.

6. ELLE GOES FOR IT

a. Makes the application video

b. Elle takes practice test after practice test and finally scores well.

7. ALL GOES WELL

a. Elle gets accepted to Harvard Law School

b. Elle arrives at Harvard and gets herself set up

c. fact that she is surprised and Elle thinks she's gained his respect. She makes a date to see Warner after her first class.

8. ALL FALLS APART

a. Elle's female professor (portrayed by Holland Taylor) picks on Elle (disrespects her) and asks Elle to leave the class because Elle is not properly prepared

b. Warner meets up with Elle, with his fiancé. Elle is devastated and feels disrespected by Warner and his fiancé.

c. Elle is denied membership in study groups, feels disrespected.

d. When finally asked to a law school party, she is told it's a costume party and shows up in a Playboy Bunny outfit. She is frustrated that she was so disrespected and made to look like a fool.

NOTE: Because it's a comedy, Elle never loses hope; she always has a comeback and always pulls herself out of her doldrums.

e. MIDPOINT: Elle does a major shift. She decides she will stop focusing on getting Warner through social means and decides to become super student to gain the respect of all her peers. Elle gets her computer; she meets a law school graduate (portrayed by Luke Wilson) and stops focusing on Warner. She gets one of the coveted internships at the law firm of Callahan (portrayed by Victor Garber), he becomes her mentor. She becomes friends with Warner's fiancé; she feels a sense of respect and acceptance.

f. Callahan doesn't take Elle seriously and her contributions and thoughts on the case are not respected.

g. Callahan finally does admit that Elle's contributions may be valid and then makes a sexual advance. Elle feels disrespected and is forced to doubt that he ever thought her work was valid.

h. Warner's fiancé withdraws her respect because she thinks that Elle is having an affair with the professor and that's why Elle is getting a chance to work on the case.

9. CRISIS

a. Elle doubts herself; is she really smart and respected or are people responding to her because she's blonde and beautiful? Should she go home and forget about law school? Should she give up? The climax reveals Elle's decision.

10. CLIMAX

a. Elle takes the lead position on the case in court and puts Callahan in his place

b. Elle finds a discrepancy in the testimony.

c. Elle gets the truth out of the witness and wins in the case for her client.

d. Elle tells Warner she doesn't want him anymore

NOTE: The how Elle solves the case remains in the comedy arena and also true to the theme; her breaking down of the testimony directly relates to her "blonde-ness" and knowledge of beauty treatments.

11. TRUTH COMES OUT

a. Elle graduates with honors

b. Elle has new friends

c. Elle has a new love

d. Elle has self-respect.

IRON GIANT

1999

book by Ted Hughes
screen story by Brad Bird
screenplay by Tim McCanlies

GENRE: Drama/Coming-of-Age/Sci Fi

DRAMATIC QUESTION: Will Hogarth be able to save his good friend, a gentle iron giant, from destruction?

THEME: Without questioning those in power, one can never accomplish the impossible.

ACT ONE: Hogarth, age 9, is an outcast at school and desperately wants the chance to have a real friend. He even tries to cage a squirrel to force the squirrel to be his friend. Act One introduces Hogarth and his loneliness. It also introduces Hogarth's single mom, a waitress who works long shifts, and her potential love interest, an odd scrap yard artist named Dean. Hogarth's squirrel does not want to be caged and at the end of Act One, Hogarth is friendless and alone at home.

ACTS TWO and THREE: What if a gun had a soul? A gigantic mobile weapon from another planet is sent to destroy Earth, but is damaged on arrival and loses its memory. This is the gentle Iron Giant. It is befriended Hogarth. Hogarth needs to keep the knowledge of Iron Giant's presence from the community for fear they might not understand he's a gentle giant. Soon the paranoid government agent Kent Mansley arrives in town and to pump up his own reputation, he is determined to destroy the giant at all costs.

Hogarth and the Iron Giant do all they can to survive, but miscommunication, ego and arrogance bring about near-tragic results.

ELEVEN STEP BREAKDOWN AND NOTES

1. HOGARTH WANTS companionship. Specifically, a pet. **WHY?** Hogarth (voiced by Eli Marienthal) is an only child and his mom (voiced by Jennifer Aniston) works night as a waitress. Hogarth and his mom live out in the country and Hogarth is lonely.

2. HOGARTH LOGICALLY TRIES TO ACCOMPLISH HIS DESIRE

    a. Hogarth adopts a little squirrel in hopes the squirrel will be his friend.

3. HOGARTH IS DENIED

    a. The Squirrel runs off.

NOTE: See how simple it is? The rest of the time in Act One is spent working on the illumination of character. The squirrel is used to bring Hogarth and scrap yard artist Dean (voiced by Harry Connick Jr.) together.

4. SECOND OPPORTUNITY FOR HOGARTH TO HAVE COMPANIONSHIP-

    a. Hogarth is watching scary movies alone at home and hears a noise. He goes out to investigate. He sees the Iron Giant and saves him from electrocution.

NOTE: We have caught a glimpse of the IRON GIANT at the top of the movie: so the audience is primed and ready for him to be part of the story.

5. CONFLICTS FOR HOGARTH ON TAKING ADVANTAGE OF THIS OPPORTUNITY

    a. Hogarth has to lie to his mom about the existence of the Iron Giant

    b. Hogarth has to hide his new friend, the Iron Giant, from everyone

    c. Iron Giant is noisy, hungry.

    d. Iron Giant has been spotted and Hogarth is anxious and the Iron Giant's future.

6. HOGARTH GOES FOR IT

a.   Hogarth puts Iron Giant in the barn; it's clear that Hogarth's decided to keep him.

7. ALL GOES WELL FOR HOGARTH, HE HAS A FRIEND

a.   Decides to bring Iron Giant to Dean's scrap yard

8. ALL FALLS APART

a.   The government agent, Kent Mansley (voiced by Christopher McDonald) moves into Hogarth's house. He's heard of the Iron Giant and resolves to "take it out".

b.   Dean can't keep Iron Giant; he is eating all of Dean's scrap iron.

c.   Iron Giant, wanting to have fun, jumps into lake and accidentally makes his presence is clear again

d.   Mansley is getting closer to finding the Iron Giant.

e.   Iron Giant witnesses a gun fired and its bullet kill a deer. He learns that guns can kill

f.   Mansley suspects Hogarth. Mansley locks Hogarth in barn and interrogates him

g.   The army arrives in town, all intent on taking out the Iron Giant.

h.   Dean figures out Iron Giant is a walking huge gun made by government and that – essentially – the Iron Giant is a bomb

i.   Iron Giant saves kids from a destroyed building but the Iron Giant spotted by the government agents

j.   The town and Hogarth's mother now supports the Iron Giant but Hogarth realizes it is too late to keep the Iron Giant safe

k.   Hogarth sees the army shoot at the Iron Giant

l.   Mansley lies, saying Iron Giant is dangerous

m. Iron Giant and Hogarth fly into the air when the Iron Giant is forced to protect Hogarth

n. Big battle in the sky

o. Iron Giant thinks Hogarth is dead. The Iron Giant, distraught, turns into huge weapon

9. CRISIS

a. Dean is going to take Hogarth to the hospital but Hogarth decides to stay to protect Iron Giant.

b. Iron Giant, angry and scared, is about to set off the bomb that is part of him. Hogarth says "You are who you choose to be."

10. CLIMAX

a. Hogarth realizes Mansley has set off a bomb and it's heading towards Iron Giant

b. Iron Giant flies up into the sky and "eats" the missile – and saves the day.

11. TRUTH COMES OUT

a. Dean and Hogarth's mom have fallen in love

b. Hogarth gets a "real" family

CHINATOWN

1974

written by Robert Towne

GENRE: Drama/crime/mystery/tragedy (This film is sometimes referred to as an example of "neo-noir".)

DRAMATIC QUESTION: Will Jake Gittes find out the truth about the Southern California water scandal and be able to bring the guilty parties to justice?

THEME: Without truth there can be no justice

ACT ONE: Sets up the protagonist, everyman Jake Gittes. Jake (portrayed by Jack Nicholson) is an ex-cop, now he is a private investigator in Los Angeles, California. The circumstances that caused him to leave the police force are never clearly stated, all the audience knows is that, in the past, an injustice was never settled (perhaps covered up?) in Los Angeles' Chinatown district. Jake is good at his private investigator job, he has clients. When Jake takes on a new client, a woman claiming she is Evelyn Mulwray, wife of powerful Hollis Mulwray (in charge of the Water Department) in Los Angeles, wants Jake to obtain proof that her husband is having an affair. Jake does the job, and he is successful. When it's revealed that this woman was impersonating the real Mrs. Mulwray, Jake's life takes a sharp turn. The respect and pride he felt in his recent success is taken away from him. Jake realizes he was duped, that the <u>real</u> Mrs. Mulwray (portrayed by Faye Dunaway) is now planning to sue him for claiming she was his client and digging up her husband's "affair".

ACT TWO: Jake is determined to find out who played him for a fool and why. The <u>mystery</u> genre is supported with the <u>clues</u> that Jake unearths about a water scandal, a murder and parentage of a young girl. The romance genre is introduced, quickly taken through its steps and dropped; the crime/mystery genres are paramount. When Jake finds out the most shocking truth about the participants in this mystery, Jake has to make a choice: do what is best for him to retain respect in the community, or settle for self-respect by doing the right thing.

ACT THREE: Jake chooses self-respect (not wanting to create a circumstance that harkens back to the mysterious goings-on in Chinatown in his past) and tragic results occur. The bleak reality of power and money being able to buy men's souls makes the story of Chinatown resonate since its first showing.

ELEVEN STEP BREAKDOWN AND NOTES

1. JAKE GITTES WANTS respect. WHY? Jake has an experience in his past (in Chinatown) where he lost self-respect. He is now building that back up and he wants all to know that he is honest and is above being bought. Jake wants "right" to win.

2. JAKE LOGICALLY GOES ABOUT GETTING RESPECT

   a. Jake dresses nicely

   b. Jake has nice offices

   c. Jake advises a client not to beat his wife because she is having an affair, he says "if you love her, let it blow over."

   d. Jake takes on case of Mrs. Mulwray, she wants her husband's affair with a young woman exposed. Jake does his job "well". He finds out about Hollis Mulwray and the Southern California water situation.

   e. Jake does his good job; he follows Mulwray and takes pictures of him with a young woman. The pictures "somehow" get into the newspapers.

   f. Jake defends his profession in barbershop claiming that he is a legitimate businessman who does a service to his clients.

3. JAKE IS DENIED A FEELING OF BEING RESPECTED

   a. Jake realizes he been set up when the real Mrs. Mulwray reveals herself and tells him she is going to sue him. Jake is made to look like a fool and this does not make Jake feel respected.

4. JAKE HAS SECOND OPPORTUNITY TO GAIN RESPECT

a. Jake decides to investigate why he was the one chosen to be made to look like a fool

5. JAKE'S CONFLICTS ABOUT TAKING ADVANTAGE OF THE SECOND OPPORTUNITY

a. Jake doesn't know who he can trust

b. Jake is not getting straight answers to any of his questions.

6. JAKE GOES FOR IT

a. Jake starts investigating

7. ALL GOES WELL; JAKE IS GETTING CLOSER TO GETTING THE RESPECT HE DESIRES

a. Jake gets information from RussYelburton, one of the head people at the water department, regarding the dispute between the orchard-growers who need to irrigate their fields and those involved in the water department who want to build a dam that would divert water to other places

b. Jake finds out a crooked ex-sheriff is working for water department; things look more fishy

c. Mrs. Mulwray tells Jake she is dropping her lawsuit against him. Jake wonders why and considers this another clue as the case gets more complex

d. Jake finds Hollis Mulwray murdered at the reservoir

e. Mrs. Mulwray hires Jake to find out who killed her husband

f. Jake gets a major clue at the morgue; a bum was found dead at the dry reservoir, but there was salt water in his lungs

g. A young boy on horse tells Jake that water comes through the reservoir only at night

h. Jake sees water gush through the reservoir at night. The clues adding up.

i. Jake is attacked at the reservoir and his nose is cut. This makes him realize he is getting closer to the truth.

j. Jake finds out that Mrs. Mulwray's father, Noah Cross, and

Hollis Mulwray used to own the water department together. Mulwray wanted the water to be publicly owned, Cross wanted it to be a for-profit business. A huge rift ensued. Jake gets Yelburton to tell him about the nightly diversion of water.

k. Noah Cross wants to hire Jake – to find the girl that Mulwray had been having the 'affair" with. Jake wonders why, but knows that he is getting closer to the heart of the mystery.

l. Jake gets clues from the library

m. Jake gets beat up in orange grove

n. Jake gets a clue that leads him to the old folks home, Jake knows the clues are getting him closer to the truth. Jake barely misses getting beat up again but Mrs. Mulwray comes to his rescue and drives him off

o. Jake goes to bed with Mrs. Mulwray

p. Jake follows Mrs. Mulwray after she gets a mysterious phone call

q. Mrs. Mulwray covers (lies) about the identity of the young girl (the one Jake thought was having an affair his Hollis Mulwray) and Jake believes her

r. Ida Sessions, the woman who pretended to be Mrs. Mulwray at the beginning of the story, is found dead. Detective Escobar wants to know Jake's involvement in the case and begins to keep tabs on Jake

8. ALL FALLS APART FOR JAKE

a. Jake wants to get Escobar to see the bigger picture in the case. He leads Escobar to water runoff site. The water does not flush into the dry area that night. Jake looks like a fool (obviously does not get respect).

b. Yelburton's men deny telling Jake about the runoff. Jake is made to look like a fool again. Escobar tells Jake to have Mrs. Mulwray in Escobar's office because Escobar suspects her of murdering her husband

c. Jake goes to the Mulwray mansion to get Mrs. Mulwray but she has skipped. Jake is incensed, she has caused him to look like a fool again

    d. Jake finds Hollis Mulwray's eyeglasses in the saltwater pond at the Mulwray house. Jake realizes Hollis Mulwray was killed here and he suspects Mrs. Mulwray is responsible.

    e. Jake finds Mrs. Mulwray at her butler's house and accuses her of lying to him and playing him for a fool. Mrs. Mulwray finally tells the truth, that she is both "mother" and "sister" to the girl because she got pregnant after her father, Noah Cross, raped her.

9. CRISIS

    a. Jake realizes the complexity of the problem and the complex and history of those involved. He knows he'll be in trouble with Escobar for not delivering Mrs. Mulwray.

    b. Jake makes his decision to do "the right thing" and lies to Escobar so he can help Mrs. Mulwray escape with her daughter/ sister and not have to be under the thumb of her father

10. CLIMAX

    a. Escobar doesn't trust Jake. Jake drives to San Pedro and hopes to ditch Escobar.

    b. Jake tries to mastermind the escape for Mrs. Mulwray and tells Cross a lie Jake realizes Cross killed Mulwray and now wonders how he can prove it

    c. Cross has crooked ex-sheriff put gun to Jake's head and demands to be taken to the young girl

    d. In Chinatown, Jake's workers are handcuffed by Escobar and his men.

    e. Mrs. Mulwray tries to escape with her daughter

    f. Noah Cross barks orders to stop Mrs. Mulwray and his granddaughter/daughter from escaping

    g. Bullets are fired

    h. Jake has to witness Mrs. Mulwray being killed

11. TRUTH

    a. Noah Cross takes the young girl (his granddaughter/daughter)

    b. Jake is told this is "Chinatown" – where bad things happen

    c. Money wins out and injustice is served

ROSEMARY'S BABY

1968

written by Roman Polanski
based on novel by Ira Levin

GENRE: Drama/horror/mystery/psychological thriller

DRAMATIC QUESTION: Will Rosemary survive her pregnancy and decide to bring her baby into the world?

THEME: Without a strong self of sense, one can lose one's soul.

ACT ONE: The normal life of the protagonist is introduced. Young married couple; "every woman" Rosemary (portrayed by Mia Farrow) and Guy (portrayed by John Cassavetes) are with a real estate agent, looking for a New York City apartment. The agent shows them an apartment in a Gothic style building on NYC's Upper West Side. The previous tenant had been an aged woman who fell into a coma and died.

It becomes clear Rosemary wants the perfect life. For Rosemary, that means a love-filled marriage, a great home and children.

The horror/thriller aspect of the film story begins right away. The apartment building and is large, cavernous and dark. There are strange clues left behind in the apartment by the previous tenant. Her best friend thinks something could be wrong in the building. Rosemary is too trusting, optimistic and eager to please to take any of these negatives seriously. When Rosemary is drugged and thinks she "hallucinates" being raped by a devilish monster, the audience is steps ahead of her. The audience knows (not all the details and they are anxious to know them) that evil is afoot and begins to root for Rosemary to quickly come to the same conclusion.

ACTS TWO and THREE illuminate the evil intent around the sick and pale Rosemary who only wants to do what is best for the baby inside her womb. Rosemary is trying to do the right thing and finds herself caught in an evil web because of her belief in the goodness of people.

NOTE: Rosemary is in almost 100% of the scenes of this film.

ELEVEN STEP BREAKDOWN AND NOTES

1. ROSEMARY WANTS the perfect life. **WHY?** She seems to be the typical upper-class young woman used to good things. She has desires that focus on creating a good home for her husband and hoped-for-children Because Rosemary is <u>typical</u>, she is a true drama heroine (an ordinary person put in extraordinary circumstances.)

2. **ROSEMARY LOGICALLY GOES FOR ATTAINMENT OF HER PERFECT LIFE**

   a. Rosemary gets her husband Guy to look at new apartments

   b. Rosemary convinces Guy to take this "perfect" apartment

   c. Rosemary makes love with Guy to please him and in hopes of getting pregnant

   d. Rosemary fixes up apartment

   e. Rosemary makes friends with girl in apartment building in the laundry room

   f. Rosemary comforts Guy when he doesn't get the part he covets in the Broadway play

   g. Rosemary tries to get out of an invitation to dinner at older neighbors, Minnie and Roman Castavet, knowing Guy won't want to spend time with them. (Rosemary is not able to dodge the invitation)

   h. Rosemary thanks Guy for having dinner with the Castavets and Guy mentions that he actually had a good time

   i. Rosemary talks about having babies

   j. Rosemary is proud of her husband being on a TV commercial

   k. Rosemary takes charm (meant to help her get pregnant) from Minnie to be "nice" but puts it away because the smell of the tannis root bothers her

   l. Rosemary tries to make her husband happy by eating the dessert that neighbor Minnie sent over.

m. Rosemary gets pregnant.

NOTE: While all these logical things are happening – the clues that make up the mystery genre are set in: a letter from a previous tenant, a door that is blocked by a big piece of furniture. Also Rosemary's friend, Hutch tells them of the building's scary history (a man supposedly conjured up the devil and got killed in the lobby), the weird charms, a girl's suicide, Guy passionately wanting Rosemary to eat a dessert she does not want and then Rosemary's hallucination of having sex with the Devil.

3. ROSEMARY IS DENIED HER SENSE OF HER PERFECT LIFE

a. Rosemary is upset that Guy admits to having sex with her when she was passed out after eating a large dinner and topping it off with the dessert Guy forced her to consume.

b. The pregnancy is causing Rosemary pain.

4. ROSEMARY'S SECOND OPPORTUNITY TO GET HER PERFECT LIFE

a. Roman and Minnie arrange for Rosemary to see a "fancy" doctor - a well known doctor who takes care of many of New York City's high society expectant mothers

b. Guy finds out that he has gotten the role her coveted in the Broadway play because the originally cast actor suddenly became blind

5. CONFLICTS ABOUT TAKING ADVANTAGE OF HER SECOND OPPORTUNITY

a. Rosemary was happy with her regular doctor but Guy seems insistent

b. Rosemary wants to make Guy happy to maintain what she considers the perfect marriage.

6. ROSEMARY GOES FOR IT

NOTE: Remember, this is a horror film so the protagonist is choosing to go down the path that will put her deeper into the circumstances of horror.

a. Rosemary lets Guy lie and tell her regular doctor that they have moved to California and that's why Rosemary will no longer be his patient.

7. ALL GOES WELL FOR ROSEMARY

a. Rosemary trusts well-known Dr. Sapirstein and starts to do as he says. She allows Minnie to give her a drink every day and she wears the smelly charm and she begins to feel better.

8. ALL FALLS APART FOR ROSEMARY

a. Rosemary starts to feel greater pain from the pregnancy.

b. Rosemary loses weight

c. Guy is avoiding Rosemary, does not want to sleep with her.

d. Rosemary gets a haircut. Guy doesn't like it.

e. Rosemary starts to crave raw beef.

f. Hutch, Rosemary's friend, comes over and tells her she looks sick

g. Roman and Minnie are invading Rosemary's life; she feels stifled

h. Rosemary notices Roman's pierced ear

i. Roman and Hutch square off and argue; Rosemary feels in the middle

NOTE: This is where Roman steals one of Hutch's gloves so he can put a spell in Hutch and put him in coma- another mystery clue.

j. Hutch falls sick and fails to meet Rosemary at an appointed time

k. Rosemary eats raw liver. When she realizes what she is doing, she freaks out.

l. Rosemary plans a party for old friends. These friends notice how ill she looks and counsel her that she shouldn't be in such pain from a pregnancy

m. Rosemary wants to switch doctors and Guy gets angry with her

n. Suddenly the pain stops. Rosemary feels baby move. She never switches doctors.

p. Rosemary packs for the hospital (*Note: Time passage here, three weeks left before the birth*)

q. Rosemary gets a phone call that Hutch has died. He has left her a book. The book is about witches. Rosemary recognizes the faces of the witches - they are the faces of her neighbors in her apartment building. Rosemary wonders what this can mean, Hutch leaves her a clue to figure out - an anagram. (*More mystery*)

r. Rosemary uses Scrabble game tiles to help her figure out the anagram.

s. Rosemary realizes Guy is against her, he's thrown out Hutch's book.

t. Rosemary throws out the smelly charm necklace

u. Rosemary goes to Dr. Sapirstein, hoping he will help her. Rosemary realizes he is one of the witches

9. CRISIS

a. Rosemary races out of Dr. Saperstein's' office. She <u>decides</u> to call her original doctor – Dr. Hill. Rosemary asks him to help her, to be her doctor once again. He tells her to come over.

10. CLIMAX

a. Rosemary thinks she's safe with Dr. Hill. He listens to her story and makes her feel as if he believes her.

b. Dr. Hill calls Dr. Sapirstein and Guy to come get her. Dr. Hill thinks she is unbalanced because of the stress of her pregnancy.

c. Rosemary races off from Guy and Dr. Sapirstein and they chase her through the dark and cavernous apartment building.

d. Guy and Dr. Sapirstein catch Rosemary. They give her a sedative.

e. Rosemary goes into labor and has the baby

f. Rosemary, post birth, is told the baby has died

g. Rosemary grieves. But then, days later, she hears the cry of a baby.

h. Rosemary hides her medication so she will be able to get out of bed

i. Rosemary opens the closet (that now is a door) and enters Roman and Minnie's apartment

j. Rosemary sees the witches gathered around a baby's crib

k. Rosemary sees her baby. Her baby has the eyes of a devil

11. TRUTH THAT COMES OUT

a. Rosemary realizes her child is the devil's child and that she was used by this coven of witches as a vessel to bring this evil into the world

b. Rosemary realizes that Guy "sold" her for his own fame and fortune.

c. Rosemary is freaking out and is about to go - but ultimately, can't deny motherly love. She wants to "be the mother" - and – at the end of the film, Rosemary asks to hold her baby

d. The witches herald Rosemary as the "mother" of the coven's future

* In most horror films, evil wins. That's why horror films are so ripe for sequels.

CASABLANCA

1942

written by Phillip and Julius Epstein and Howard Koch
based on play *"Everybody Comes to Rick's"*
by Murray Burnett and Joan Allison

GENRE: Drama/War/Romance

DRAMATIC QUESTION: Will Rick come to understand and accept why Ilsa left him in Paris and will he become an active part of his own life again?

THEME: Without coming to grips with the past, one cannot move forward.

ACT ONE: The story opens with a voiceover, giving the audience the knowledge they need about the state of the world at the time World War II is raging; refugees are fleeing war-torn Europe to come to Africa where they hope to find flights to Portugal, a country from which they can find passage to freedom and safety in the New World. One of the routes is through Casablanca in French Morocco in North Africa. The Germans are present in the Casablanca but they do not officially occupy it.

The PLOT kicks in right away; two German couriers have been murdered and the visas (letters of transit) they had been carrying have been stolen. These letters of transit would allow two refugees to gain passage to Portugal; the letters of transit are very special, they are non-rescindable and signed by Charles DeGaulle. The letters of transit could be sold for a very high price.

The Germans are pressuring all as they try to control the city of Casablanca. The local police force, led by Inspector Renault (portrayed by Claude Rains) is cooperating with the Germans. There is an Allied Underground fighting against the Germans.

The city is tense; the streets are filled with pickpockets and desperate people trying to sell anything to be able to pay for favors that could lead to their passage to freedom.

The one haven in the city is RICK'S CAFE. All are welcome; Germans, French, refugees and locals. The owner, Rick (portrayed by Humphrey Bogart), has a reputation for being neutral, for not taking sides in the war. He does not mix with customers. He's a loner and has cut himself off from all emotions.

This film stands out because Rick, the protagonist, does not appear for the first ten minutes of the film, but he is the topic of many conversations. Once introduced, Rick's normal life is quickly set up. He's American-born, arrived in Casablanca from Europe and has no allegiances." *I don't stick my neck out for nobody…*" is his favorite phrase. The inciting incident breaks Rick's habit of neutrality - a criminal and one of Rick's customers, Ugarte (portrayed by Peter Lorre), asks Rick to hide the stolen letters of transit and Rick, knowing of their importance and value, agrees. The Germans storm Rick's Café and arrest Ugarte. No one knows that Rick now holds the letters of transit in a secret place.

Once the PLOT is laid out, the film becomes all about characters - their wants/needs/fears/goals. In ACT TWO, the romance genre takes over the film story when Rick's past love, Ilsa (portrayed by Ingrid Bergman), walks back into Rick's life. Ilsa broke Rick's heart, jilted him in Paris, and he has never recovered. It is now this romance that forces Rick's change – from cold and uncommitted to a man now ready to engage in the world and in the fight against the enemy.

ELEVEN STEP BREAKDOWN AND NOTES

This film is a good example of a character that thinks he wants one thing, but the audience knows he <u>needs</u> something else to bring about a beneficial change.

1. RICK BLAINE (portrayed by Humphrey Bogart) **WANTS** to not get emotionally involved in life. WHY? He feels he was jilted in a love affair and made to look like a foolish romantic. ***BUT WHAT RICK REALLY <u>NEEDS</u> IS TO RE-CONNECT WITH LIFE.***

2. RICK LOGICALLY GOES FOR WHAT HE <u>THINKS</u> HE WANTS

   a. Rick stays by himself

   b. Rick makes it clear to a local woman who wants a relationship with him that she means nothing to him

c. Rick not swayed by pressure from the Germans to join their side

d. Rick is not swayed by the French police captain to show allegiance to his side

e. Rick does not drink with the customers

f. Rick does not "save" Ugarte from arrest

3. RICK IS DENIED HIS DISCONNECTION

a. Sam, Rick's only close friend, plays a song on the piano that brings back painful memories for Rick

b. Rick sees Ilsa, the woman who broke his heart, years ago, in Paris

c. Ilsa is with Laszlo, a Resistance leader, a man Rick respects

d. Rick, his deep hurt surfacing, gets drunk -

FLASHBACK: PARIS. IT IS NECESSARY FOR THE AUDIENCE TO SEE THIS GREAT LOVE AFFAIR AND THE KIND OF MAN RICK USED TO BE: HE WAS WARM, GENEROUS, COMMITTED TO TAKING SIDES IN THE WAR EFFORT, HE WAS CAPABLE OF GREAT LOVE. We find out that Ilsa, during the time of the flashback, thinks the "the man in her life" is dead and that she is free to fall in love with Rick.

e. Back to the present in the film: When Ilsa comes to the café late that night to explain her actions, Rick insults her, accusing Ilsa of lying to him, of sleeping with a lot of men and pretending that Rick had been special to her. Angry and frustrated, Ilsa walks out of the café.

f. Rick finds out the next day that Ilsa is married to Laszlo

g. Ilsa won't forgive Rick for his insults the previous evening

h. Rick's Café is ransacked by Captain Renault's men who are looking for the letters of transit. It's getting more difficult for Rick not to take sides in the war.

4. SECOND OPPORTUNITY FOR RICK TO GET WHAT HE NEEDS

NOTE: In a film with this structure, this is usually where the NEED takes over from the WANT.

    a. Ilsa lets Rick know the truth about why she left him in Paris. He starts to understand that she did (does) care for him. Ilsa's situation is complicated because of her husband, Laszlo, and his commitment to anti-German activity. She doesn't want to hinder Laszlo's work.

    b. Rick wants Ilsa back, and it's clear to him that she wants to be with him also.

5. CONFLICTS FOR RICK TAKING ADVANTAGE OF THE SECOND OPPORTUNITY

    a. Rick respects Ilsa's husband, Laszlo, and his leadership in the Resistance

    b. It would be dangerous for Ilsa to stay in Casablanca with Rick

    c. The Germans are getting more aggressive as the war heats up

6. RICK GOES FOR WHAT HE NEEDS: CONNECTION

    a. Rick helps a young Bulgarian couple (lets them win at the roulette table) so they can get passage to Portugal without the young woman having to sleep with Captain Renault. Her story makes him understand Ilsa more (all elements of the film story work to help illuminate the story of Rick and Ilsa).

(NOTE: This is an example of writing a scene that REFLECTS on the story and allows us see the change in Rick, but not in an "on the nose" way.)

7. ALL GOES WELL: RICK IS STARTING TO CONNECT

    a. Rick's employees have seen Rick do a good thing for the young Bulgarian couple and rejoice that he has taken a side against Renault's sexual harassment of a young woman.

    b. Rick and Renault begin to talk politics - Renault assumes Rick is as greedy and out for himself as Renault is, but Rick is really talking to gain information.

    c. The Germans sing their national song in Rick's Café and Rick allows Laszlo to lead others in the French national song.

d. Laszlo comes to Rick to ask for the letters of transit. Rick says no. He says if you want to know why – ask your wife. Rick knows that by saying this, Ilsa will come to see him again and Rick also hopes to force Ilsa to make a choice between the two men.

e. Ilsa heads to Rick's Cafe when Laszlo goes to underground meeting.

f. Rick tells his maitre'd not to tell him where he is going (but Rick knows he is going to underground meeting)

g. Ilsa asks Rick to give Laszlo the letters of transit. Rick says no. Ilsa calls Rick on his selfishness and his cowardice. She pulls a gun on him because she wants to help save her husband. Rick still won't give her papers. Ilsa breaks down and declares her love for Rick. The complete story of why Ilsa left Rick in Paris comes out; she had thought Laszlo was dead and just before she was to meet Rick to exit Paris, she found out that Laszlo was alive and injured – and needed her. She didn't send word to Rick because she thought Rick might come after her – and that would put Rick in danger of being arrested.

h. Ilsa admits her deep love for Rick and of her fears that she can never leave Rick again.

8. ALL FALLS APART

a. Rick struggles – should he believe Ilsa?

b. The German general wants Rick's Café closed. Renault closes café.

c. Rick finally sees he is being forced to take sides in the war – and in love. Neutrality is no longer possible.

9. CRISIS

a. Ilsa says Rick must do the thinking for both of them. Rick now has a decision to make: Should he do all he can to ensure he gets to be with the woman he loves or to support the Resistance against the Germans?

10.CLIMAX

a. Laszlo comes to Rick's Café, injured. Ilsa is still upstairs. Rick tells his maitre'd to take Ilsa home without Laszlo seeing her.

b. Laszlo tells Rick he knows that Rick is in love with Ilsa. Selfless, wanting Ilsa to be safe, Laszlo tells Rick to use the letters of transit to take Rick and Ilsa out of Casablanca.

c. Rick tells Renault he is using the transit papers for himself and Ilsa - that Rick doesn't care about Laszlo's fate. Rick makes Renault think that Rick will set Laszlo up so Renault can arrest Laszlo and put him in a concentration camp.

d. Renault buys Rick's plan and comments that Rick has fewer scruples than he does.

e. Rick plays the set up for the arrest of Laszlo. At the final moment, Rick pulls a gun on Renault and forces Renault to call the airport so that Laszlo and Ilsa can fly out on the plane without trouble.

f. Renault double-crosses Rick and calls the German general

g. At the airport, Rick tells Renault to fill in the names on the letters of transit; write Laszlo and his wife. His actions surprise Ilsa, she thought that Rick had decided that Rick and Ilsa should be together.

h. Laszlo, understanding that Rick has finally taken sides in the war, says, "*Welcome back to the fight.*"

i. Laszlo and Ilsa head to the plane.

j. The German general and his men show up to stop Laszlo's exit.

k. Rick shoots the Germans

l. The plane takes off with Laszlo and Ilsa on board

m. The French police show up, Rick faces arrest

n. Renault makes his decision, and decides to back Rick. Renault does not tell the French police that Rick shot the Germans.

11. TRUTH COMES OUT FOR RICK

a. It is clear Rick has decided to take sides in the war, that the fate of the world takes precedence, for him, over his personal happiness. He has re-connected with life.

b. Rick is joined by Renault, *"Louis, I think this is the beginning of a beautiful friendship…"* and the two walk off into the fog. It's clear they will be joining the Resistance fighters against the Germans.

SCENARIOS YOU MAY ENCOUNTER AS YOU TAKE YOUR SCRIPT INTO THE MARKETPLACE

Here are a few scenarios of situations you may experience when you take your script into the marketplace, followed by questions that may arise.

Scenario: You have written a killer spec script and an agent is excited to send it out into the marketplace. The script goes out, there is interest but no studio or production company steps up to buy or even option your script. That's the bad news. The good news? Many executives and producers now want to take "a meeting" with you.

Question: If the film production companies think my spec script is great, why don't they want to buy it and produce it?

Answer: First of all, keep your eye on the positive. They think your script shows talent. They want to meet you. Film executives may read twenty or more scripts a week and only request to meet one writer. The "meeting" is an important part of a successful screenwriting career.

Okay, it's still frustrating. Let's investigate possible reasons the production entity is not buying your script and putting it right into production.

1. Budget. One reason could be the price of producing your film. Each production company is looking to fill a niche. Each company has a businessperson who has done all the mathematical calculations necessary to determine what financial plan is the most fail-safe for the goals of the company. Many production companies will have decided to only produce films that cost over 50 million dollars - or over 100 million dollars. Or films that cost 10 million or less. Or films that could be made for 2 million dollars or less or any other dollar amount decided upon by the production company. Some studios will only do films that can open wide (in thousands of theatres) and their business people tend to think that means the film should be wildly expensive and use only top box-office actors and high production values. Other companies will target the small art houses and hope for a word-of-mouth hit. If your film does not feel big-budget-enough or low-budget-enough or medium-budget-enough, a company may pass on the purchase of your script. However, they are interested in you as a writer. Producers and development executives will only take a meeting if they think that at some point in the future they would consider being in business with you.

2. Another reason a film company can "love" your script but not want to produce it? Actor availability. There is a group of "bankable" actors. These are actors that ensure a film will attract a certain audience base. This group is always changing, but some of the actors that may be in the group are Matt Damon, George Clooney, Clive Owens, Cameron Diaz, Julia Roberts, Meryl Streep, Tobey McGuire, Jake Gyllenhaal, Scarlet Johanneson, Reese Witherspoon and a few others. Having a bankable actor can make the production company feel a level of confidence that reviewers and audience will pay attention to the film when it is released. Of course if the film does not work, not even a great or famous actor can ensure a huge take at the box office, but the chances of recouping an investment is greater with a "name" actor attached to the film. So, if your script, no matter how fabulous, isn't constructed to attract talent of a certain caliber, its purchase might not be pursued. Yes, some name actors will lower their fees if they love a project or want to work with a certain director, but these projects tend to be put together through personal relationships. Talent agents rarely encourage their "stars" to do low-budget films because the agency takes ten percent of the paycheck. Ten percent of a small paycheck does not pay the company's rent or agents' salaries. There has to be a great deal of trust that the project will be well managed and artistically solid for an actor to commit to two or three month of their year. Remember, actors are professionals, take pride in their projects and have to think of their own future in the marketplace.

3. Another reason a film company may decide not to produce your spec script even though they say it's the best thing they've read for eons? It's not a film story they have been invested in since its inception. Studios and production companies have projects in development. This means they have already paid money for the writing or rewriting of projects they hope will eventually make it down the production pipeline. An executive has an investment in getting a film she convinced her bosses to option or buy, developed and shepherded onto the screen – this could enhance her career. She may want to make sure a prior investment works out before she takes on a new project.

4. Your project could be of a similar genre or story area to a project already being developed by the production company.

5. There may not be any development funds left to invest in a new project. Most production companies or studios have budgets for development. Once those funds are spent, they may have to wait for their next fiscal year to invest in new projects.

The writer rarely knows the details of the decision process of why some scripts languish or some get bought or why some scripts find their way into production. Production companies will have personal or working relationships with certain directors or actors or producers. Quid pro quo deals are made all the time; you do this for me and I'll do this for you. Marketing concerns (name value of attached talent) play a big part of decisions. Assessing the quality of a script is always subjective – one person in the company could be pushing for your script and another person (perhaps one with more power) may not respond to the script in the same way.

Keep your focus on the positive. You are beginning to meet "the players". Make each meeting count. Relationships are very important in the film business, make sure you make the most of every opportunity.

Question: When meeting with an executive or producer, after they make it clear they are not going to buy or option my script, what do we talk about?

Answer: Their other projects. Ask what they have in development. Ask what they may be looking to put into development. They may tell you their mandate (10 million dollar films aimed at the family audience or the teen audience or 20 million dollar horror films or…). They may ask if you have any other scripts or ideas for scripts. Arrive for the meeting with at least three ideas – hopefully pretty worked out. Be prepared to pitch. Be prepared to listen to their feedback – and whether you agree with their ideas or not (no need to tell them whether you do or not, just go with the flow) – let them know you appreciate their time and you'll consider their input.

Question: Does a screenwriter ever get a job out of these "meet and greet" meetings?

Answer: Yes. It's not commonplace, but you could get lucky. The best of all meeting scenarios? The film executive has a project and she is in a position to hire a writer for that project. She tells you about it, you spark to the idea, you toss in a few questions or ideas and it is decided you are just the writer for that particular project. Or perhaps the reason the executive wanted to meet you is because she really responded to the dialogue in your script and she needs someone to do a dialogue rewrite on a film that is slated for production. Or she thinks the action sequences in your script are exciting and she wants you to punch up that area of one of the scripts they have in development. Again, this is not a commonplace occurrence unless you are a writer with a strong track record. You should enter your "meet and greet" meetings with more simple expectations: I will make a new contact, I will learn more about this production company and what the company is looking for in their projects. I will be able to add this company to the list of production entities that will read my next spec script or hear a pitch on a new idea.

Question: What's the best thing to do while trying to get a spec screenplay produced?

Answer: Write another script. You must always be working on new material.

Scenario: Your script has found its way into a buyer's hands and an offer has been made for its purchase. You don't have representation (agent, manager or lawyer) and you are not sure of the next step.

Question: Should I negotiate the price, points and/or perks for myself?

Answer: No. There are too many variables that need to be addressed in the sale of your literary property. There are a few options you can pursue.

1. If you have a screenwriting friend or acquaintance that has an agent or manager, ask if he would be willing to ask his representative if they will look at the deal that has been presented to you. Chances are - if there is money involved, the representative will talk to you. You, of course, must be willing to pay a percentage of the deal as a fee for the representative's help (usually 10%). In most cases, a representative's help will be worth it, this is her business and she will know the ins and outs of it. This project can forge a relationship that will be helpful in your next projects. A screenwriter needs a well-trained and well-connected advocate and respected representation in the business.

2. If you don't have someone to make an introduction to an agent, manager or entertainment lawyer, make a call to the Writers Guild of America (East or West coast office). They will point you to a website that lists agents and managers. A good place to start is http://www.donedeal.com . Make some "cold" calls to literary agencies and explain your situation. You may get an agent on the phone. If you don't, go to the next agency on your list. If the deal is valid and there is real money about to change hands, you will eventually find a representative to talk to you.

3. Always remember this is not the only script you will ever write and hopefully not the only deal you will ever sign. Think long-term. Use this experience to find representation that you respect and, hopefully, stick with for a long time.

Scenario: You do not live in the larger cities where you have access to production companies – cities like Los Angeles, New York, London, Chicago, Austin, San Francisco, Hong Kong or another city with a large or burgeoning film community.

Question: How do I get my script into the hands of people who might want to put my script into production?

Answer: Contests and festivals. There are many script contests and festivals. Find the ones that are best for your script (some target the horror genre or action genre or other genre, others target stories suited for low-budget or…). Some contests charge a fee for submission, some are free. Entering a screenwriting contest is a way to get a script noticed. If you happen to win or place in a contest, make sure the agents that you have targeted get a quick note to alert them to the news. Many agents/managers will only consider taking on new clients who have done well in scriptwriting contests.

Consider going to one of the major film cities to take a week-end or week-long seminar in some area of filmmaking. It could be a writing seminar, it could be a production seminar. You will meet other people whose interests match your own and you will strengthen your contact base. The film business is based on relationships; you may make a friend or create a contact that could lead to representation or to a meeting with a film production executive. You could meet someone with aspirations to produce or direct, that someone could turn out to be a person of talent, ambition and resources and your script could be the project that sparks a business relationship.

If you live in an area that offers seminars or writers groups, find one that appeals to you. Again, you will be making contacts and you will be finding other people as passionate as you are about screenwriting. You will also be working on your craft. Remember, a writer is constantly learning.

There are screenwriters groups on the internet. Search out a good one, be a loyal member, find a group of writers you with whom you click. Caution: Don't let your contribution to others' work take too much time away from your own work.

Scenario: Your script has garnered attention in a screenwriting contest. Untried producers want to option it and work to get it into production. The fee offered isn't large enough to attract an agent or manager or lawyer's attention, but you want to pursue this possibility.

Question: What is the length of time I should consider for an option on my literary property?

Answer: The screenwriter wants a short option, six months to a year. This is enough time for you to assess the validity of the as-yet-untried producers and their ability to move your script towards production. The producers will want a longer option because it does take time to get financing, talent and the proper crew in place and they don't want to put forth a lot of effort only to lose their option and control of the property. You will have to negotiate the time frame, but keep in mind that once you accept the terms of the option, you cannot send out your script or try to find other production possibilities until the option as lapsed.

If, at the end of the option period, you feel that progress has been made towards production of your screenplay, you can renew the option. Many producers will want to keep the renewal possibility solely in their hands (they will ask for the initial option and also an option to renew for the same or larger fee). Consider insisting that the option renewal is a part of the contract that requires the agreement of both parties.

Putting together a film production takes time and a lot of energy. This is not the time to be impatient. Producers are often working with no compensation and will only see profit if and when the film goes into production. Appreciate the work that people are putting into getting your script before the cameras. At the same time, assess the validity of the efforts. There is no reason to keep your script out of the marketplace if you feel there is little hope for progress with a certain group of producers.

Question: How much should the screenwriter charge for an option?

Answer: The price will vary from $1.00 to as high as someone will pay. No matter how much the agreed-on price is, get the terms of the deal in writing. No matter if you are working with friends or strangers, get the specifics of the agreement in writing. This will *save you embarrassment, misunderstanding and heartache down the road.*

Some option deals will have certain goals that serve as assessment tools. Example: If financing is 50% in place by a certain time, the option can be renewed. Or if a certain talent is attached by a certain time, the option can be renewed. Or if the cameras are rolling by a certain date, a purchase price (as opposed to the option price) goes into effect. There are seminars and books on various option and production deals. If you have to consider the variables of how to sell or option your own literary property without a professional's help, it's a good idea to educate yourself.

Scenario: The screenwriter has one or five or ten screenplays that are ready for production. Some are optioned, some are not.

Question: What should the screenwriter be doing while he waits for his work to find its way into production?

Answer: Write. Continue to make contacts. Write. Search out others who are interested in the business and share knowledge. Write.

SHORT GLOSSARY OF SCREENWRITING TERMS

Let's make sure we are using the same terminology. The definitions below are of terms that every screenwriter needs to know; you want to be able to use the "short-hand" when talking to your fellow writers and studio types and story development executives. You also want to be able to go through your work and ask yourself, have I used all the tools available to tell my story?

ANTAGONIST: The character who gets in the way of the hero (see protagonist); this character can be actively trying to stop the protagonist because of conflicting goals or it can be a character who, by nature, acts as a stopping block. Sometimes the antagonist is called a nemesis, sometimes a "bad guy," sometimes the "evil force," sometimes the "villain." *Examples: Voldemort in the* **HARRY POTTER** *films (wants to destroy Harry because Harry stands in the way of Voldemort attaining ultimate power and controlling the world) is a very different kind of antagonist than Tony Blair in* **THE QUEEN** *(in order to keep the Royal Family from seeming cold and uncaring, Tony Blair wants Queen Elizabeth to show respect and emotion in the days after the death of Princess Diana) – but both are antagonists because they are working to stop the protagonist from achieving a goal.*

ANTI-HERO: A protagonist who does the wrong things for the right reason. This could be a character that acts in a dishonorable way to achieve honorable goals or who is forced to (or finds herself in circumstances where) underhanded actions is necessary. *Examples: Michael in* **GODFATHER,** *Munny in* **UNFORGIVEN.)**

ARC: A story that has a complete arc will have a beginning, middle and end. To create a satisfactory story arc a writer must take his characters and/or state of the world and through a change. (See Character Arc and Character Development.)

"B" STORY: A supporting subplot of the screen story that will directly affect the outcome of the "A" story. There can be more than one "B" story in a screen story, there can be "C" stories that take up less time, but still have an arc.

BACKSTORY: The events that make up the life of the character up until the moment the film story begins. These events bring the character to his or her readiness to take on the action of the story and answer the question <u>why</u> is the character acting and reacting to the forces of the story.

BEATS: Those silent moments within scenes that are charged with emotion; humorous or dramatic. Actors take beats within their scenes, directors and editors create beats in scenes to make sure an emotion or meaning is successfully conveyed.

BOX OFFICE MOJO: Internet site for detailed film box office information. http://www.boxofficemojo.com

BUTTON: Usually the last line in a scene that signals its completion. Often used in comedy scripts, as in a final word or line that "buttons" the joke.

CHARACTER ARC: The change in your character from the beginning of the screen story to its conclusion. *Examples: A character goes from shy and retiring to being able to stand up for himself. A character goes from egotistical and completely self-serving to realizing that helping others has rewards also.*

CHARACTER DEVELOPMENT: Your main character will go on a journey in your story; starting at point A and ending at point Z. Or B. Or H. (It all depends on how much your character changes.) A character <u>must</u> change or you run the risk of your story being static. A character can grow from irresponsible to responsible, from naive to wise, or from fearful of love to willingness to take the risk of emotional commitment. Emotional growth is most important. Physical growth (as in a sports story) should always go hand in hand with emotional growth. The story you tell <u>must</u> force the character to take a hard look at himself and, in doing so, create the environment for the change to occur.

CLIMAX: The most exciting and important part of your story. The climax is usually in Act Three, when your main character is fighting against all odds to achieve her goal. There can be no turning back. All is at risk. In the climax, the Antagonist and opposing forces are at their most dangerous. The climax can be emotional, it can be physical, and it can be both. It should bring about a catharsis. This is the result of all the story points adding up to push the main character into a final commitment to her goal that energizes and makes it impossible to turn back.

CATHARSIS: When your character experiences a revelation brought about by his actions, usually in a moment of great stress. This revelation, in most cases, brings about a new acceptance or new understanding of self or situation and allows the main character to realize that she is forever changed.

CONFLICT: <u>"Drama is conflict and conflict is drama."</u> Read that sentence out loud over and over. It is the crux of screenwriting and should become a saying that is imbedded in your mind as you write. Without conflict your story will, in most probability, be boring and static. It's the excitement of opposing forces that make for great story. The hero rises to a great challenge and faces antagonists and obstacles – whether he succeeds or fails, the effort includes great conflict. The antagonist should be as strong, brave, and smart as the protagonist. They should be worthy adversaries. Friends and allies should cause problems and disagreements. Physical obstacles should always be present. Anything that creates conflict, makes things more difficult for your protagonist should be present in your screenplay. *Remember: NOTHING SHOULD BE EASY.*

CONFRONTATION: Characters facing fears, enemies, obstacles or any kind of conflict.

COVERAGE: Production companies and studios receive a great number of scripts each year. They hire readers to write synopses of those scripts. The reader will write coverage – summarize the story, assess the writing skills, and give an opinion on the commercial possibilities of the story. This coverage is sent to a development executive with a recommendation: Consider or Pass. The executive will, in most cases, only choose to read the script if the coverage interests them.

CRISIS: Usually found at the end of Act Two when your main character finds himself in the deepest darkest hell imaginable. All seems lost. There seems to be no way out. The hardest decision must be made. Should the protagonist go forward and risk all, put himself in even greater danger (physical or emotional) or should he choose to play it safe, give up or die or walk away? This is the moment when your main character shows if he's a man or a mouse – if he is going to enter the climax and fight for what he truly needs or wants.

DEUS EX MACHINA: A Latin phrase referring to the use of an improbable character or unconvincing event used to resolve the plot. Example: The hero, in the climax of the film, is up against all odds and his success is in question. Suddenly an angel or powerful person appears (daddy or the boyfriend or the cop or some character who is not indigenous to the story) appears to "make things right." In most cases, the writer wants to avoid the use of a deus ex machina. In most cases, the protagonist needs to be responsible for the determination of his future. By using a deus ex machina, the writer is taking the outcome of the film story out of his protagonist's hands.

DEVELOPMENT EXECUTIVE: The person at the film studio or film production company who will read your script or hear your pitch or help (or not help) you get your film made.

DIALOGUE: The words the characters speak in the story.

DOUBLE-BIND: The main character faces an emotional or physical "either-or Example: The need to choose between family and career. Or having to choose between lying to make things seem better, or telling the truth and stirring up possible havoc. Or choosing between two very viable love interests. Double-binds are good to explore in your scripts. *Remember, NOTHING SHOULD BE EASY!*

DRAMA: Portrayal of the human struggle to maintain value and give meaning to the actions taken in life.

DRAMATIC QUESTION: The main question presented by the character and plot that the writer poses in the story. *Examples: Will the protagonist find redemption without putting himself at risk? Will the heroine find love while not believing in its existence?*

ELEVEN-STEP STORY STRUCTURE: A breakdown of story, focused on character.

EPIPHANY: A character's intuitive leap of understanding, when he "gets it" in a sudden burst of perception. This can happen when a strong action occurs or when he hears a certain word or sees a certain visual or other cue that signals a revelation.

FLAW: An imperfection in a character's make-up. What makes a character <u>human</u>. Flaws can be physical or emotional; sometimes both. Examples or emotional flaws could be: insecurity, low self-esteem, dangerous pride, a nervous nature, too fearless, agoraphobic, etc. Every good protagonist and every antagonist should have a flaw that will make the task of reaching the goals more difficult. – especially during the climax of the film story. Other supporting characters may also have (should have) flaws.

FORESHADOWING: Visual, action, dialogue or event that hints at situations or story points to come. Foreshadowing can be as miniscule as a passing inference or a passing visual. Foreshadowing can be a more blatant (a noose in the background of a shot featuring the protagonist, a comment such as "like father like son"…). Don't overdo foreshadowing – you don't want your audience to be ahead of you –

FORMAT: The proper arrangement of headings, slug lines, action lines, character names, dialogue and page numbers on the page that make up a professional-looking screenplay.

GENRE: The type of story you are telling; is it a drama, comedy, thriller or horror film? Is it a western, bio-pic, or sci-fi story? Audiences will, in most cases, choose which films they wish to see depending on their genres. You need to make sure you know the basic criteria of each genre.

HANDLES: The additions to dialogue in hopes of making it sound more "natural" or character specific. *Examples: "Well,..." "Oh,..." "Just in case, ..." "Don't'cha know, " "Hey, dude..." "Whatdya think? etc.* Be careful of the overuse of handles. They can slow down the pace of a story. Not every character in your film should use the same handle.

HIGH CONCEPT: A story idea that can be pitched and understood in one sentence or less. *Examples: **TWISTER** (A tornado wreaks havoc, tornado chasers to the rescue.), JAWS (A shark attacks Martha's Vineyard, a new sheriff who is afraid of water must lead an unlikely crew of shark-chasers and save the town.)* Other high concept films include ***GLADIATOR, TITANTIC, BIG***, FINDING ***NEVERLAND, GOOD NIGHT GOOD LUCK, PIRATES OF THE CARIBBEAN, THE SIMPSON MOVIE***

HOOK: An idea, sequence, character action expressed near the top of the film that brings the audience into the story and makes them want to know what the outcome of the story will be.

IMDB: Internet source for film credits, box office, reviews and industry news. http://www.imdb.com

INCITING INCIDENT: What happens that sends your main character on his new journey. What has happened that will take him out of his "normal circumstances" and propel him into new experiences.

LOGLINE: Two to three sentences that synopsize what the screen story is about, focusing on character arc and theme. Example: **GODFATHER** is a drama about Michael, the resourceful and determined youngest son of a powerful Mafia leader who has decided to break away from the family to live a legitimate life, the "American Dream." When there is a murder attempt on his father and his family comes under attack, Michael goes on a journey to protect his family and discovers that without a sense of family honor he cannot find peace.

LOW CONCEPT: A story idea that can only be understood with detailed description. There are stories that deal with intricate character or plots and must be explained in detail to understand. Examples: *NETWORK, CHINATOWN, THE ENGLISH PATIENT, AMERICAN BEAUTY, ADAPTATION, SIDEWAYS, LITTLE MISS SUNSHINE, SMOKING ACES…*

MISDIRECTION: The writer uses misdirection to guide the audience in a direction that will (hopefully) illuminate the story, but not necessarily answer the most immediate question posed by the character or plot. Example: *CHINATOWN; Jake Gittes find eyeglasses in the saltwater pond at Mrs. Mulwray's house. The audience (as well as Jake) is led to believe that this points to Mrs. Mulwray as a murderess.* Only in following the misdirection does Jake find out the truth.

MOTIF: That prop, object, place, event that holds an emotional meaning to your main character. It could be a recurring element in your story that can become an emotional benchmark. Think music, a catch phrase, a necklace, park bench, car or something that helps reveal the character's changing emotional state. The audience can recognize it as a symbol.

NEW NORMAL: Following the resolution, it is time to give the audience a sense of where the character is headed. A sense of the future for the protagonist at the completion of the story.

OBSTACLE: Obstacles can be large or small (emotional or physical) problems that are put in the path of the protagonist and antagonist that hinder their progress in attaining their goals. Obstacles are the bones of the story. Your main character needs to overcome many obstacles in order to become a hero or heroine.

OPTION: 1) Payment for the privilege of using a literary piece or true-life event (newspaper, book, poem, short story, biographical story or event) for a certain length of time. *Note: Options of less than two years are pretty useless, due to the time it takes to write and/or get a buyer interested in the project.* Every option will be different, both in price and length of time. 2) A person (usually a film producer or director) will pay for the option on a spec screenplay while they work to gather financing for the production of the project. The price is negotiable, starting at $1.00 and going up to whatever the market will bear. *Note: If someone does want to option your spec screenplay, it is in your best interest to limit the option time to six months or a year. Depending on the progress of the optioner's efforts, they may want to pay another fee to keep the option for another short period of time. You should reserve the right to decide whether you want to re-option the project. Keep* *in mind that independent film deals move slowly, production plans rarely get fully financed in a short period of time. You need to assess the amount of progress and the optioner's commitment to the project.*

OUTLINE: A document used by the writer to lay out the basic structure his film story. The Eleven Step Story Structure template can be used as the base of an outline; the Eleven Step breakdown can be expanded to include important events, emotions, plot elements that can be built into each section of the classic story template. An outline is a tool used to keep a writer on track and on story. (Note that a treatment is a polished outline that can be used as a sales tool or as a document submitted to a producer/studio/executive for approval before the writer goes to script. (SEE TREATMENT.)

PITCH: The verbal presentation of a film story. A good pitch should be no more than ten minutes. It should concentrate on the protagonist's growth and journey. Start with the set up the world, a description of the main characters and their motivations. Use the Eleven Step Story Structure as a "cheat sheet," this will ensure that you hit the major story points and show the arc of the story. Feel free to be creative, you can bring in simple visual aids if available. Remember, keep it short. Be ready for questions. If pitching to a development executive, it's a good idea to have two or three projects ready to pitch just in case your initial story idea treads on projects already in development.

PLOT POINTS: The events that move the plot forward in the film story.

PLOT TWIST: The driving force of the film takes a sudden and unexpected turn. This turn either opens up into new territory or shuts down a path or character in an unexpected way.

POLISH: The final work done on a screenplay. A polish may be needed to get the script ready to be sent into the marketplace or it may be needed to prepare the script to be the final blueprint used in production.

PREMISE: The story you are exploring with your character. A premise usually begins with "*What if….*" *Example:* **LITTLE MISS SUNSHINE** *unfolds under this premise; What if an eccentric, dysfunctional family, each with personal problems, is forced to take a road trip to help the youngest member fulfill her dream of winning a beauty pageant?*

PRODUCER: A person who works to get your film made. There are <u>creative</u> producers who concentrate on selling and gathering finances for a project and making sure all the elements of production are in place. There are line producers who concentrate on proper use of the budget while it is in production.

PROTAGONIST: The main character with whom the audience will invest and join on an emotional journey; the person with whom an audience is most likely to identify. This <u>active</u> character propels the action of the story forward. This could be the good guy, the hero or the anti-hero (a character that does the wrong things for the right reasons). It's important that all protagonists have a strong need or goal. Stories that explore the criminal or that character with dark, evil intent as the main character feature the "bad guy" as the protagonist. In most cases, even these bad guys need one or two redeeming traits or you will be in danger of losing your audience.

PUBLIC DOMAIN: A book, article, or literary piece that is available for adaptations due to the length of time from its original publish date. Every literary piece will have its own "strings attached" and should be checked into on an individual basis – but as a rule-of-thumb, if the original publishing date is 100 years old or more, chances are the piece does not have to be optioned or purchased and can be adapted by any and all. *CAUTION: Check each literary piece's provenance. Don't assume anything. A writer DOES NOT want to spend the time to adapt a story without KNOWING the screenplay will be able to be sold/produced someday.*

QUERY LETTER: A letter written in hopes of interesting a buyer or writers' representative in your film script. *Note: Most writers' representatives (agents, managers) will pay attention to the results of screenwriting contests. If your script wins or places in a contest, always mention this in a query letter.*

RESOLUTION: Usually at the end of the film when it is time to tie up loose ends, to explain the previously unexplained.

REWRITE: The work a screenwriter does after completing the first draft of a screenplay. The rewrite is designed to focus story, character arcs and illuminate theme.

REVELATION: A character comes to understand life, a person, a situation or himself in a new way.

REVERSAL: Everything seems to be going well for your character and then quickly shifts to become an adverse situation. Or, conversely, everything seems to be going poorly and suddenly takes an upswing. You will want a few good reversals in your story – will help give it an ever-changing motion.

RISING ACTION: The tempo of your story begins to go a bit faster. Typically you want your story to grow in intensity and pace. Perhaps the tension is growing, perhaps there is an intense prelude to a fight, or to a love scene…

RUNNER: A series of repeating actions or words that have no plot arc in themselves. A runner can help show time passage, add comic relief, and even serve to aid an "epiphany." A runner can be "repeated as needed" in a screenplay. (Example: *KRAMER VS KRAMER* has three breakfast scenes that show the change in the relationship between father and son. *KICKING AND SCREAMING* features the protagonist's growing obsession with coffee. *UNFORGIVEN* uses the various construction phases of the Sheriff's new home to help show the passage of time.)

SCREENPLAY: The film script. The work the actors and directors and film crew use as a guide to create a film.

SCRIPT READER: A person who works at a studio or production company who reads scripts and recommends (or not) them to a Development Executive or Producer. (See Story Analyst and Coverage.)

SEQUENCES: A series of scenes that move the film story forward. Because film is a visual, <u>moving</u> art form, a writer needs to lead the reader (audience) through the life of the characters in the story. The organization of these scenes should form a beginning, middle and end in themselves and each sequence <u>should move the story or character arcs forward</u>. *Example: A character (Bill) arrives at work late, smart-mouths the boss, spills coffee on the client, kicks in his computer screen and is fired. Each of those events makes up a sequence that could be entitled: Bill gets himself fired.*

SET UP: The time taken to portray the various elements of your story. One must set up the world (real, surreal), the time (past, present or future), the essence of your main character and supporting cast, the tone (ironic, straight-forward, or…) and the genre (horror, farce, comedy, drama, romance or…) of your story.

SLUG LINE: The heading in a screenplay that tells the reader where a scene is taking place as well as the time of day. (Example: EXT. PINK'S ROADHOUSE – NIGHT)

STEP SHEET: A breakdown, by location, of the scenes in a film story. This is a shorthand way to convey what's happening scene by scene in each act and can be used as your outline. This can help you focus on what you need to accomplish in each scene; dialogue can come next. (Example: EXT. PINK'S ROADHOUSE – NIGHT. Judy breaks up with Rick. Rick, in a rage, smashes her car and is taken away by police.)

STORY ANALYST: A person who works at a studio or production company who reads scripts and recommends (or not) them to a Development Executive or Producer. (See Script Reader and Coverage.)

STORY EDITOR: A person who helps shape and polish stories and scripts for productions. Usually a term used in television.

SUBTEXT: The unspoken intent of an exchange between actors. Subtext refers to what a character <u>doesn't</u> say, but clearly feels or desires or wants to say. A good actor will play the subtext of a scene. A good writer will not want to write "on the nose dialogue" (saying everything the character is thinking), but construct circumstances so that an audience understands the intent of a character.

THEME: Theme is the unifying moral or emotional premise that you, the writer, are exploring in your story. What is the story exploring? What are you, the writer, trying to say? Theme usually relates to the main character's revelation or to what the main character learns in the story. No need to try to be original here; themes are, in most cases, universal human truths. A simple way to figure out a theme is to try fill in the blanks: Without _____ there can be no _____. (Example: *OTHELLO;* without trust, there can be no peace. *JERRY MCGUIRE;* Without taking risks, one can never really know oneself. *MEN IN BLACK;* Without accepting there are things we will not understand, one will never truly understand the world. *MILLION DOLLAR BABY;* Without truly connecting to another person, one will never find peace. *LITTLE MISS SUNSHINE;* Without the support of family, one can feel very alone.) Note that audiences may find a different theme in your movie than the one you intend. It's "all in the eye of the beholder."

TICKING CLOCK: A story element that sets up a sense of time running out for the protagonist. This is used to accelerate tension and excitement, usually in Act Three.

TREATMENT: A document, 8 to 12 pages in length, that relays the film story in prose style. The treatment focuses on the protagonist's goals and character arc. The theme of the story should be apparent, as well as tone and genre. The most important plot elements should be included. This is not a step sheet or outline of the entire film story, a treatment is, in most cases, considered a sales tool; therefore the task is to highlight the main characters and the broader strokes of the plot that contribute to the character arc.

WGA: Writers Guild of America. The WGA is a union to which TV and film writers belong. The union has offices in NYC and Los Angeles; the union manages pension and health benefits, residual fees and aims to be a support group as well as a source of legal advice. The union holds conferences and classes for writers, some you don't have to be a member to attend. The union has a <u>mentor program</u>. The classes the WGA holds are good places to meet working and aspiring writers who one day may be in the position to hire you. http://www.wga.com

Check out these additional titles from GGC Publishing:

Gardner's Guide to Screenplay: From Idea to Successful Script by Jule Selbo

Making Great Television: Four Essential Ingredients (Gardner's Guide Series) by Dee LaDuke

Gardner's Guide to Writing and Producing for Television by Dee LaDuke and Mark Alton Brown

Gardner's Guide to TV Sitcom Writing: The Writer's Road Map by Marilyn Webber

Gardner's Guide to Animation Scriptwriting: The Writer's Road Map by Marilyn Webber

Gardner's Guide to Television Scriptwriting: The Writer's Road Map by Marilyn Webber

Gardner's Guide to Feature Animation Writing: The Writer's Road Map by Marilyn Webber

Gardner's Guide to Screenwriting: The Writer's Road Map by Marilyn Webber

Gardner's Guide to Creating 2D Animation in a Small Studio by Bill Davis